The Prudent Investor's
Guide to Hedge Funds

The Prudent Investor's Guide to Hedge Funds

Profiting from Uncertainty and Volatility

James P. Owen

John Wiley & Sons

New York • Chichester • Weinheim • Brisbane • Singapore • Toronto

Library of Congress Cataloging-in-Publication Data:
Owen, James P.
      The prudent investor's guide to hedge funds : profiting from uncertainty and volatility / James P. Owen.
         p. cm.
      ISBN 0-471-32336-5 (cloth : alk. paper)
      1. Hedge funds.   I. Title.
   HG4530 .O94 2000
   332.64'5—dc21   00-043587

Printed in the United States of America

10   9   8   7   6   5   4   3   2   1

*This book is dedicated to
my wondrously talented, witty, and effervescent
(not to mention beautiful) wife, Stanya,
who is the light of my life.*

She also writes all my dedications.

Contents

Acknowledgments

It's been said that there are two kinds of people who should never write a book: those who know nothing about the topic, and those who know everything. Luckily, when I began writing this book two years ago, I fell somewhere in between. Knowing how much I didn't know, I made sure to assemble a top-notch team of collaborators to help me pull this project off. If this book is successful it will be due to our collective efforts. My deepest thanks go to:

> Harvey Shapiro (New York City), an experienced financial writer who has written for *Institutional Investor* and the *New York Times*, who did much of the initial research, contributed enormously to early drafts, and gave us the benefit of his vast store of Wall Street knowledge.

> Brigitte LeBlanc, LeBlanc & Company (Mill Valley, California), writer extraordinaire, who helped shape the flow and structure of the book, sharpened the writing, and was always there to provide wise and objective counsel. She is a truly gifted collaborator.

> Kristine Detwiler, CFA, CPA, The Detwiler Group, Inc. (Cornelius, North Carolina), who did the invaluable and exacting work of digging up data and writing about the more technical aspects of hedge fund investing. She also critiqued manuscripts, checked facts, crunched numbers, and was on top of every detail. This book could not have been completed without her.

I'd also like to express my appreciation to the incredible team at John Wiley & Sons, Inc.: Pamela van Giessen, senior editor, who had faith in the project and guided it through all the intricacies of the publishing process; Robin Factor, managing editor; Alexia Meyers, associate managing editor; and Jennifer MacDonald, senior editorial assistant. Special thanks to the team at Cape Cod Compositors for their high degree of professionalism. I'm grateful to John T. Willig, Literary Services Inc. (Barnegat, New Jersey), for successfully bringing the idea to John Wiley & Sons and for his support throughout the project.

For his thorough and penetrating critique at the early stages of the book, I'm also indebted to Ralph A. Rieves of Farragut Jones & Lawrence (Colorado Springs, Colorado), managing editor of the *Journal of Investment Consulting*, published by IMCA, the Investment Management Consultants Association, Inc.

In the course of the project we called upon many industry professionals to contribute insights and data. Three of them went to extraordinary lengths to assist us and are deserving of special thanks: Ted Caldwell of Lookout Mountain Capital (Lookout Mountain, Tennessee), who has forgotten more about the Jones Model than most industry professionals will ever know, and Tim Flaherty and Steve Henderlite of Dillon/Flaherty Partners (Seattle, Washington), who were amazingly patient and articulate in explaining the intricacies of event-driven, arbitrage, and balanced long/short investing. Bill Lawrence and Don Halldin of Meridian Partners (Albany, New York and Orlando, Florida) were also helpful in clarifying the nuances of fund-of-funds investing.

I wish to thank my former associate, Cindy Flaherty (San Francisco), for sharing her knowledge of the legalities of hedge fund investing, and two of my colleagues at Broadmark Asset Management: Dan Barnett, chairman and chief executive officer, and Chris Guptill, president and chief investment officer, for their thoughtful and incisive comments on the manuscript.

Finally, I wish to acknowledge the efforts of my son, Win, and daughter, Allegra, who diligently proofed the manuscript for speling misteaks.

Preface

This book isn't for Bill Gates, Warren Buffett, or anyone named DuPont, Rockefeller, or Getty. If you're on the *Forbes* list of the 400 richest Americans, you certainly don't need my advice. Nor is it for the middle-income family saving to buy a house or pay college tuition; the investment philosophy espoused in this book simply doesn't apply.

You will benefit from this book if you are:

- A physician, attorney, or other professional with your own retirement plan.
- A corporate executive who has built up substantial personal assets.
- An entrepreneur who has recently sold a business.
- An individual who has come into a sizable inheritance.
- Anyone nearing retirement who plans to live off the income from an investment portfolio.

In short, I wrote this book for the serious individual investor who wants not only to protect and preserve capital, but to earn consistent, competitive portfolio returns year after year, through good times and bad. That is, for people like me.

When I began my career on Wall Street some 30 years ago, it wasn't with the idea of becoming a captain of industry or the richest guy in town.

I had one goal: to accumulate enough assets so that by the age of 60, I would be able to turn my portfolio over to capable investment managers and concentrate on lowering my golf handicap. As it turned out, I met my goal three years early, and in 1997, I retired from my partnership in a very successful traditional money management firm. I had enough of a nest egg to be able to live comfortably off the return generated by my portfolio—or so I thought.

My only remaining task was to find the right investment talent to help me meet my specific investment objectives. I thought that wouldn't be too difficult. After all, if anyone knew the money management community, I surely did. In the course of my career, I had created and run the very first investment management consulting department formed by a major Wall Street brokerage house; I had served as vice president of one of the leading investment management firms in the country; and ultimately, I became a partner in a traditional money management firm that grew from $100 million to over $8 billion in assets under management during my 15-year tenure there. Along the way, I cofounded the Investment Management Consultants Association (IMCA); I wrote a financial best-seller, *The Prudent Investor: The Definitive Guide to Professional Investment Management*; and I even served as associate producer of the PBS TV series, *Beyond Wall Street: The Art of Investing*. I knew the investment management industry backward and forward.

Yet three years after I "retired," I am back working full time at a hedge fund, overseeing the management of assets for my family and a group of private investors. Why? It's not that I needed to work in order to put bread on the table. Rather, after considerable research and soul-searching, I reluctantly came to the conclusion that no traditional money manager could give me the kind of performance I was seeking—15 percent annual returns, with no down calendar years.

Given the financial markets' uncertainty and volatility, it was difficult to find any traditional managers who gave me the confidence that they could meet my 15 percent hurdle over each of the next three to five years. And it was virtually impossible to find any who convinced me that they could also deliver on the second objective—no down years. With all the personal contacts and information sources I'd built up over 30 years in traditional money management, I couldn't find any investment manager who I believed could achieve both of my objectives. If I had, I wouldn't be writing this book about alternative investment strategies.

But the fact is, no traditional money manager using conventional tools and strategies would ever hold out the prospect of substantial annual returns with no down calendar years. Not one mutual fund would ever dare put both those goals in its prospectus. And no traditional separate account manager would suggest that was what he or she was offering. For reasons I'll explain, traditional money management simply isn't capable of achieving the kind of consistently positive returns that I and, I suspect, a lot of other affluent investors are seeking.

Luckily, I found another way. And that's what this book is about. I'm going to explain why traditional investment management may work very well for giant corporate pension funds and multibillion-dollar university endowments. It has also helped millions of Americans to accumulate assets toward long-term goals, such as retirement or paying for college. But it no longer serves the interests of those individual investors who have *already* created wealth and are now most concerned with earning consistently attractive returns year in and year out, no matter what the market is doing.

In this book, I'm going to argue that conservative high-net-worth investors who want to be certain their portfolios will support them and their family in retirement should put significant portions of their money into hedge funds. Now, I know that at this point you may be staring at the page in disbelief. Hedge funds? Didn't this guy Owen ever hear of Long-Term Capital Management, the giant hedge fund that fell to earth in 1998, setting off a multibillion-dollar financial crisis?

Ah, yes, LTCM. I know it well. I also know something too few investors realize: LTCM is an example of one very specific and distinct segment of the hedge fund universe. Other hedge funds use completely different approaches. In fact, some hedge funds are among the most conservative investments an individual could make. As Thomas Schneeweis, a professor of finance at the University of Massachusetts at Amherst and a hedge fund expert, wrote in the *Journal of Alternative Investments* in 1998,

> There are many lessons to be learned from LTCM: 1) diversify, 2) high return investments are also potential low return investments, and 3) trading in illiquid secondary markets is potentially disastrous in extreme market conditions. These are, of course, lessons that are true for all investments, and have nothing to do with the fact that LTCM was a hedge fund.

I also know all about hedge fund guru George Soros and his billion-dollar bets on the British pound and the Japanese yen. But what I also know are the facts and figures on myriad hedge fund strategies, and that many hedge funds have lengthy track records of generating attractive, consistent returns.

Perhaps the most important thing to know about hedge funds is that they are a bottle into which all sorts of wine may be poured. Hedge funds are not a kind of investment, but rather a mechanism for making investments in the same sense that mutual funds are a mechanism. As in the case of mutual funds, the vehicle called a hedge fund is not inherently speculative or conservative, large or small, aggressive or passive. It is simply a framework, a legal structure, through which a pool of money can be marshaled and then invested in an almost endless assortment of ways.

In the pages ahead, I will expand on why traditional, mainstream investment management has diverged from the needs of many individual investors, and I will explain why hedge funds can better provide what these investors seek. I will explore which kinds of hedge funds are best suited to helping investors achieve the kind of consistent—and consistently good—returns they need to sustain a comfortable retirement. And I will describe how individuals can invest directly in individual hedge funds or gain exposure to an array of hedge fund strategies through a fund-of-funds approach.

So, I invite you to put aside, at least temporarily, any preconceptions you may have about hedge funds, take careful note of my emphasis on conservative investing, and hear me out. I hope you'll find the case I'm going to make persuasive. At a minimum, I think you'll learn a lot about the surprising and sometimes mysterious world of hedge funds.

JAMES P. OWEN
Montecito, California

Three of the world's most successful and renowned money managers are traveling on the same private jet en route to an international monetary conference. Tragically, the jet develops engine trouble, quickly loses altitude, and goes down over the Bermuda Triangle. There are no survivors.

In an instant, the three world-class money managers are standing before God, who is sitting on His throne. There at the gates of heaven are Peter Lynch, the market-beater who made Fidelity Magellan a household name; Sir John Templeton, the legendary founder of the Templeton funds; and George Soros, the most daring and successful hedge fund manager of them all. In all His majesty, God tells them, "I'm going to ask each of you just one question. How you answer will determine where you spend eternity."

"Peter," God intones, "what do you believe?"

Awestruck, Peter Lynch stammers, "Well . . . I'd have to say that I believe growth stocks should be a big part of every investor's portfolio."

"Fine, my son," God replies. "Come sit here at my right hand."

"What do you believe?", God repeats, turning to Sir John, who reflects a moment and then answers, "If truth be told, I believe above all in diversifying into international and emerging markets."

"That's fine, my son," God beams. "Come sit at my left hand."

"And you, George," the voice of God booms out. "What do you believe?"

Without a second's hesitation, Soros replies, "I believe you're sitting in my chair!"

PART I

WHY CONSERVATIVE INVESTORS SHOULD KNOW ABOUT HEDGE FUNDS

Chapter 1

What's Wrong with Traditional Money Management?

"Let the trend be your friend."

If you believe this old Wall Street adage, it's time to cozy up to stock market volatility. During the past couple of years, the U.S. stock market has witnessed its highest volatility since the 1930s. And all indications are that this unwelcome new neighbor may hang around for a while. As the *Wall Street Journal* put it early in 2000, "Today's stock market quietly has acquired the attention span of a two-year-old."

Some say the market's violent ups and downs are the early warning signs of a full-fledged bear market. Others argue that this kind of volatility just goes hand in hand with an aging, but still vigorous bull market. No matter which view you embrace, it's hard not to get jittery when stocks start gyrating wildly. Any day of the week now, you may find that the Dow Jones Industrial Average has swung 100, 200, or even 300 points in either direction. The prices of individual stocks can fall 20 or 30 percent in one hour simply because they missed some analyst's earnings forecast by a couple of cents a share.

You can argue that we emerged from the 1990s with such lofty stock market levels that a 200-point movement in the Dow is small in percentage terms. In a statistical sense, that's true, but in absolute terms, a triple-digit move in the Dow is still a sizable dislocation in the market. Market volatility is not only scary these days, it feels like it is getting more violent. That's disturbing to people who want and need stability in their investment portfolios in order to maintain stability in their lifestyles.

So what's an investor to do? Clearly, it's naive to assume that the market's extraordinarily high, 20-percent-plus annual returns of the past five years will continue indefinitely. That's a stretch, even for someone who still believes in Santa Claus and the tooth fairy. But with inflation tame and long-term Treasuries yielding only 6 percent, going to 100 percent cash doesn't make much sense, either.

It's my view that in times like these, traditional money management simply isn't capable of achieving the kind of consistently attractive returns that conservative high-net-worth investors want.

WHAT I BELIEVE

By any yardstick, professional money management has been immensely rewarding during the past decade and a half. Through mutual funds, 401(k) plans, and separately managed accounts, millions of investors have been able to participate in and benefit from the longest bull market in U.S. history.

It's been exceptionally rewarding for money managers, too. Just 20 years ago, there were only 500 mutual funds; today there are over 10,000 stock, bond, and money market funds with total assets exceeding $7 trillion. And the 100 largest investment management firms collectively manage upwards of $5 trillion. In short, professional money management—particularly *equity* management—has become a major growth industry.

However, after a successful 30-year career in traditional money management, I am convinced that many basic tenets of the industry are outdated. I reached that conclusion based partly on my own experience. In January 1983, I joined a start-up money management firm with just $100 million in assets under management. I felt the prospects for our business were good. The Federal Reserve's monetary policies had finally broken the back of inflation, and plenty of solid, blue-chip companies were selling at prices that were ridiculously low relative to their earnings, dividend yields, and price-to-book values.

As it turned out, my timing couldn't have been better. We happened to be just five months into a major bull market that has continued for nearly two decades. Back in the early 1980s, all you had to do to earn steady, competitive returns was buy high-quality stocks and hold them. Operating with the wind at our backs, our firm built an impressive track record and grew to more than $8 billion under management by the time of my retirement. Our experience mirrored the rising fortunes of an entire industry.

However, it has become crystal clear to me that if you're a traditional money manager today, you're operating with the wind full in your face. That's not to say I'm predicting the end of the bull market, or that stocks will plunge dramatically anytime soon. My point is that the character of the market has changed fundamentally from what it was 20 years ago. In stark contrast to the benevolent climate my colleagues and I enjoyed for so long, we're now in far more turbulent times. Traditional money managers are struggling to deal with a market characterized by record valuations and unprecedented volatility.

After years and years of steadily rising stock prices, only a confirmed Pollyanna can be confident that stocks will keep endlessly moving higher. Of course, there are those who insist that the Dow will reach 36,000 or some similarly ambitious number in the near future. And there are those who maintain that some "new paradigm" is at work in the economy or the stock market, rendering traditional notions of value useless and irrelevant. Maybe so. But while these theoretical discussions are interesting, you have to ask yourself: What if the optimists are wrong? Do I really want to wake up one day to find that the market has tanked and my portfolio has lost a significant portion of its value, wiping out years of bull market gains? Or do I want to hedge my bets and be prepared for whatever the markets have in store?

As money managers try to cope with a difficult and uncertain environment, they are also being challenged by the sheer volume of assets flooding the market. Many managers simply have more assets than they can handle. They may find themselves trying to put large sums of money to work in markets or niches that can't absorb all that investment. Or they may have more assets to invest than solid ideas to invest them in. To get in and out of their increasingly larger positions, they may also need more liquidity than the market can provide.

Moreover, I believe we're now in a stock picker's market. At these valuation levels, managers can't simply hope to ride the wave; to do well, they need to be genuinely skillful at selecting specific investments. The irony is that for the last quarter century, conventional Wall Street wisdom has often denigrated the very concept of superior stock picking. Attention has centered instead on techniques for asset allocation and portfolio construction. As a result, pure stock picking is a skill at which fewer and fewer traditional managers excel.

THE BREAKDOWN OF THE OLD ORDER

Few would deny that traditional money management has worked well in the past. But faced with this new order of things, it isn't working so well anymore. Old tenets such as "buy and hold" and "there's safety in diversification," once held as gospel truth, no longer can be counted on to carry the day. And investors are the ones taking the hit. According to Morningstar, Inc., only 7 percent of diversified domestic equity mutual funds managed to beat the S&P 500 index during the second half of the 1990s. In other words, traditional management isn't delivering on its implied promise to beat the market, leading many investors to wonder if they're getting their money's worth from active management fees.

That kind of performance might be okay if traditional strategies were providing protection against major market declines. But they're not. When, for example, the stock market dropped 19 percent during 1998's summer correction, 73 percent of actively managed mutual funds plunged even farther. Just imagine what could happen in a real bear market, like the Armageddon of 1973–1974.

The record shows that traditional management has performed very well during normal times—meaning periods when the market is rising at a moderate pace and multiples are expanding. But when the S&P 500 is selling at 25 times earnings and it's not uncommon for the Dow to make a weekly move of 300 to 400 points either way, it seems clear that these aren't normal times. It's no exaggeration to say that today we're in uncharted waters. Faced with extreme volatility and valuation levels through the last half of the 1990s, traditional managers have been lagging the market on the upside and doing worse on the downside, giving investors the worst of both worlds.

It's no wonder that many investors have been tempted to liquidate their actively managed portfolios and shift everything into index funds—until, that is, they stop to ponder just what would happen to their index funds in the event of a major downturn, let alone a protracted bear market. It's certainly true that index funds gave millions of Americans a low-cost way to profit handsomely from the bull market. Yet it's equally true that index funds are the one investment instrument *guaranteed* to go down right in lockstep with any market decline. So much for capital preservation.

AN OUTDATED MIND-SET

It may seem unfair to blame traditional money managers for failing to adapt to such an erratic market. After all, turn on any business channel, and you can see panels of renowned experts jousting over their divergent theories of what's really happening in the stock market and why. But to say that traditional managers are having trouble adapting to changing times gets right to the crux of the problem.

Over the past half century, mainstream money managers have become increasingly united in embracing a specific, codified set of principles and beliefs. They are guided by a canon that has been formulated by academics, elaborated by investment professionals, and cemented by large institutional investors and consultants. Taught in every business school, these principles have become so embedded in the money management industry that practitioners could go through their entire careers without ever questioning them, or the assumptions behind them. Debate may rage over process or methodology, but rarely over the bedrock principles themselves. The tenets of traditional money management add up to a rigid and all-pervading mind-set—a way of viewing the market that I believe has become outdated.

At this point, maybe I should interject that I'm not the only one who believes traditional money management is deeply flawed. In his 2000 book *Hazardous to Your Wealth: Extraordinary Popular Delusions and the Madness of Mutual Fund Experts*, Robert Markman, president of Markman Capital Management, noted, "Much of the multitrillion dollar investment industry is built on half-truths, incorrect interpretations, flawed data, unrealistic expectations, and absurd contradictions. No wonder portfolios based on accepted doctrine have not produced the results intended."

In the next chapter we'll discuss the tenets of traditional money management in more detail, looking at their historical roots as well as their consequences. For now, I want to focus on a single key principle— the one which, more than any other, shapes the goals, aspirations, and mind-set of traditional managers.

THE CULT OF RELATIVE PERFORMANCE

One hundred years ago, every investor believed in absolute return. The only number that mattered was the annual percentage earned on invest- ments, and the goal was to earn positive returns every year. To anyone who cared about building wealth, this was just common sense.

But as we'll see in Chapter 2, the advent of Modern Portfolio Theory (MPT) and the rise of giant institutional investors brought a complete shift in investment thinking. Since the 1960s, mainstream money man- agers have measured success in terms of *relative performance*—that is, how their performance compares to an arbitrary benchmark such as the S&P 500 stock index.

At first blush, this seems a reasonable tenet to embrace. Why shouldn't investors want performance that's better than the market aver- ages, especially when they're paying the tab for active management? In- deed, investing for relative performance is all well and good in a year when stocks are up 20 percent. But what happens when stocks are *down* 20 percent? That's when an investment manager can brag to a client, "Look at what outstanding performance we've had! Your portfolio is down *only* 18 percent."

Investing for relative performance is a philosophy that says, "What matters isn't whether you make or lose money this year, but how well your investments perform relative to your benchmark." Thus, losses are viewed as acceptable—in fact, inevitable—whenever the market goes down. That's just part of the game.

Of course, sustaining major losses isn't the end of the world for some- one running a multibillion-dollar pension fund. Even if the market plunges, he can afford to sit tight, stay calm, and just ride it out. But what if you're a 55-year-old who has built up a stake of several million dollars and wants to live off the annual return? One thing's for sure: *You can't pay the bills with relative performance.*

For big institutional investors, the emphasis on relative performance does make sense. After all, they're investing OPM—Other People's

Money—ostensibly with a long time horizon, defined by Modern Portfolio Theory as a minimum of 25 years. They know that markets continually fluctuate and that investment styles move in and out of favor. And they realize that in every year of this relative performance derby, there are bound to be winners and losers. *Everybody* can't beat the market, because collectively major institutions virtually *are* the market.

From this perspective, as long as they don't lag too far behind the market averages ("tracking error" in institutional parlance), they will do fine over the long haul—that's the relative performance game in a nutshell.

The trouble is that the institutional mind-set has permeated every facet of the investment world, trickling down even to the retail side of the industry. Thus, the same techniques and strategies used to invest a multi-billion-dollar pension fund are applied to a $1 million personal portfolio—yet the goals, the time horizon, and the sensitivity to losses are entirely different. In other words, what's good for General Motors may not be good for you. For affluent individuals, there *is* a better way: Invest with an absolute return objective—that is, with the goal of achieving attractive, positive returns year in and year out, regardless of what the market is doing. This is the single principle that most separates nontraditional managers from their traditional counterparts.

KEEPING WHAT YOU HAVE

In these times of extreme stock market volatility, the biggest problem with the relative performance game becomes frighteningly clear. For institutions and individuals alike, the focus on beating the market has become so single-minded that the goal of capital preservation—the bedrock notion of prudent investing—has virtually fallen by the wayside.

In fact, I believe that capital preservation and relative performance have become mutually exclusive. Traditional managers may pay lip service to preserving capital, but in the real world, they are under such pressure to outperform the market and keep up with their peers that they have little choice but to push capital preservation down the priority list.

So what if valuations are at an all-time high and the market's red flags are up? If a traditional manager takes a defensive stance by raising cash and ends up missing out on a market rise, he or she—not the manager who loses money in a major market decline—will likely be fired for underperformance. Taking a big hit in a market downturn is to be expected; that just comes with the territory. Compounding the danger is the industry's focus on short-term results, despite all the talk about long-term investing.

When the next extended downturn will come is anybody's guess. Clearly, the market's risk/reward profile looks much different today than it did at the start of this bull market. And historically, after each 10-year period in which price-earning ratios have averaged 20x or more, the next decade's equity returns have been dismal.

But whether the bear market rears its head in 10 days or 10 years, the time to prepare for it is now. Ask yourself one question: Would I rather underperform the market when times are good, or risk losing a substantial chunk of my money in a major bear market? The simple fact is that you can't have it both ways. No manager can deliver *both* superior relative performance in a bull market *and* superior absolute performance in a bear market. Those are two completely different goals requiring different investment approaches and even different mind-sets.

When it comes to making the trade-off, I know where I stand. First and foremost, I'm seeking no down calendar years. And I'm more than willing to give up some of the dramatic upside potential of a bull market in order to lower the risk of big losses in a market wipeout. In short, I'll pick capital preservation over the relative performance chase every time.

WHY CAPITAL PRESERVATION SHOULD BE PARAMOUNT

Personally, I've always felt that the pain of losing $100 is greater than the joy of winning $100. Why? It's really a matter of simple math. Say you've invested a million dollars with the goal of earning a 15 percent annual return over any three-year period. In year one, you meet your goal, but in year two the market goes down and you lose 15 percent. What rate of return do you have to earn in the third year to keep pace with your goal? You may be surprised. (See Table 1.1.)

NOT A GOOD FIT

Collectively, the tenets of traditional money management work well enough in the early and middle stages of a bull market. The rising tide lifts all boats, and ideally your portfolio will even go up more than the market. Some would say that if you don't beat the market, you're not getting your

Table 1.1   **Losses Are Hard to Make Up**

	Annual Return	Value of Investment	Annual Return	Value of Investment
Year one	+15%	$1,150,000	+15%	$1,150,000
Year two	+15%	$1,322,500	−15%	977,500
Year three	+15%	$1,520,875	+55.6%	$1,520,875

Based on a $1 million initial investment and a 15 percent annualized return objective.

money's worth from your active managers—but remember, that's not the biggest problem.

The real danger is that traditional investment managers lack the mind-set and the tools to cope with downturns in the market. If and when markets are volatile or trending down, your investments will act like a small boat bobbing on the open sea. However, in such situations, it's not the managers but their clients who get seasick.

Moreover, if the market really starts drawing water, the traditional approach is in big trouble. Traditional money managers don't pull the plug when the market drops 15 or 20 percent—that's just a correction and they're supposed to stick to their avowed style. The market can be down 30 percent or more before they even begin to think about taking some defensive action.

Much of traditional money management is based on various theories of investment that make great theoretical sense and often work just fine for institutions with an infinite time horizon. These are sound principles for theoretical portfolios where life is measured in "bell curves" and "long tails" and "two-sigma events." Trouble is, if you're not theorizing about a portfolio but rather living (or planning to live) off the returns, traditional approaches don't necessarily serve your needs.

In the next chapter, we'll look at how this state of affairs came to pass, in order to understand the reasons for the hegemony of traditional investment management today. And in the chapter following that, we'll begin examining alternative investment approaches—a critical exercise for any investor who doesn't want to be invested 100 percent long in stocks when the next bear market comes.

Chapter 2

How Did Investment Management Go Astray?

It wasn't always this way. Investment managers used to be cognizant of the downside risks that investors faced. And they were mindful of the need to deliver consistent returns that were keyed to some absolute level, reflecting their individual clients' specific financial needs and aspirations.

To understand how this mismatch between the goals of managers and clients came about, we need to look at the historical development of the investment management industry in the United States, and in particular the crucial changes that took place in the 1960s. What we will find is that in the last three or four decades, the dramatic changes in financial markets have been interwoven with equally dramatic changes in the intellectual foundations of investment management and in the culture and practices that guide that activity. The emphasis on relative performance turns out to be a handmaiden of the marketing culture that has come to dominate the industry.

THE "PRUDENT MAN" STANDARD

The investment management industry in the United States dates back at least to the beginning of the nineteenth century. Early on, individuals took on the task of managing the wealth of others. Their putative clients were either widows and orphans who lacked any knowledge of financial matters or churches and colleges that were accumulating endowments from departed congregants and graduates. These managers were typically lawyers or bankers, the people in the community thought to have the financial knowledge and probity to handle other people's money.

From the outset, the investment management profession was guided by three principles.

- The first was fiduciary responsibility: An investment manager was to be a fiduciary, acting solely in the best interests of the client. The money could not be diverted to meet the needs of the manager or the manager's other clients, or to serve any other purpose except advancing the client's own interests.
- The second was preservation of capital. Once money had been accumulated, the primary goal was making sure it stayed accumulated. While it was invested to earn a return, the overarching objective was not to see how much you could earn but how securely you could maintain the money. Intellectually, and sometimes legally as well, pools of capital were viewed as being composed of principal and interest, and while more interest was nice, the key was maintaining the principal.
- Interwoven with this was a third principle, the emphasis on prudence. A fiduciary preserved capital by investing prudently. This was codified into law as far back as 1830 when the courts resolved the case of *Amory v. Harvard College* by ruling that a fiduciary must act as a "prudent man" would be expected to act. That was interpreted to mean that the fiduciary should seek a reasonable return but preserve capital and avoid speculation above all.

It should be noted that in this ruling, and in many others since then, the courts have wisely avoided specifying what constitutes an appropriate investment in any particular circumstance. The courts have never held that the test of an investment is its outcome—whether it made money. Rather, since this historic decision in 1830, the courts have said the appropriateness of an investment is measured in terms of the a priori reasonableness of the strategy itself, rather than the ex post facto results. The doctrine has since been updated to the more politically correct "prudent person" rule, and in some complex situations, the standard is what a "prudent expert" would do.

With prudence established as the standard to which fiduciaries must adhere, for years bank trust departments invested almost exclusively in high-grade bonds and blue-chip stocks. Investment services were sold not on the basis of the results that could be expected, but the degree of safety provided, "safety" being defined as capital preservation. Over the course of the twentieth century, however, the creation of pension plans, the rise of institutional investors, and the development of Modern Portfolio Theory were to completely change the investment landscape.

WHAT PENSION FUNDS LEARNED

It is easy to forget that pension funds and, indeed, retirement itself, are relatively new concepts. For most of human history, people worked as long as they were physically able and then depended on relatives to support them. The idea of retirement barely existed until the nineteenth century; Otto von Bismarck set up the first pension plan in Europe some 140 years ago. In this country, it wasn't until 1900 that the Pennsylvania Railroad introduced the first pension program that covered hourly wage earners as well as salaried employees. And it took years before the idea really caught on.

The U.S. government did its part by creating the Social Security system in 1934, but the Great Depression and World War II slowed the struggle for private pensions. The Ford Motor Company set up its first pension plan for rank-and-file workers only in 1949; it took until the late 1950s for substantial numbers of employers to offer pensions as a standard employee benefit, along with medical insurance.

Once an employer agreed to pay lifetime pensions, the next question was how to pay for this benefit. In the earliest days of pension plans, smaller employers typically purchased annuities from life insurance companies, freeing the employer from both the administrative burdens and the financial risks associated with guaranteeing a future stream of payments whose duration was uncertain. However, larger employers often concluded that they didn't need the insurance companies. Why turn over money to an insurance company when it could be held in the company's coffers to help bolster the balance sheet? Thus, most of the larger early pension plans operated on the pay-as-you-go model, and few companies set aside any significant reserves to cover future obligations. Those that did typically invested in their own bonds.

A pivotal event occurred in 1923 when the Morris Packing Company failed, taking its pension plan down with it. The weakness of pay-as-you-go plans became even more apparent after the stock market Crash of 1929 and the onset of the Great Depression. Amid the nation's economic travail, those businesses that managed to stay afloat found themselves struggling to make good on their promise of a lifetime pension.

After the end of World War II, as more and more of the nation's largest industries began to set up plans, there was a rapid growth in the funding of pension plans, meaning that companies began putting money aside to pay future benefits.

As this money began to pile up, industrial executives were increasingly inclined to look outside their companies for investment management services. After all, they were in the business of making widgets, not investments. Some companies hired insurance companies to manage this money. Others went to the trust departments of regional or money-center banks; in many cases these banks were already providing the companies with a range of commercial services, so it seemed only natural to give them the job of managing pension assets as well.

These institutions were often run by men who had been profoundly affected by the 1929 Crash and invested pension assets as conservatively as possible. Because these managers were usually responsible for investing all or most of the money in a pension fund, they frequently ran a "balanced fund," which gave them the freedom to shift money among various debt instruments and blue-chip stocks in a risk-averse fashion.

Like generals fighting the last war, however, these investment managers were on guard against events that didn't happen. Their overriding caution did provide a safe haven against market declines. Ironically, though, they were blind to a different kind of risk: They failed to anticipate the long-term impact of inflation. According to Ibbotson Associates, the Chicago investment research firm, between 1935 and 1954 long-term corporate bonds earned an average annual return of just 3.4 percent—a figure *below* the average annual inflation rate of 3.5 percent. Thus, while fixed-income securities were universally regarded as safe and conservative, they did not even hold their own against the pace of price increases over the course of nearly two decades.

Meanwhile, over the same period, large-cap stocks delivered an average annual return of 13.1 percent and small-cap stocks rose a whopping 16 percent per year on average. The disparity between stock and bond returns finally hit home in the early 1960s, as the stock market recorded double-digit gains in four of the decade's first five years.

The nation's largest corporations saw the purchasing power of their pension assets erode even as the nominal assets grew to sizable sums. Moreover, their dismal investment returns meant that companies would have to contribute more money from their earnings in order to meet current and future pension obligations. Obviously, something had to give.

It didn't take long for investment priorities to shift. In corporate treasuries and in investment management organizations across the country, a new generation was taking the reins, and for them, the stock market's impressive rise after World War II loomed larger than the 1929 Crash. Many began championing the view that investing more heavily in common stocks was the only way to stay ahead of inflation and keep pace with rising pension obligations.

THE RISE OF MUTUAL FUNDS

While insurance companies and bank trust departments clung to their traditional ways, a new wave of institutional investors was gaining visibility: mutual funds. The mutual fund industry had its beginnings in 1924 with the founding of Massachusetts Investors Trust. By 1941, the industry had some $500 million in assets. And in the 1950s, investors attracted by the bull market in stocks began turning over substantial sums to the industry. Those running the nation's mutual funds were not striving simply to preserve capital, as old-guard investment managers had done, but to multiply it. And rather than looking back to 1929, when many of these managers had not yet been born, they took note of the fact that stocks earned money in 17 out of the 20 years from 1942 through 1961. And as George J. W. Goodman, aka "Adam Smith," wrote in his 1969 best-seller, *The Money Game*:

> The salesmen of mutual funds noticed that when they spread the literature from all the funds before prospective customers, a lot of the customers weren't interested in nice, balanced diversified funds any more. They wanted the funds that had gone up the most, on the idea that those were the funds that would keep going up the most. So the assets of the Dreyfus Fund and Fidelity Capital and Fidelity Trend grew by hundreds of millions of dollars, and all the salesmen everywhere called up the mutual-fund management companies and said, "Give us more of these funds that perform like Fidelity." Thus was performance born, out of

distrust for fixed income, out of suspicion of the erosion of the dollar, out of the capital gains available from the companies that had some sort of lock on something, technological or otherwise.

Performance-oriented mutual funds did not simply bring another approach to investing; they brought a whole new culture. Previously, investment managers took your money only if you passed muster. Investing was a bit of a sideline for both banks and insurance companies, and both sought to emphasize their seriousness of purpose and commitment to preserving capital. That image was important to their *real* business—taking deposits and selling insurance.

Mutual funds had a very different model: They got paid specifically for managing money, and the more money they managed, the more they made because their fees were based on assets under management. No matter who you were, your capital was welcome. What the mutual fund business model most closely resembled was the vacuum cleaner: The goal was to suck up as much money as possible. How to do that? The answer was to offer something distinctive. While the banks virtually reeked of safety and security—you could easily imagine the words "preservation of capital" engraved on the stone pillars outside their cathedral-like halls—those were difficult qualities to pin down. Think about it: How do you prove that you can preserve something better than anyone else? But investment performance—now there was something you could get your arms around. What's more, it was something the mutual funds' more old-fashioned competitors didn't trumpet; indeed, they viewed any type of promotion as downright gauche.

In short, mutual funds brought the sheen and dazzle of marketing to the formerly staid world of investment management. In an effort to attract a steady flow of new assets, mutual fund companies ran full-page newspaper ads, sponsored television shows, and conjured up images of lions coming out of subway entrances. They emphasized brand names and brand extensions, taking their cue from Procter & Gamble and Colgate-Palmolive. There was no waffling on their unique selling proposition: Give us your money and we'll give you the highest possible returns. The approach wasn't far removed from the techniques used to sell mouthwash or shampoo: Buy our product, and your life will be enriched.

Bank trust officers held their noses in disgust, but upstairs, the banks' senior managers watched money in low-interest savings accounts and no-interest Christmas savings clubs walk, if not run, right out the door. Billions were soon winging their way to Boston, Baltimore, and other major mutual fund stomping grounds.

Once performance fever took hold, there was no stopping it. Individual investors weren't the only ones who swapped success stories around the watercooler, vying to see who could claim the most impressive returns. Pension fund executives began to think that injecting a bit more growth into their portfolios might be wise. Meanwhile, several universities had turned small endowments into large ones by investing aggressively. And soon, as "Adam Smith" notes,

> The trustees of other universities were coming into the great trust companies which handled their endowments and saying, "Rochester has come from nowhere to the fifth-richest university, and Wesleyan is building new buildings all over the place, and they did it with Xerox, find us another Xerox."

Meanwhile, this competitive spirit was further whipped up by the emergence of a new cottage industry—an industry whose sole purpose was comparing and ranking money manager performance to the third decimal point. By the late 1960s, A. G. Becker and Merrill Lynch had begun to compile and sell performance data to the pension industry, as did the Frank Russell Company, then a small brokerage firm headquartered in Tacoma, Washington. By promising anonymity and making aggregate results available to all who participated in their surveys, the data collectors succeeded in convincing a growing cadre of investment managers to provide detailed performance data. This way, every manager and client could see just how their quarterly results stacked up against those of their peers. The race was on.

PHILANTHROPY WEIGHS IN

In the mid-1960s, the increased focus on performance received a further boost from what might have seemed an unlikely source: the Ford Foundation. The mighty Ford Foundation, then the nation's largest philanthropic organization and one of its biggest investors as well, was headed by McGeorge Bundy, a former Harvard dean who had come to national attention while serving as national security adviser to President John F. Kennedy during the early days of the Vietnam War.

Using his Ford Foundation post as a bully pulpit, Bundy argued that college endowments and foundations should invest more aggressively in stocks in order to achieve higher returns. In 1969, the Ford Foundation published a report called *Managing Educational Endowments*, which called for heavier weighting in equities and an emphasis on growth stocks rather than blue chips. The report noted, "The record of most American colleges and universities in increasing the value of their endowment through investment management has not been good." And it added, "We believe the fundamental reason is that trustees of most educational institutions, because of their semipublic character, have applied a special standard of prudence to endowment management which places primary emphasis on avoiding losses and maximizing present income." This "special standard of prudence" noted by the report was, of course, precisely what the endowment trustees thought they were supposed to pursue.

The report highlighted what it called "the adverse consequences of the failure to establish the clear-cut objective of maximum long-term total return, which we believe should be the primary endowment objective of every Board of Trustees." It concluded:

> We believe the total return can be increased sufficiently to permit both a larger annual contribution to operations and greater long-term growth. Another result, in our opinion, will be a significant increase in the safety of the endowment over the years ahead.

To be sure, the blue-ribbon panel included some dissenters. For example, Howard R. Bowen, then the president of the University of Iowa, wrote:

> The report may underemphasize risk. It is true that in the past several decades, many investments considered by some standards to be risky have paid off. It does not follow that under other conditions the same policy would be as rewarding. Who can be sure that the conditions of the next two decades will be the same as those of the past two? No one knows for sure.

And James H. Lorie, a professor of finance at the University of Chicago's Graduate School of Business and director of its Center for Research in Securities Prices, noted in a passage that later proved to be prophetic:

The report states that trustees should seek to maximize the long-run total return on endowments. Many competent studies indicate that such an objective subjects the investor (the endowed institution) to great uncertainty as to the value of its portfolio in the short run.

When the Ford Foundation spoke, endowments listened. However, the foundation's timing as an investment adviser couldn't have been worse. As Christopher Knowlton would later write in *Fortune*, "No sooner had colleges loaded up on stocks than the Dow Jones Industrial Average crashed from 985 in 1968 to 631 in 1970," a loss of 36 percent. During the next three years the market rebounded, only to tumble even harder in 1973 and 1974, when the Dow plunged 45 percent and the Ford Foundation's endowment went tumbling with it. From a peak of $4.1 billion, the foundation's assets dwindled to $1.7 billion. Grants awarded by the foundation fell from $197 million in 1973 to $75.8 million in 1979, and, taking inflation into account, the real value of its giving fell by a stunning 70 percent.

Mutual funds didn't fare much better. Although by "the late 1960s, the aggressive, performance-oriented managers of mutual fund portfolios began to be regarded as folk heroes," as Peter Bernstein observed in his 1996 book, *Against the Gods: The Remarkable Story of Risk*, "it took the crash of 1973–1974 to convince investors that these miracle-workers were just high rollers in a bull market." Bernstein notes that while the S&P 500 fell by 43 percent from December 1972 to September 1974, the funds run by two of the industry's highest-profile managers, the Manhattan Fund, and the Hartwell & Campbell Fund, fell by 60 percent and 55 percent respectively.

But by this time, the die had been cast. The Ford Foundation had helped to popularize and legitimize the performance game among endowments and foundations, just as aggressive young financial officers and money managers were convincing corporate investors to focus on return instead of risk.

Though investment managers' confidence was understandably shaken and their clients traumatized by the bear market of 1973–1974, an evolving body of economic thinking stepped into the breach, helping them to rationalize what had happened. According to Modern Portfolio Theory, investment risk wasn't something to be avoided at all costs, as earlier generations of investors had thought, but something to be accepted and "managed."

MODERN PORTFOLIO THEORY

The concepts and theories that are generally grouped under the heading of Modern Portfolio Theory were first outlined in a doctoral dissertation written by Harry M. Markowitz at the University of Chicago in the early 1950s. Markowitz and William F. Sharpe, another brilliant thinker, put forward a number of ideas about the ways investors should approach markets and think about risk. These ideas would both transform the profession of investment management and earn their creators the Nobel prize in economics some four decades later.

Modern Portfolio Theory was grounded in the observation that the various asset classes—stocks, bonds, and so on—not only performed differently, but had different risk characteristics. Markowitz and Sharpe showed that by quantifying and balancing the returns and risks of various asset classes, investors could construct a diversified investment portfolio that would provide the maximum expected return for any given level of risk or, alternatively, the minimum level of risk for any expected return. When combining asset classes, the trick was to make sure that they were not correlated—that is, that their prices moved in different patterns, and in response to different economic and market factors.

Prior to MPT, investors generally followed one of two approaches in choosing stocks: fundamental analysis or technical analysis. Those in the former camp carefully analyzed the results achieved by a business and its prospects going forward, investing in those companies that seemed poised to grow faster than the economy or appeared to be undervalued relative to their intrinsic worth. Those in the second camp, the practitioners of technical analysis, carefully examined changes in securities prices and sought to find patterns in a stock's historical movements. They would then analyze the current market for signals that a historical pattern might be recurring, investing with the hope the pattern would play out much as it had in the past. Often called chartists, these technical analysts surrounded themselves with charts sketching out various patterns, which often took familiar shapes such as head-and-shoulders, saucers, and so on.

By the 1960s, however, academic researchers began harnessing the early generations of computers to produce increasingly thorough and efficient analysis of the huge volumes of stock price data being gathered at the University of Chicago's Center for Research in Securities Prices. This data, showing the daily price movements of every listed stock going back to 1926, revealed a number of things.

For starters, researchers advanced the view that the stock market could not be characterized in terms of recurring price patterns. In fact, they said, the historical data showed that stock prices followed a "random walk." That didn't mean prices moved randomly—they responded to events. But the nature and timing of such events *was* random: At any point in time there could be good news, or bad news, or no news. Backing their arguments with hard data, the researchers essentially held that technical analysis was worthless.

Based on their investigations, the researchers also concluded that the markets were highly efficient. They didn't mean that the financial markets process transactions and pieces of paper effectively, but rather that all the readily available information affecting a stock's value was quickly reflected in its price. If that were true, it meant that fundamental analysis was not worth much, either. In essence, they held that because professional investors accessed the same information from the same sources, investments based on conventional wisdom were bound to get conventional results.

Having debunked investment managers' efforts to pick winning stocks, the proponents of MPT offered a new paradigm: The key factor in investment success was not the selection of individual investments, but rather the broad asset allocation strategy being pursued. In other words, it was far more important to be in the right asset classes than the right stocks. Thus, an investor's most important task was to formulate an asset allocation policy, based on the risk and return characteristics of each asset class, and then construct a portfolio with the optimal blend of asset classes and investment styles, according to one's objectives.

Eventually, virtually all large institutions and money managers adopted asset allocation as the driving force in their investment programs, and ultimately this approach became standard throughout the retail side of the industry as well. More than mere categories for grouping investments or analyzing performance, asset classes became the universal building blocks for investment portfolios.

A MIXED LEGACY

Modern Portfolio Theory did much to help investors understand the nature and sources of risk associated with the management of investment portfolios. It lent academic credence to the commonsense notion that an investor could safely take additional risks to boost portfolio returns, so long as the new investments presented different and offsetting risks. And in preaching the need for broad diversification among asset classes to reduce the variability of returns, the believers in MPT sounded a cautionary note that investors bedazzled by bull market returns needed to hear.

But as often happens when a theoretical construct is applied in the real world, MPT with its emphasis on asset allocation has had some consequences its creators may never have foreseen or intended—the prime one being the industry's unrelenting drive toward specialization. Once investors began constructing portfolios on the basis of asset classes, it followed that the assets in each class should be managed not by a generalist, but by a firm with specialized expertise. The same reasoning was applied to the style categories developed within asset classes and to the subclasses developed within style categories on the basis of market capitalization.

Soon large institutional investors had perhaps two dozen style boxes into which their managers had to fit neatly. Meanwhile, mutual funds were springing up in an equally wide array of categories, enabling individual investors to employ complex asset allocation schemes of their own.

The notion of manager specialization is certainly sensible enough, as is the attempt to balance out the performance of varying asset classes and investment styles over long time periods. Consider the classic equity management styles—value and growth being the two primary examples. All have produced reasonably competitive results over the long term—which is why they've remained popular—but none has worked well *all* the time. With the constant shifts in economic and market cycles, every style has been out of favor at times, producing lackluster results or even substantial losses for months, sometimes years on end.

The trouble is that styles have become so tightly defined—and investors and consultants so insistent on unvarying adherence to these rigid styles—that how well managers perform in absolute terms is generally considered less important than how well they fit their given asset class or style category. The prevailing practice today demands that traditional managers do little or nothing to adapt their investment style to changing market conditions, for fear of throwing the client's entire asset allocation scheme out of whack.

Thus managers have little choice but to stick with their investment disciplines, for better or worse. And if their performance suffers, so be it;

for the manager whose style is out of favor, the prescribed response is simply to wait patiently for more hospitable times to come around again.

Once money managers were hired to protect and grow assets; today they're hired to fill a slot on an asset allocation style chart. Those who can't be pigeonholed aren't even considered, and those who veer from their avowed style or fail to meet their benchmarks risk getting fired. So in this context, losing money isn't that bad; in fact, since it's viewed as unavoidable, it's not really a transgression at all. For investment managers, "style drift" has become the ultimate sin.

The issue of manager specialization—or overspecialization, depending on your point of view—was the subject of lively debate at the May 2000 annual conference of the Association of Investment Management and Research (AIMR), one of the traditional money management industry's leading forums. Reporting on the session in its August 7, 2000 issue, *Pensions and Investments* magazine found noted investment researcher Steve Leuthold, chairman of the Leuthold Group, Minneapolis, to be among those decrying the "narrow mandates" that can straitjacket equity managers. "Specialization has been carried to such extremes in the investment management business that it really does severely limit the manager's ability to make common-sense judgments regarding portfolio structure," Leuthold told the AIMR conferees.

Pointing to huge gaps in the performance of investment styles in recent years, Leuthold suggested that managers should be allowed to depart from their avowed styles when stocks they'd normally buy are overpriced. Moreover, he said, they should be able to hold onto rising stocks that style dictates might require them to sell—for example, a value stock that becomes a growth stock. He even ventured the opinion that managers should be free to enhance performance by putting a sizable portion of portfolios into cash, if they wish.

Peter L. Bernstein, a best-selling financial author and president of the New York–based economic consulting firm that bears his name, took a similar tack, questioning why managers should be yoked to narrowly defined, often shifting benchmarks that may be faulty themselves. *P&I* cites one of Bernstein's recent client papers as declaring, "One of the many troubles with using these indexes as benchmarks is that they are floating crap games."

Needless to say, many plan sponsors and consultants shrink from such heresies; others agree that specialization has become a serious problem, yet balk at the idea of freeing managers from stylistic constraints. Still, as *P&I*

observes, "pressure to loosen the 'equity manager's straitjacket' . . . is building."

ONE SIZE FITS ALL?

Another fundamental problem with the industry's blanket adoption of asset allocation principles is the failure to distinguish between the needs of institutional and individual investors. For institutions investing on a large scale and over a long time horizon, capturing returns from asset classes, rather than from stock selection, is a pragmatic approach. Orchestrating investments at the asset-class level is a far more efficient way of investing large asset pools than trying to select individual stocks, particularly if your time horizon is 20 or 30 years.

It's a different story, though, for affluent individuals. At this level of investing, it's quite possible to achieve superior investment returns with a concentrated portfolio of 25 to 35 really outstanding companies. And think about it this way: How many families on the Forbes 400 list attribute their wealth to a really smart asset allocation policy? Yet today almost every traditionally oriented financial planner and consultant unhesitatingly tells his or her clients that asset allocation accounts for as much as 94 percent of portfolio returns.

On the subject of asset allocation, traditional money managers have been afflicted with tunnel vision for some time now. As a result, stock picking has become so deemphasized and devalued on Wall Street that it's almost a dying art. To say that this limits the investment strategies and opportunities a manager can pursue is a gross understatement. With their thinking framed by the asset allocation paradigm, traditional managers look up through a telescope and react as though they were seeing the entire investment universe.

SETTING THE BAR TOO LOW

Another legacy of Modern Portfolio Theory is the assumption that markets are highly efficient. And once again, at the level of the large pension fund manager or giant mutual fund complex, this is undoubtedly true. There is a limited number of stocks with sufficient liquidity and market capitalization to meet the needs of those with billions to invest, and as a result traditional managers—especially those using large-cap strategies—tend to follow the same well-defined universe of stocks as their peers.

Yet there are clearly areas of the market that are rife with inefficiencies and provide opportunities that are open to anyone who is willing to ferret them out and can invest at a more modest scale than the giant institutions. As Warren Buffett once put it, "I'd be a bum on the street with a tin cup if the markets were always efficient."

For instance, inefficiencies can often be found at the cusp of economic and technological change, whether it be a subtle refinement to a single manufacturing process or the emergence of a whole new industry. New technologies arise, industries retool, consumer habits and buying patterns shift—and in our information-driven society, the pace of change is only accelerating. So while a traditional manager might fear changes that could upset a strategy based on historical market patterns, one who is more flexible and forward-looking sees change as the source of opportunity.

Inefficiencies also arise from the one market variable that no computer model or market theory can fully account for: investor psychology. Few managers are so completely rational and objective that they can factor out all emotion when markets are moving rapidly and millions of dollars are at stake. Their actions may be tinged by optimism or pessimism, complacency or fear, especially in times of heightened volatility. The market constantly reflects the influence that emotional reactions and investor perceptions can have on stock prices—and this is another source of opportunity in itself. Indeed, to a manager willing to play the contrarian, the widely held belief in a rational, efficient market can be an advantage in itself. "The more people think markets are efficient," George Soros once observed, "the more inefficiencies there are."

Yet the belief that markets are efficient has helped dictate the course of mainstream investment methodology. Original, fundamental research was once considered the sine qua non of professional equity management, but today is seen as adding little value to the investment process; in fact, it's widely viewed as irrelevant.

Seeing scant prospects of profiting from little-known information or unique insights, professional managers have sought other sources of advantage. Increasingly, they have embraced the use of quantitative, "black-box" strategies that model the statistical relationships between market variables. What all these approaches have in common is that they bank on the assumption that the patterns of market behavior observed in the past will hold true going forward. In essence, it's investing by looking in the rearview mirror, rather than at the road ahead.

It's important to note that the belief in market efficiency not only has shaped the methods employed by managers, consultants, and clients, but has defined their aspirations as well. If you are interested in only a certain universe of stocks, and they're the same stocks your peers are following, there is little hope you can gain any meaningful edge over your competitors. Incremental return—a small margin above the market average or benchmark—is the best you can hope to achieve. This view holds particular sway among large institutional investors and managers, and with good reason: They and their peers hold such a high proportion of the country's investable assets that they virtually *are* the market. But is there any good reason why a forward-thinking, nontraditional manager must be limited by what the market is doing? Not in my book.

ERISA'S STAMP OF APPROVAL

The U.S. Congress did its part to reinforce the theories and assumptions underlying Modern Portfolio Theory. In 1974, Congress enacted the Employee Retirement Income Security Act (ERISA), legislation introduced after several failing companies, most notably Studebaker-Packard and the Penn Central Railroad, left pension funds bereft of the funding needed to make good on promised employee pension benefits. The ERISA legislation imposed stricter funding rules on pension funds, created the Pension Benefit Guaranty Corporation, and prohibited self-dealing and other abuses.

In addition, ERISA laid out a variety of tests regarding the handling of pension responsibilities and redefined what constituted prudent investment management. The original concept applied the test of prudence to each investment. But in a nod to MPT and the new emphasis on the role that diversification could play in ameliorating risk, the legislation took the view that an investment's prudence had to be judged within the context of the total portfolio. Thus, an investment that might not be deemed prudent on its own could meet that test if it were part of a portfolio of investments viewed as prudent overall.

In several other ways, ERISA codified into law the processes and procedures being advocated by Modern Portfolio Theory. Thus, any investment managers who hadn't already been steeped in MPT in business school found their ERISA clients (and their attorneys) willing and eager to fill that gap in their education.

THE GROWING ROLE OF CONSULTANTS

The enactment of ERISA also helped expand the role of investment management consultants, who soon became prime keepers of the MPT flame. Whereas institutional investors once looked to investment managers as their main source of outside investment expertise, they now required another kind of expert advice. Faced with the task of evaluating, hiring, and continually monitoring a broad array of managers, assessing each one within the context of a distinct investment specialty and manager universe, pension plan sponsors and other institutional investors needed help just to keep their asset allocation policies on track.

Furthermore, pension executives noted that when the U.S. Department of Labor censured plan sponsors, it was never on the basis of investment results and outcomes. Rather, the DOL assessed whether plan sponsors had engaged in due process and careful, disinterested deliberations. Institutions quickly realized that they could shield themselves from liability by documenting that they had well-established decision-making processes in place and, better yet, that expert consultants had helped them make all of their important investment decisions. The result was a dramatic rise in the prominence and role of investment consulting firms through the 1980s and 1990s.

These firms collected and analyzed reams of data on investment managers. They knew all about investment processes, disciplines, personnel, and results. And they could advise their clients on which managers provided the best fit with their precisely spelled-out objectives. To be sure, the clients made the final decisions, but by functioning as gatekeepers the consultants came to wield enormous, make-or-break power over investment managers. Yes, the clients made the decisions—but they did so based on the short lists that consultants gave them.

The rise of consultants was one more factor further entrenching the specialization and relative performance orientation of money managers. To earn their fees and make their services indispensable, consultants applied a systematic, analytical approach to every aspect of the investment process. With their asset allocation charts, their tables full of carefully calculated performance numbers, and their elaborate investment style matrixes, consultants gave clients much more than information and advice. What they provided was science.

In this way, consultants abetted the transformation of money managers from strategic partners who helped shape investment policy to narrowly focused hired hands employed to do one job, and one job only. While the institutions and their consultants made the big-picture decisions, money managers functioned as asset-class job shops. Is it any wonder traditional managers complain that their services have become a commodity?

THE LOGICAL EXTREME: INDEXING

One of the ironies of the industry's overriding focus on relative performance is that more often than not, investment managers fail to pass the test they have imposed on themselves. Each year a substantial percentage of mutual funds and money managers—up to 90 percent in some years—prove incapable of outperforming the market. Most managers cluster somewhere slightly below the market averages, and after adding in fees and costs, consistently trail the market.

The seemingly lackluster results of so many managers shouldn't be surprising. Institutional investors have grown so dominant in the market that it is statistically impossible for a majority of them to beat the market averages. In Lake Wobegon, perhaps, all the children can be above average, but in real life, half of any group must inevitably be below average.

Recognizing the futility of attempting to consistently beat the market, by the end of the 1970s a number of managers concluded that "if you can't beat 'em, join 'em." Thus arose a whole new, passive investment approach. The idea was that rather than seeking to outperform the market, managers could create "synthetic" portfolios that precisely mirrored the market through all its fluctuations. In this way, managers could guarantee that their results would be just as good as the market's—no better, to be sure, but no worse, either. What's more, since it was much cheaper for managers to invest passively than it was to maintain large research and stock-picking operations, the savings could be passed on to clients.

With Wells Fargo Bank leading the way, managers rushed to create index funds in the mid-1970s, and legions of investors flocked to this new, lower-cost alternative. By the end of the 1990s, about a quarter of all institutional funds were indexed, and individual investors had poured billions of dollars into the index funds set up by Vanguard and other leading mutual fund companies. Indeed, by the beginning of the year 2000, Vanguard's S&P 500 Index Fund was running neck and neck with Fidelity's Magellan Fund for being the nation's largest mutual fund.

Indexing created a vitriolic debate in investment circles, which continues unabated today. Some insist that indexing is by far the most sensible and efficient way to profit from the stock market's long-term growth; others complain that the indexers' willingness to settle for average performance sets the bar much too low. But in any case, it's clear that the rise of indexing, and indeed the entire indexing debate, only further entrenched the view that comparing returns against the market is the sole meaningful test of investment skill. It's also obvious that while indexing lets investors capture market returns at low cost, it does absolutely nothing for someone concerned about volatility or a serious market decline.

SO WHAT'S THE PROBLEM?

In Chapter 1, I explained why traditional money management's single-minded focus on relative performance is a poor fit with the needs and goals of many individual investors—particularly affluent investors, who have a large enough stake to know that their first priority is keeping the assets they have.

This chapter showed how mainstream money management came to operate the way it does today. In large part, it was the evolution of pension plans and the rapid growth of mutual funds that led the money management industry to adopt a beat-the-market mentality—a world view that defined success in terms of market averages and replaced the goal of capital preservation with the attitude that "some years you win, some years you lose." The industry's aggressive marketing of investment services only heightened the emphasis on short-term results.

Meanwhile, Modern Portfolio Theory arose from academia, becoming the foundation of a rigorous, systematic investment approach geared to balancing the risks and returns from varying asset classes over time periods of 25 years or more. While MPT was driven by the needs and circumstances of large institutional investors, it quickly came to dominate thinking throughout the investment industry. The belief that most returns are driven by asset allocation decisions rather than security selection, the assumption that markets are efficient, the notion that incremental return is the best one can hope to achieve—all these MPT-derived tenets have become so embedded in the money management profession that few ever even think to question them.

There is a common thread to all these historical developments. They have shaped a mind-set—the one I've labeled "traditional money management"—which assumes that investors and money managers alike are held captive by the market's cycles. But here's the real point: Not only do traditional managers behave as though their destinies were irretrievably tied to the market's overall direction, they embrace principles and methods that virtually guarantee that this is the case! When managers stick to a rigidly defined investment style no matter the cost, when they fail to defensively raise cash in a flagging market, when they believe that capturing the returns from a given asset class mix is the very best they can do—in all these cases, they are fulfilling the prophecy that says that losses are to be expected whenever the market goes down.

Fortunately, there are some very successful money managers who reject traditional thinking, breaking free of hidebound theories and practices. And although they are a small minority in the scheme of things, their numbers are growing.

As we'll see in the next chapter, nontraditional investment approaches have increased in popularity over the past several years, giving high-net-worth investors a growing set of alternatives to an outdated investment paradigm.

Chapter 3

The Growing Appeal
of Alternative Investments

Once you understand that traditional money managers are inevitably captive to the market's ups and downs, it's easy to see why interest in alternative investments has been growing—especially among investors who are primarily seeking consistent, attractive returns. In simplest terms, alternative investments are a category of investments defined mainly by what they are not—that is, not correlated with mainstream stock and bond markets. And according to an ongoing survey by Goldman Sachs and Frank Russell Company, U.S. pension funds, endowments, and foundations have more than quadrupled their exposure to alternative investments over the past decade.

LEADING THE WAY

The trend toward alternative investing has been most evident in the world of endowments and foundations ("eleemosynary" investors, in professional parlance), which tend to have goals similar to those of many wealthy investors. Foundations and endowments need to generate a fairly high and predictable level of total return every year to meet operating obligations and fund capital improvement programs, while at the same time continuing to grow assets over the longer term. When you think about it, their investment needs parallel those of an affluent individual who wants to maintain a certain lifestyle through retirement. Both kinds of investors seek consistently high absolute returns.

So it's not surprising that institutions such as Harvard, Yale, Princeton, and Stanford Universities were early in investing a substantial portion of their assets in ways that didn't tie returns to the vagaries of traditional stock and bond markets. The Yale University Endowment, with more than $7 billion in assets, was one of the first to pursue alternative investment approaches. (See Table 3.1.) In its 1999 investment report, Yale detailed its shift away from traditional domestic assets and toward alternative investments:

> Over the past decade, Yale has reduced dramatically the Endowment's dependence on domestic marketable securities, reallocating assets to nontraditional asset classes. In 1989, approximately 70 percent of the Endowment was committed to U.S. stocks, bonds, and cash. Today, the diversifying assets of foreign equity, private equity, absolute return strategies, and real assets dominate the portfolio, representing nearly 75 percent of the Endowment.

In his new book, *Pioneering Portfolio Management*, David F. Swensen, manager of the Yale Endowment for the past 14 years, elaborates on the benefits and results of the tilt toward alternative investments:

> Aside from reducing dependence on the common factor of U.S. corporate profitability, the asset allocation changes ultimately exposed the portfolio to a range of less-efficiently priced investment alternatives, creating a rich set of active management opportunities.
>
> In spite of a systematic reduction in exposure to domestic equities during one of the greatest bull markets ever, the Yale endowment produced extraordinary returns. Measured from the bottom of the U.S. market in 1982, Yale's return of 16.9 percent per annum stands in the top 1 percent of institutional funds. Stated differently, had the university generated returns equivalent to the average for institutions of higher education, endowment assets would be $3.3 billion lower as of June 30, 1999.

Table 3.1   Yale University Endowment
Asset Allocation, June 1999

Domestic equity	15.1%
Fixed income	11.1%
Absolute return	21.8%
Foreign equity	11.1%
Private equity	23.0%
Real assets	17.9%
Total	100.0%

Source: The Yale Endowment: 1999 Update.

Just as impressive is the example of Notre Dame. As highlighted in a September 13, 2000 *Wall Street Journal* profile, chief investment officer Scott Malpass has used a strategy incorporating alternative investments to grow Notre Dame's endowment fund from $2.2 billion to $3.5 billion in just one year. Chalking up a 57.9 percent return for the 12 months ending June 30, 2000, Malpass undeniably had a phenomenal year, but that was no flash in the pan. The fund's gains have averaged an impressive 29.1 percent over the past three years, outperforming the S&P 500 by 9.4 percent annually! According to the *Journal*, this track record is due in large part to Notre Dame's strong commitment to alternative investing.

IN SEARCH OF DEFINITIONS

Exactly which kinds of investments fall into the "alternative" category? As is often the case with evolving disciplines, the definitions and boundaries concerning alternative investments aren't always clear. Even the experts sometimes disagree.

In their 1999 book, *The Handbook of Alternative Investment Strategies*, the editors, Thomas Schneeweis and Joseph Pescatore, put it this way: "Investments that provide unique risk and return properties not found easily in traditional stock and bond investments are often classified as alternative investments."

Venture capital, private equity, leveraged buyouts, and oil and gas are all generally accepted as being alternative investments, as are farmland and timberland. While many investment professionals also include real estate, others don't. Portfolios of conventional, publicly traded stocks and bonds also qualify as alternative investments *if* they are constructed and managed in nontraditional ways. That's why hedge funds are generally included in any listing of alternative investments.

A DISTINCT CATEGORY

A fundamental question is whether, in aggregate, alternative investments constitute a separate asset class. One can easily argue that they don't, on the basis that the asset class would include such a diverse variety of investments that it would be difficult to generalize about its risk/return characteristics. According to Yale:

> The definition of an asset class is quite subjective, requiring precise distinctions where none exist. Returns and correlations are difficult to forecast. Historical data provide a guide, but must be modified to recognize structural changes and compensate for anomalous periods. Finally, quantitative measures have difficulty incorporating factors such as market liquidity or the influence of significant, low-probability events.

However, from a practical point of view, alternative investments are often treated as an asset class insofar as endowments and foundations in particular target them for allocation of a certain portion of assets. And if you're really sophisticated, you may carve out room for allocating a portion of your fund to specific investment categories such as private equity or venture capital as asset classes unto themselves, establishing set portfolio allocations to these specific categories.

But on one point there is no debate: A growing number of institutions and individuals believe their portfolios must include alternative investments if they are to be truly diversified.

There is a burgeoning alternative investment community with its own organization, the Alternative Investment Management Association (AIMA), which was founded in 1990, has a membership of more than 200 investment management organizations, and produces an ambitious array of conferences, surveys, and newsletters.

The field has also become fertile ground for academic and commercial investment researchers, and boasts its own publication: the *Journal of*

Alternative Investments, published by Institutional Investor, Inc., a leading financial publishing company. That's not to mention the growing list of books published on the subject. And, of course, web sites abound.

But regardless of whether alternative investments are viewed as an asset class or as a category covering a mixed bag of investment vehicles, the critical point is that they substantially broaden the horizons for investors, expanding both the types of investments that can be made and the range of strategies an investor can pursue. Most important, they provide a way investors can break free of market volatility and the fear that a major bear market is lurking somewhere over the horizon.

AN ACCELERATING TREND

It was after the market turmoil of the late 1960s and early 1970s that institutional investors started testing the waters of alternative investing, in the hope of smoothing out the ups and downs of the financial markets while also enhancing their overall investment returns. Typically beginning with real estate, venture capital, and private equity, early adopters included such prominent institutions as the Harvard and Yale endowments and a few corporate investors such as the General Electric pension fund. It turned out to have been a fortuitous move. In a 1995 profile in *Institutional Investor* magazine, GE Investments, the investment management arm of General Electric—it manages the company's pension fund as well as funds for outside clients—reported that over the previous 10 years private equity had been its best-performing asset class.

Foundations and endowments spearheaded the trend, due not only to the nature of their investment objectives, but also to the fact that they were often headed by wealthy individuals who were receptive to a more entrepreneurial, opportunistic brand of investment thinking. In the 1980s, some institutional investors began adding timberland and farmland to their asset allocation mix. And by the 1990s, they were venturing into hedge funds.

The numbers show that investors today are not only continuing to expand the diversity of their alternative investments, but greatly increasing the amount of assets committed. Since 1992, Goldman Sachs, and Frank Russell Company have been surveying a number of U.S. pension funds, endowments, and foundations regarding their exposure to alternative investments. These institutions, each of which has assets of more than $3 billion, were estimated to have an aggregate investment in alternative investments equal to $12 billion in 1986 and $36 billion in 1990. Successive surveys have found their exposure in this arena climbed to $58 billion in 1995 and $91 billion in 1997. The 1999 edition of the survey found total alternative investments for the year ending June 30, 1999 had climbed 67 percent in two years, to $152 billion.

In the 1999 survey, covering 189 funds, 61.4 percent reported holding alternative investments, and their average allocation to this area had risen from 6.3 percent of assets in 1997 to 7.3 percent in 1999. When broken down by type of institution, the survey found that endowments and foundations had an average of 13.8 percent of their assets invested in alternative investments, compared to 7.3 percent for corporate pension plans and 5.5 percent for public employee retirement plans.

The 1999 version of the survey also polled 90 of the largest pension funds in Europe for the first time, and the 61 respondents said they had allocated 3.5 percent of their assets to alternative investments, up from 1.9 percent in 1997. Alternative investments may still represent a relatively small fraction of overall investments both in the U.S. and abroad, but the upward trend has been strong across the board.

THE PURSUIT OF PERFORMANCE

In *Alternative Investing,* a 1998 report published by AIMR (the Association for Investment Management and Research), Charles G. Froland, a managing director at the General Motors Investment Management Corporation (which manages GM's vast pension fund), neatly sums up why there is an increasing interest in alternative investments: "Alternative investment strategies have come to play an increasing role in investment portfolios, partly because of a promise of high returns and partly as a way to find refuge from the swings in fortune of the more traditional markets."

It's true that return data for some types of alternative investments can be sketchy, since they may involve assets that are not publicly traded and may change hands infrequently, thus making them difficult to appraise or evaluate. Nonetheless, the data that exist show why performance-minded investors are increasingly "thinking alternative."

For example, one analysis of the risks and returns of an alternative investment portfolio, consisting of venture capital, distressed securities, and buyout funds, showed it outperforming a traditional portfolio of stocks, bonds, and cash by a substantial margin over the 1991–1996 period. The results of this study, conducted by Thomas Schneeweis and Richard Spurgin, were published as a white paper, *Alternative Investments in the Institutional Portfolio*, by the Alternative Investment Management Association in 1998. As Table 3.2 indicates, the alternative investments returned 28.7 percent over the five-year period, versus 16.2 percent for the S&P 500, 18.4 percent for the Russell 2000, and 8.3 percent for the Salomon Brothers Corporate/Government Bond Index.

These returns offer a powerful argument in favor of adding alternative investments to a traditional portfolio of stocks and bonds. Indeed, Schneeweis and Spurgin concluded:

The analysis supports previous results that conclude managed futures, hedge funds, and traditional alternative investments such as REITs, commodities, and private equity should be added to stock and bond portfolios. The study also shows that hedge funds and managed futures belong in a diversified alternative investment portfolio.

Table 3.2   **Returns on Traditional versus Alternative Assets, 1991–1996**

Traditional Assets	*Annual Return*
S&P 500	16.2%
Russell 2000	18.4%
Salomon Brothers Corporate/Government Bond Index	8.3%
Real Estate Investment Trusts (REITs)	17.9%
Treasury Bills	5.0%
Alternative Assets	
Leveraged Buyout	22.3%
Venture Capital	33.3%
Distressed	24.0%
Traditional Alternative Portfolio*	28.7%

Source: Thomas Schneeweis and Richard Spurgin, *Alternative Investments in the Institutional Portfolio*, Alternative Investment Management Association, 1998.
*Traditional alternative portfolio is an equal-weighted blend of Wilshire venture capital, distressed, and buyout.

REDUCING MARKET RISK

The other key attraction of alternative investments is that they generally have a low correlation with the stock and bond markets that comprise the core of most sizable portfolios. Alternative investments either are driven by different forces than the stock and bond markets, or are driven by the same forces, but in different directions. As a result, when stocks zig, many of these other investments zag.

The low correlations reflect the fact that many alternative investments are participating in markets that move independently of stocks and bonds. Whatever might be going on at a given publicly traded company, its stock price is often affected by the direction of the market to one degree or another. But the prices for oil or timber or cattle are shaped by supply-and-demand forces in the global commodities market, not by the S&P 500. Nor do stock market trends and events necessarily have much influence on a given portfolio of real estate or venture capital investments.

As Swensen points out,

> Even though for short time periods, diversifying financial assets ... may show high correlation to marketable equities, over reasonable investment horizons assets driven by fundamentally different factors produce fundamentally different patterns of return.

A similar point can be made regarding portfolios of conventional securities that are managed using nontraditional strategies and tactics; the results can be radically different from what the mainstream market is providing. The most clear-cut example is short selling (i.e., selling securities you don't own in the hope that when you buy them back later the price will have declined). When the market goes up, by definition the short portfolio goes down, and vice versa.

In a general sense, of course, all investments are ultimately influenced by larger economic trends and developments. For instance, if the economy is booming, real estate prices may rise more rapidly and people will be more eager to invest in new ventures. Conversely, if the economy is mired in recession, it will likely have a dampening effect on all markets sooner or later. But markets aren't all affected by broad economic trends to the same degree or at the same time, and their movements may even be in different directions. Moreover, even when the economy is just comfortably cruising along, the performance differentials between markets can be substantial.

As Schneeweis and Pescatore note in *The Handbook of Alternative Investment Strategies*, alternative investments' low correlation with the market and its movements indicates that many may be regarded as offering "unique risk and return trade-offs" not easily available through traditional investments. The main conclusion: Alternative investing "enables investors to reduce the long-term uncertainty in their final investment value."

Thus, if alternative investments zig when the mainstream markets zag, the effects of market downturns will be modulated. Depending on the investments and strategies employed, gains may be modulated, too. But for investors who care more about building a secure future than about beating the market, the modulation is the critical thing.

Luckily, with the growth of alternative investing, investors who don't want to put all their eggs in the stock market have a wider range of possibilities than ever before. And while this investment category used to be out of reach for all but the most fabulously wealthy, ($5 million or $10 million investment minimums being the norm), that has changed dramatically in recent years. Although minimums are still beyond the reach of the average investor, firms such as Goldman Sachs and Morgan Stanley Dean Witter have packaged alternative investments in ways that make them accessible to many more investors. Some of the newer products carry minimums that are as low as $250,000.

WHICH ALTERNATIVES MAKE SENSE?

The evidence indeed suggests that alternative investing does provide a way of reducing some of the uncertainty of the financial markets. The question is, which specific alternatives should you choose? One practical problem is that investing in a widely diversified portfolio of alternative strategies is beyond the means of most high-net-worth investors. It's also true that each alternative investment category and strategy has its own characteristics, limitations, and constraints. For example, investments in oil and gas and real estate have proven to be highly cyclical. Others, such as commodities and managed futures, are fundamentally speculative. Still others are difficult to evaluate and monitor without a high degree of expertise in a given industry or technical discipline.

In addition, the performance of many alternative investments is hard to track. It's difficult for an investor to know what his or her holdings are worth at any point in time because it is difficult for the fund manager to accurately value the underlying investments. Venture capital and private equity are, by definition, investments in nonpublic companies whose share prices cannot be found in a newspaper listing. A few years after making an investment, the fund may take a company public or sell its private equity stake to another company; only then do the fund managers and investors really know what the investment was worth. The lure, of course, is that when an investment is successful, the payoff can be huge. Private equity is one of the few ways you can turn a million dollars into 5 or even 10 million, as long as you're willing to take the risks and be patient.

This brings up what is perhaps the biggest problem with most alternative investments: their lack of liquidity. They require investors to tie up their money for extended and sometimes indefinite periods of time. In the case of timberland, for example, it could be a decade or more before investors even begin to see a return on their investments. When it comes to private equity and venture capital, there is a life cycle to the investments, and anyone who invests in a company during its early stages cannot realistically expect to get their money back or receive any payoff for a half-dozen years or more. Indeed, it may take months or two to three years before the fund managers are actually able to channel investors' money into particular ventures.

For many institutional investors, of course, this "Rip Van Winkle" approach isn't a problem. They are looking for the best results they can get over a period of 25 years or more. To any individual investor who plans to live off portfolio returns, however, locking up a large sum of money for a half dozen or more years is untenable. There's also the safety-net issue. Even if they don't need the income, many investors are justifiably afraid that something could happen during that period—either in the economic environment or in their own lives—that will cause them to need that money. Being unable to gain access to their own funds is a risk they may not want to take.

ZEROING IN ON HEDGE FUNDS

In all my research covering the entire range of alternative investments, I found only one vehicle that offers the opportunity for attractive, consistent returns without serious constraints on liquidity. I'm talking about hedge funds. In comparison to other alternative investments, investors can get in and out of most hedge funds with relative ease. Virtually all hedge funds permit withdrawals on at least an annual basis, most on a quarterly basis, and some even on a monthly basis.

While some hedge funds may invest in arcane areas of the market or utilize quantitative strategies that are difficult to fathom, many invest in familiar listed securities and use strategies any reasonably sophisticated investor can understand.

It's no surprise that in this climate of heightened market uncertainty and volatility, there has been a strong surge of interest and investment in hedge funds. As recently as 1990, according to Cerulli Associates, there were about 2,000 hedge funds worldwide, with total assets of about $45 billion. By 1999, there were an estimated 6,100 hedge funds worldwide with assets totaling $355 billion. As you can see, hedge funds have shot up markedly in terms of both the numbers of funds and assets under management.

Historically, most of the assets invested in hedge funds have come from high-net-worth investors, a phenomenon I'll discuss in later chapters. Having spearheaded the larger trend toward alternative investments, foundations and endowments have also been prominent hedge fund investors. In recent years, corporate pension funds, too, have increasingly looked to hedge funds as a way to reduce their overall portfolio risks. Weyerhauser, Eastman Kodak, and IBM are among the growing list of corporate investors that have set allocations to hedge funds. From their point of view, however, hedge funds pose one serious problem. The hedge fund industry simply cannot absorb the many billions in assets that corporate investors throw around. This is because many hedge fund strategies are most successful when applied to a relatively modest volume of assets—say, up to $500 million or so. This effectively keeps many institutions from investing anything more than a tiny fraction of their portfolios in hedge funds, if they do it at all. But this translates into an *advantage* for affluent individual investors, who continue to dominate this sector, accounting for an estimated 80 percent of hedge fund assets under management today.

WHAT THE NUMBERS SHOW

Given the events of the past few years, it's fair to question whether any of these hedge fund investors really knew what they were getting into. In the late 1990s, the global markets were buffeted by financial crises in Asia, Brazil, and Russia. A number of hedge funds tallied spectacular losses, some folding entirely. And all this culminated in the infamous mega-meltdown of Long-Term Capital Management. While history shows that traditional investment management has failed to protect investors' capital during market downturns, the obvious question is whether hedge funds have done any better.

In fact, the evidence suggests that they have. During the third quarter of 1998, for example, when the average equity mutual fund fell 15 percent, the average hedge fund fell just 6.1 percent, as measured by the Van U.S. Hedge Fund Index. More importantly, the Van U.S. Hedge Fund Index was still *up* 1.9 percent for the first nine months of the year, while the average domestic stock fund was down 7.1 percent. And in 1994, the most recent calendar year in which the average domestic stock mutual fund posted a loss, falling 2.2 percent, the Van U.S. Hedge Fund Index gained 1.4 percent. These are by no means isolated examples, as we'll see in Chapter 5, which reviews the performance record of hedge funds in some detail.

But the nagging question remains: What about LTCM? If some hedge funds sustain huge losses, how can hedge funds be held out as a source of consistently positive returns? The answer is that LTCM is just one out of more than six thousand hedge funds. As we shall see in the next chapter, hedge funds are an extraordinarily diverse investment category. Indeed, many hedge funds have little in common beyond their legal structure. Judging all hedge funds by the experience of Long-Term Capital Management is like judging an ethnic group by the behavior of any one member.

A DIFFERENT DRUMMER

The more you know about hedge funds, the more you discover that within this very broad investment category are opportunities to earn consistent, attractive returns with safe and liquid investments. While some hedge funds pursue exotic niche strategies incomprehensible to anyone without an advanced degree in mathematics and others invest in highly risky securities, many hedge funds invest in precisely the same kinds of stocks and bonds traditional investment managers choose—only hedge funds do it in different ways.

One fundamental difference is that conservative hedge fund managers invest with an eye to earning absolute returns, regardless of what the market is doing. And for high-net-worth investors, that can make all the difference in the world.

PART II

WHAT HEDGE FUNDS HAVE TO OFFER

Chapter **4**

What Exactly *Is* a Hedge Fund, Anyway?

One of the ironies of hedge funds is that they're run by people who are often described as brilliant and who have mounted some of the most intellectually sophisticated investment strategies conceivable. Yet collectively they have failed to produce a widely accepted definition of the very investment vehicle they use. The result is that hedge funds are known more for their mystique and mythology than anything else—a state of affairs that runs counter to the interests of investors and hedge fund managers alike.

Many investors who could benefit from hedge funds are missing out because they think this realm of investing is too speculative, too exotic, too pricey, or too controversial. And hedge fund managers are missing out because they're getting less attention from prospective investors than they deserve. Whenever the stock market is rocked by some financial crisis or goes into extreme gyrations, it seems as though hedge funds get at least part of the blame, even though the aggregate assets of all the hedge funds in the world don't match the dollars invested with the nation's half-dozen largest mutual funds.

GROWING POPULARITY

The origins of the hedge fund mystique are clear. For many years, hedge funds were part of a distant, rarefied landscape populated by very, very rich people. Some had old money, some had new money, but they all had lots of it. To paraphrase Ernest Hemingway's famous remark to F. Scott Fitzgerald, the rich were very different from you and me; they invested in hedge funds.

But all that has changed in recent years. As I explained in the previous chapter, more and more institutional investors are putting money into hedge funds. And although hedge funds are not exactly being sold at the corner market, there has been an equally dramatic surge in the number of individual investors, many of whom are affluent without being superrich.

One reason for this has been the growing media interest in hedge fund activities. Who hasn't heard of George Soros, the brilliant and audacious hedge fund manager who bet billions on the British pound and the Japanese yen in his high-flying currency plays? Or Julian Robertson, who in 1999 was labeled "one of the 20 most powerful people on Wall Street" by *Worth* magazine? Or Jeff Vinik, the hedge fund manager whose ignominious fall from grace at Fidelity obscured a stellar record. Over the prior 10 years he achieved "an average 29 percent per year return with scarcely any down quarters," according to a recent issue of *Forbes*—a track record eclipsing that of *every* mutual fund.

These days, the media have good reason to see hedge funds in a more positive light. As the century came to a close, memories of Long-Term Capital Management's 1998 blowup were superseded by reports of strong 1999 results from many hedge funds. In a March 2000 article entitled "Hedge Funds: An Industry Comes of Age," *Bloomberg* magazine trumpeted the "stellar results delivered by the hedge fund industry" in 1999 and noted that "striking returns" were achieved by hedge funds across many investment categories. The cause for their enthusiasm could be seen in black and white: The Hennessee Hedge Fund Index rose 32.6 percent for the year, far outpacing the S&P 500's 21 percent gain.

So it's little wonder that affluent individuals and institutions alike are channeling assets into hedge funds at an accelerating pace. As a headline in the February 7, 2000 edition of *Pensions & Investments* put it, "Hedge funds are back and everybody has to have one."

SEEING PAST THE MYTHS

Despite all the good press hedge funds have been receiving of late, the reality remains that even among dedicated readers of *Barron's*, *Forbes*, or the

Wall Street Journal, there are probably very few investors who can accurately explain what hedge funds are all about. Even among actual hedge fund investors, many have taken the plunge clueless as to what strategy the fund is pursuing or what risks are being incurred. Yet many of those who could benefit from hedge funds steer clear, either because they lack sufficient information or because they're scared off by hedge funds' reputation for high-octane investing.

Hedge funds *are* confusing. For starters, the industry has its own jargon—a kind of "hedge-fund-speak" that's almost incomprehensible to the uninitiated. Attend any hedge fund conference and you'll hear spirited debates over such topics as "high-water marks," "drawdowns," and "hurdle rates."

In their structure, hedge funds are completely different from the mutual funds familiar to millions of investors. Hedge funds domiciled in the United States usually take the form of a limited partnership; those based outside the United States (known as "offshore funds") may be set up as corporations or investment companies and may be listed on stock exchanges.

And in terms of the strategies they pursue, hedge funds come in a dizzying array of flavors. In comparison with the me-too approach characteristic of mutual funds, hedge funds operate in a free enterprise zone where managers can pursue virtually any strategy they might choose or devise. Some hedge funds are exotic, investing in distressed securities, emerging-country debt, or arcane forms of arbitrage. Others are fairly plain-vanilla, investing in domestic, publicly traded securities. They may be specialized niche or sector players, or make a handful of concentrated bets across many industries. In fact, there are probably almost as many hedge fund strategies as there are hedge fund managers.

A STRUCTURE, NOT A STRATEGY

So there's good reason for all the confusion. While the attributes of 401(k) plans, IRAs, and assorted other investment vehicles are rigorously defined by law, there is no standard legal or regulatory definition of a hedge fund.

The single most important thing for investors to understand is that the term "hedge fund" refers not to the investment *strategy* a manager pursues, but rather the investment *structure* that is used. Hedge funds are private, limited partnerships restricted to "accredited" investors, meaning folks with substantial means.

Because they are private—that is, not offered to the general public—hedge funds as a rule don't come under the spotlight of the U.S. Securities and Exchange Commission (SEC). They have the freedom to invest in whatever they choose and to employ nontraditional investment techniques that mainstream money managers either can't or typically don't employ, either because of regulatory constraints or investor perceptions. Moreover, the majority of hedge funds are philosophically oriented toward absolute returns, opting out of the relative performance game.

The more you know about hedge funds and their history, the more you discover that the image of flamboyant, dice-tossing speculation is the exception, not the rule. The fact is, the very concept of hedge investing grew out of an effort to *lower* investment risk.

A PIONEERING APPROACH

What is generally considered to be the first hedge fund was created on January 1, 1949, by Alfred Winslow Jones, a decidedly unlikely financial pioneer. Jones had dabbled in everything from diplomacy to journalism before starting his fund, and his views led some people to label him a socialist.

A. W. Jones was born into an American family in Melbourne, Australia, and came to the United States when he was four. After graduating from Harvard in 1923, he traveled widely as a steamship purser. In the early 1930s, he served as a vice consul at a U.S. embassy, and during the Spanish Civil War he reported on civilian relief efforts for the Quakers. In 1941, Jones received a Ph.D. in sociology from Columbia University, and his dissertation, *Life, Liberty and Property*, became a widely used sociology text. During much of the 1940s, Jones was an editor at *Fortune*, and he also wrote for its sister publication, *Time*, and other magazines.

The genesis of Jones's next career—as a fund manager—seems to have been the research he did for an article published in the March 1949 issue of *Fortune* entitled "Fashions in Forecasting." Jones was struck by the fact that every Wall Street expert he interviewed said it was impossible to predict the market's direction with any consistency. For Jones, the light-bulb went on.

Intrigued by the forecasters' lack of success, Jones set out to create an investment strategy that would largely take market direction out of the picture, so that performance would depend primarily on stock-picking skills. His idea was brilliant in its simplicity. Jones systematically balanced long investments in undervalued stocks with short positions in overvalued stocks. In this way, he effectively neutralized his market exposure and hence his risk. He also applied moderate leverage to further increase profit potential on the long side.

These techniques weren't original in themselves; what *was* unique, though, was the way in which he combined them. Jones's innovation was to take two tools that had been used mainly for speculative purposes—short selling and leverage—and merge them to create a fundamentally *conservative* investment approach designed to systematically produce positive returns in both up and down markets.

NEUTRALIZING THE RISK

Consider the basic idea of short selling—something traditional managers generally shun. Confining themselves to the long side of the market, traditional managers buy a stock at $30 and hope to sell it at some point in the future for $40, $50, or more. But what if you find a stock that's selling at $30 that seems poised for a fall—maybe a big fall?

Short selling is a way to take advantage of that insight. It operates much as long investing does, only in reverse. In simplest terms, to short a stock you sell shares that you don't own, but "borrow" from a brokerage firm, with the expectation of buying the same stock later at a lower price. You subsequently close out the transaction by buying shares on the open market and using them to replace the borrowed ones you sold. If the stock has declined in price, as you hoped, you make money. But if the position goes against you and the stock you shorted has gone up in price, then of course you lose money when you close out the trade.

This may sound risky—and it is, if you sell short *exclusively*. But that's not what we're talking about here. Jones used short selling to hedge a long portfolio against a general market decline, applying stock-picking skills to make profits on both the long and short sides.

Leverage is likewise a double-edged sword, enabling an investor to compound the results of an investment for better or for worse. Assume, for instance, that you invest $1,000 to buy 100 shares of a $10 stock. If the stock goes up to $12, you've made a 20 percent return. But if you had borrowed and invested another $1,000, you'd have boosted your return to 40 percent (minus transaction fees and interest on the borrowed funds) without putting any more of your own capital at stake. If your investment declines in value, the use of leverage will boost your losses, too: You'll owe all the money you've borrowed plus the additional loss.

Before Jones came along, short selling was used largely by speculators and not by serious, respectable investors. Similarly, leverage was seen as a speculative way of achieving higher returns while adding a layer of risk. Jones's breakthrough was to perceive that a basket of shorted stocks could serve as a hedge against a drop in the overall market. He also saw that a skilled investor who had taken steps to control market risk could afford to apply a judicious amount of leverage, thereby netting even more return from good stock picks. (See Table 4.1.)

Jones recognized that there are two primary sources of risk in an equity portfolio: stock selection and market risk. He designed his system to maximize the impact of stock selection and limit the impact of market risk. The central thesis of Jones's investment approach can be summed up in this formula:

$$Net\ market\ exposure\ (\%) = \frac{Long\ exposure - Short\ exposure}{Capital}$$

But to understand fully how Jones's system worked, it's best to use an example. Say you start with $1,000 in capital. Using Jones's techniques, you would borrow some money—say, $100—so you could purchase shares valued at $1,100. But then you would also short shares valued at $400.

So while your gross investment would be $1,500 (the $1,100 long position plus the $400 short position) or 150 percent of your capital, your net market exposure would be only $700 ($1,100 minus $400). Thus, your portfolio would be 70 percent "net long." This means that only 70 percent

Table 4.1   **Why Short Selling + Leverage = Lower Market Risk**

$100 original investment + $25 leveraged buys	$125 long investments − $75 short investments
$125 long investments + $75 short investments	$50 net market exposure (which equals 50% of capital)
$200 market opportunities	

of your portfolio would be exposed to an overall market decline. Furthermore, in the event of a general downturn, the gains from your short positions would help offset the losses from your long investments.

But this is not to say that Jones tried to take market trends entirely out of the equation. Although he valued stock picking over market timing, he did not seek to completely neutralize his market exposure by equally balancing long and short positions. Rather, he increased or decreased his net market exposure based on his assessment of the strength or weakness of the market.

For instance, in the example just described, $700 of the total $1,500 in investments is unhedged, while $800 is "inside the hedge" ($400 in long investments balanced by $400 in short positions). The hedged portion of the portfolio is constructed so that it is market neutral, meaning long positions offset short ones no matter which way the market moves.

THE BEGINNING OF A TREND

The Jones fund was innovative in one additional way: It used an incentive fee structure by which Jones earned 20 percent of the profits he generated for his investors. Also noteworthy is that Jones was philosophically committed to investing his personal assets in his fund, and always reinvested his own profits and fees. In this way, his interests were completely aligned with those of his investors—a legacy that shapes the way hedge funds operate today.

Jones organized his fund as a private partnership in order to have maximum latitude and flexibility in constructing its portfolio. He set up the fund as a general partnership in January 1949 and three years later converted it to a limited partnership. Jones also went on to hire other portfolio managers, each of whom had responsibility for a portion of the overall portfolio. And the company continued after his death, under the leadership of his son-in-law, Robert L. Burch III.

After A. W. Jones created the first hedge fund in 1949, others began adopting the private partnership model he had used, although the industry grew slowly at first. In the mid-1950s, other incentive-based partnerships sprang up, including one called Buffett Partners, a fund set up in Omaha by a youthful investor named Warren Buffett. (Wonder what ever happened to him?) But it's important to note that not all of these so-called hedge funds actually hedged their investments in the sense that Jones did.

Many of these new funds used long-only strategies that owed more to Graham & Dodd than to A. W. Jones.

Jones, meanwhile, operated out of the limelight for some 17 years, but ultimately was acknowledged as the founding father of the hedge fund industry. In an April 1966 *Fortune* article entitled, "The Jones Nobody Keeps Up With," Carol J. Loomis reported that even after Jones's incentive fees, over the previous five years his fund had soundly trounced the Fidelity Trend Fund, the best-performing mutual fund for that period, by 44 percent. And over the previous 10 years, it had beaten the Dreyfus Fund, the best-performing mutual fund for that period, by an astounding 87 percent! The Loomis article sparked a surge of interest in hedge funds on the part of both investors and money managers, as the former saw the potential for attractive returns and the latter a chance to be richly rewarded for their investment skills.

THE BOOM YEARS

It took a few more years, however, before the hedge fund industry really took off. In the early 1960s, total hedge fund assets under management stood at about $2 billion, according to Cerulli Associates, and by the end of the 1960s, when George Soros created his Quantum Fund, there were still fewer than 150 hedge funds. But by 1990 there were nearly 2,000 hedge funds with total assets of more than $45 billion. By 1997, according to Cerulli, hedge fund assets reportedly surpassed $300 billion.

Of course, since hedge funds are exempt from registration requirements, all the available figures on hedge funds must be taken as estimates, and the estimates vary widely. As shown in Figure 4.1, according to Hedge Fund Research, the worldwide hedge fund market has grown from approximately $39 billion in 1990 to just over $475 billion at the middle of 2000. Early in 2000, Cerulli estimated the number of hedge funds at 6,100 and their total assets under management at more than $355 billion. Other sources estimate total hedge fund assets at anywhere from $300 billion to over $400 billion. On one thing all the sources agree: Hedge funds have become a major industry unto themselves.

TODAY'S HEDGE FUNDS

However many thousands of hedge funds have been created, they all owe a debt to Alfred Winslow Jones—some because they have adopted various

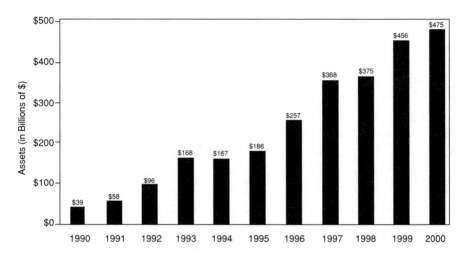

Figure 4.1 **Growth of Total Hedge Fund Assets 1990–2000**
Source: Hedge Fund Research, Inc. 1990–1999 data as of December 31; 2000 data as of June 30.

elements of his strategy, others because they have used the same partner-ship structure. But because hedge funds have evolved with few legislative or regulatory constraints, over the years they have branched out in many different directions. Thus, Jones's successors have used his structure and approach as a jumping-off point, adapting and modifying it to pursue an almost endless variety of investment strategies.

All hedge funds do, however, have certain characteristics in com-mon. First, they continue to be *private* investment vehicles. They are not offered for sale to the general public, and are therefore exempt from many SEC requirements. Operating on the assumption that investors of sub-stantial means are capable of evaluating investment risk, the SEC gives hedge funds more latitude than, say, mutual funds, because they are de-signed specifically for "sophisticated" investors, not the man (or woman) on the street.

Despite their overall exemption, hedge funds must nonetheless sat-isfy certain disclosure requirements in offering their securities (something we'll discuss in detail in Chapter 11), and they must comply with SEC an-tifraud provisions and state solicitation rules.

But there is a trade-off for hedge funds' relative freedom from regu-lators. Because they are not registered with the SEC, hedge funds are prohibited from advertising or broadly marketing their products. This means that they become known primarily by referrals and reputation.

What hedge funds gain in the bargain is broad discretion over what they invest in and how. Hedge funds are free to take both long and short positions, to concentrate assets in a small number of holdings, and to use leverage to any degree they choose. Unlike mutual funds, which are highly regulated and restricted in their use of nontraditional investment tools, hedge funds can invest in a wide array of markets using virtually any investment strategy. Of course, a hedge fund is under no compulsion to employ any of these tools. It may completely avoid leverage, steer clear of derivatives, or run the kind of broadly diversified, long-only portfolio associated with mutual funds. The point is that hedge fund managers have all these tools at their disposal, and the freedom to use them as they wish.

In his book, *Pioneering Portfolio Management,* Yale endowment chief investment officer David F. Swensen explains the value of nontraditional investment techniques:

> Market efficiency drives returns on market-like portfolios to the average, causing conventional portfolios with conventional ideas to produce conventional results, a poor outcome for active investment managers. . . . Excess returns stem from out-of-the-mainstream positions that achieve recognition in startling surprise to ordinary market observers. By identifying the unexpected consequence before it occurs, successful investment managers realize superior returns from exploiting superior insights.

AN EXCLUSIVE CLUB

One way that hedge funds *are* restricted is in the number and type of investors they can accept. Section 3(c)(1) of the Investment Company Act of 1940, which regulates investment advisers, exempts investment funds that do not make a "public offering" and have fewer than 100 investors. Hedge funds not only limit themselves to 99 investors, but are also open only to "accredited" investors as defined by Regulation D. For many years, accredited investors were defined as individuals with an income of $200,000 a year for the past two years ($300,000 per year for couples) and a reasonable expectation of continuing to earn that amount in the future. Alternatively, individuals can be "accredited" if they have a net worth of at least $1 million; for institutions, that accreditation threshold is $5 million.

In 1996, however, the National Securities Markets Improvement Act was enacted, creating a second set of standards. Section 3(c)(7) of the Investment Company Act stipulates that partnerships can have up to 499 investors so long as each individual is "qualified" by having a *liquid* net worth of at least $5 million. To participate in these larger funds, institutions must have at least $25 million in assets.

I should point out that the concept of relaxing regulation for vehicles limited to "accredited" or "qualified" investors is employed in other contexts, and not just for hedge funds. Certain other securities offered only to investors of substantial means are also exempt from various registration and disclosure requirements, such as certain bonds issued in the United States by foreign entities.

THE PRICE OF ENTRY

Even if there weren't accreditation requirements limiting hedge fund investments to the wealthy, the funds' own account minimums would have the same effect. Hedge funds virtually all require what most would consider a high account minimum—sometimes as low as $250,000, but more often $500,000 or $1 million. That's a far cry from mutual fund minimums, which are often $1,000 and may be as low as $250. And for hedge funds, a $1 million minimum isn't even considered all that high; managers with established track records commonly set minimums of $2 million or even more.

A fledgling hedge fund may open its doors with a minimum on the bottom rung of this scale, say $250,000. But once the fund has one or two successful years under its belt, it will inevitably raise the minimum to at least $500,000, if not more. And why not? If your ultimate goal is to run a hedge fund with $100 million in assets and you're limited to 99 investors, realistically, you can't get there with a $250,000 minimum, even with spectacular performance.

But that's not to say there are no alternatives for those who just want to get a toe in the water. Investors wishing to invest smaller amounts can often participate through various "feeder fund" structures or funds of funds, which pool assets from a number of investors to meet the minimum hedge fund requirements.

Hedge funds also limit the times when investors can get in or out—

another difference from mutual funds, which are "open-ended," meaning investors can buy new shares or sell existing shares back to the fund at the current net asset value at any time. In contrast to this "continuous offering," hedge funds open to new investors only at specified intervals, such as once each quarter. Moreover, while most mutual funds try to attract as much money as possible, hedge funds often reach a targeted dollar amount and then permanently close to new investors, since their goal is to *optimize* performance.

And as far as U.S.-based hedge funds are concerned, investors can only redeem their interests by selling them back to the partnership under procedures spelled out in the fund's offering documents. (This does not hold true, however, for many offshore hedge funds, whose shares may be listed on stock exchanges and traded like those of a public company.)

There's one more limit placed on the liquidity of hedge fund investments: Many funds impose an initial "lock-up period," typically one year in length, during which shares cannot be redeemed without a penalty fee. After that, most hedge funds permit the withdrawal of funds on a quarterly basis; however, there may be a "notice period" of as much as 60 days required before the investor can actually redeem funds. This practice evolved because some hedge funds invest in thinly traded securities and private placements, and therefore cannot always generate cash on short notice. Similarly, because their holdings may not be "marked to market" every day as by law mutual fund holdings must be, some funds specify that investors who decide to withdraw all of their funds will initially get back only 90 percent of their estimated value, with the remaining 10 percent held back until the fund's audit is completed.

Because most U.S.-based hedge funds are organized as limited partnerships, the tax consequences of any investments flow through to the investor. This means that all tax-related events, such as realized capital gains or losses, will figure into each investor's own tax calculations. So unlike mutual funds, hedge funds do not have any "embedded" capital gains liability. This raises questions of tax efficiency for investors, which we'll address in later chapters.

WHO INVESTS?

Because of hedge funds' high investment minimums and somewhat restricted liquidity, the universe of hedge fund investors is essentially limited to two groups: high-net-worth families and institutional investors. By far the largest group of hedge fund investors is comprised of affluent individuals, who currently account for more than 80 percent of hedge fund assets. Until the end of the 1980s, investors in hedge funds were almost exclusively high-net-worth investors. In the 1990s, however, this circle began to expand as institutional investors started to participate in hedge funds. And while hedge funds have attracted their share of mega-rich clients, today their prime market—high-net-worth families—includes many executives and professionals who definitely qualify as affluent but wouldn't be considered fabulously wealthy by today's standards.

Given U.S. demographic trends, it's not surprising that hedge funds have been booming. According to Charles Schwab Corp., there are now 6.1 million American households with a net worth of $1 million to $5 million, and over the past five years this group has grown at a rate of 40 percent annually.

A DIFFERENT KIND OF INCENTIVE

A key area of contrast between hedge funds and traditional money management is fee structure. If you run a mutual fund, for example, the way you succeed is by attracting assets—the more, the better. Traditional management fees are calculated as a percentage of the amount of assets under management, regardless of how well or how poorly your investments perform.

Hedge fund managers charge an asset-based fee, too, typically 1 to 2 percent per year. But that's not where the real motivation lies. For hedge funds, the principal source of compensation is the annual performance fee, a charge that's typically 20 percent of the profits. This incentive fee, often called the "carried interest" or "carry," is usually paid quarterly, but sometimes annually.

Hefty as a 20 percent performance fee may sound, it still has to be earned. Sometimes hedge funds specify a "hurdle rate"—a level of return that must be achieved before the manager's profit participation begins to kick in; often the Treasury bill rate is used. Another common provision is for a "high-water mark," which stipulates that if managers incur net losses in a given year, they must recoup those losses before they begin earning their performance fee the following year.

The performance-fee system has more implications than one might think. One consequence is that talented hedge fund managers don't have to run billions of dollars to do well. That's an extremely important point, given the fact that many investment strategies are most successful when applied to a smaller account base rather than a very large one. The mutual fund industry is rife with examples of managers whose outstanding success eventually led to failure, as their funds attracted more assets than the manager could effectively handle. The larger the fund, the more liquidity becomes an issue and the more limited the universe of stocks suitable for investment. So in money management, at least, smaller is often better. That's why topflight money managers will leave high-profile mutual funds with billions in assets in order to run their own hedge funds, often opening their doors with only modest amounts of money to manage.

For their part, sophisticated investors often like the idea of a fee structure with incentives built in. They don't mind paying someone a share of whatever profits they're getting, recognizing that with performance-based fees, what they're paying for is results. Think about it: Managers do well only when investors are doing well, and investors naturally get the lion's share of the returns.

Of course, the way hedge fund managers become truly wealthy is by making handsome returns on their own money—that is, by being their own clients. While the size of their investments may vary widely, the general partners in a hedge fund *always* commit a substantial share of their personal wealth to their own funds. This is in sharp contrast to mutual funds, where members of the board of directors often have only a nominal investment in the fund, and no one expects individual fund managers to invest alongside their shareholders.

With hedge funds, the general partners share in both the upside potential and the downside risks. The fact that the financial interests of the fund's general partners and their investors are closely aligned makes their relationship a true partnership. And while even the most successful mutual fund managers are usually employees of a fund management company—hired hands, if you will—most hedge fund professionals are owner/entrepreneurs.

In fact, you could sum up the differences by saying that hedge funds are far more entrepreneurial than any mutual fund. While mutual fund complexes are often giant organizations with their own hierarchy (and bureaucracy), most hedge funds operate with staffs of only a dozen or so people. And when a star manager leaves a high-paying mutual fund job, it's often to set up shop as a hedge fund—the one place where you can do things your own way and control your own destiny.

Swensen observes that "small, independent firms reside at the opposite end of the spectrum from large subsidiaries of financial service conglomerates," drawing a clear contrast between the two:

> By pursuing safety and avoiding controversy, bueaucratic structures systematically screen out the market opportunities likely to yield superior returns. Bureaucracies deal poorly with the constantly changing market environment, failing to address even elementary active investment management problems.

In Swensen's view, the advantage of smaller, more entrepreneurial firms is that they "emphasize people, putting plans and structures in a secondary position." His conclusion:

> Small independent firms with excellent people focused on a well-defined market segment provide the highest likelihood of identifying the intelligent contrarian path necessary to achieving excellent investment results.

On Wall Street the "talent flight" from big investment firms to upstart hedge funds happens every day; yet there's very little, if any, flow of people going in the other direction. What makes hedge funds such a magnet for skilled investment talent isn't just the money; it's the chance to "stand up and be counted" and be rewarded based on the results. When you invest in a hedge fund, it's that entrepreneurial drive that you're really paying for.

BEHIND CLOSED DOORS

Central to the hedge fund mythology is their image of being secretive, with their dealings and methods held strictly under wraps—and this is one aspect of the myth that's not entirely wrong. Unlike mutual funds and other investment products that are sold to the general public and governed by extensive disclosure requirements, hedge funds are under no obligation to tell the world what they're doing. They're subject to only minimal reporting standards, and it's not as though you can look up their price in your morning newspaper. A hedge fund often reports performance only on a quarterly basis, and even a fund's own investors may not be able to learn the exact nature of its current investments.

Hedge funds usually do report their top 10 holdings and show the sector weightings for the overall portfolio. They may also indicate what percentage of their investments is held in long versus short positions. But hedge funds never, ever report their specific short positions for an eminently sensible reason: Other investors could make hay with that information, goosing the price of a shorted stock, thereby forcing the fund to buy it back at a higher price and potentially incur a major loss.

Moreover, some hedge funds pursue proprietary strategies that they are loath to share with other investors. Remember, their sole competitive advantage comes from their intellectual property—the unique set of decision rules, instruments, models, and strategies that they've evolved and must safeguard at any cost, just as the formula for Coca-Cola is locked away in a vault rather than emblazoned on each bottle.

Then too, some hedge funds make rapid and sizable movements in and out of thinly traded securities. In such cases, secrecy is imperative to avoid front-running by other investors. Knowledge of a fund's intentions could have a significant impact on the prices at which the fund is able to buy or sell securities.

So if hedge funds tend to be closemouthed, it's not only due to the lack of disclosure requirements. It's also because their investment results could be seriously undercut if their methodology were widely known. Hedge funds must also avoid running afoul of the SEC by offering any public comments or disseminating any information that might be construed as a come-on to potential investors—that is, marketing.

In addition, hedge funds often cater to wealthy families who are assiduously shy of publicity. Dependent on word of mouth and referrals to attract new investors, hedge funds avoid any appearance of being loose-lipped. So they tend to be as quiet about their investors as they are about their investments.

A DISTINCT CULTURE

It all adds up to a culture that's very different from what you'll find in mainstream money management firms. Mutual funds, for instance, have a *marketing* culture—the more money they bring in, the more fees the management company collects. So with few exceptions, mutual funds continually seek new money, either from current investors or from new ones. While there may be limits to how much money can, in fact, be successfully deployed with certain strategies, as we've noted, relatively few mutual funds seem to worry about little things like that.

So how do mutual funds attract more money? Usually by achieving high visibility among the general public. Good performance certainly plays a role; an additional star in the Morningstar ratings can lead to millions of new dollars coming in the door. But so does heavy advertising and extensive public relations efforts. Being part of a well-known family of funds, such as Fidelity, Vanguard, or Janus also helps; branding is just as important to the mutual fund business as it is to the purveyors of consumer goods. That's why the mutual fund industry spends as much as $1 billion a year on advertising. This does not include such marketing efforts as direct mail, literature, and promotions, which are also hugely expensive, or the enormous fees paid by funds for "shelf space" in mutual fund supermarkets.

In contrast, hedge funds have a *performance* culture. It's the investment returns—not the flow of new money—that drives compensation for hedge fund managers. And they raise additional assets largely through the discreet dissemination of their track records through a small community of sophisticated investors, consultants, and financial advisers. With no need to reach the general public, they focus on that very small segment who are willing and able to invest six- or seven-figure sums on the basis of a strong reputation and a compelling story. And remember, because they have only 99—or at most, 499—investor slots to fill, they can be selective in deciding whose money they accept.

GROWING VISIBILITY

But as the number of affluent American households continues to grow and the market for hedge funds broadens, hedge funds are becoming more visible. *Barron's*, for instance, runs excellent, substantive interviews with hedge fund managers as a regular feature. And in the wake of the Long-Term Capital Management collapse in 1998, there are encouraging signs that the hedge fund industry has become more willing to offer greater transparency.

For example, in December 1999, the *Financial Times* began offering "near real-time information on the performance and risk profile of hedge funds" through a new web-based service called PlusFunds.com, with the sponsorship of Standard & Poor's and Ernst & Young. The *Financial Times* described this service as an attempt "by the hedge fund industry to increase the data it gives investors, while keeping the detailed breakdown of their portfolios secret." Initially, only 35 hedge funds had agreed to disclose information to PlusFunds.com, but its executives predict that those numbers will grow, partly because fund-of-funds managers will pressure the funds in which they invest to participate. As Ben Borton of Hedge Fund Research recently told one reporter, "We are seeing more managers willing to provide more information about their strategies, portfolio holdings, and risk-management processes."

Another recent development has been the creation of hedge fund indexes. In 1999, Tremont Advisers teamed up with Credit Suisse First Boston to create the CSFB/Tremont Hedge Fund Index, and in February 2000, Hedge Fund Research launched another index with Zurich Capital Markets. While not likely to steal any thunder from the Dow Jones Industrial Average, the S&P 500, or the Russell 2000, these indexes will shine a bit more light on the industry.

Historically, it's an industry that has operated without the usual professional trappings of associations, conventions, and newsletters. That, too, is changing. The Hedge Fund Association was formed in autumn 1997, providing a forum through which members can take collective action to burnish their image and put forth accurate information on their industry. One of the first things the association did was to create an Internet site at www.thehfa.org.

Thus, bit by bit, the veils that have obscured the truth about hedge funds are lifting, and many of the old myths are fading in the light of day.

SOURCES OF INFORMATION

When seeking information, it should be noted that there is no one official source that collects and interprets hedge fund statistics. As a result, a cottage industry has emerged to fill this gap. The three most widely used providers of databases are Hedge Fund Research (HFR) in Chicago, Managed Account Reports in New York, and TASS International Research, a London-based division of Tremont Advisers. And there are some other groups that collect their own statistics, such as the Hennessee Group in New York and Van Hedge Fund Advisors International in Nashville. But many sources, such as Boston-based Cerulli Associates, get their primary data from the three main collectors.

One caveat to prospective investors is essential: The quality of any hedge fund data is open to question. Its value depends on how willing hedge funds are to provide timely and accurate information, and whether data collectors independently verify the information they are given.

In an essay entitled "Technology's Impact on Hedge Fund Investing," Stephen McMenamin of the Jefferies Group quoted Nocola Meaden, chief executive officer of TASS International Research, who said, "The big players reluctantly give us their numbers. We have seven people who make outgoing calls to remind them. You might say we are professional naggers." (McMenamin's essay may be found in *Evaluating and Implementing Hedge Fund Strategies*, published in London in 1999 by Euromoney Books.)

In some cases, the reluctance of hedge funds to report on their holdings, returns, or policies reflects inertia; in other cases, there may be an aversion to providing information when funds are doing poorly. All in all, the supply of information about the hedge fund universe is vastly smaller than the information flow in most other parts of the financial world.

SNAPSHOT OF THE INDUSTRY

Measured against the colossal scale of traditional money management, it's clear that hedge funds still occupy just one tiny corner of the investment universe. Today an estimated 6,100 hedge funds exist worldwide—yet that's far less than the number of mutual funds in the United States alone. At the beginning of 2000, it was estimated that hedge funds had some $355 billion in total assets under management—but that's less than the combined holdings of the half-dozen largest U.S. mutual funds.

Still, looking at the industry itself, the picture that emerges is one of rapid and dynamic growth. The recent explosion in the number of hedge funds reflects developments on both the supply side and the demand side. An upsurge in personal wealth, much of it generated by dot-com and other technology companies and by history's longest-running bull market, has greatly expanded the ranks of high-net-worth households, the principal source of hedge fund capital. And as I noted earlier, many institutional investors have turned to alternative investments, including hedge funds, as a way to expand their opportunity set.

On the supply side, there has been no shortage of investment managers eager to launch or join hedge fund organizations, thanks to the independence and the potential rewards they offer. Meanwhile, the major Wall Street brokerage firms that serve as "prime brokers" for hedge funds have made it easier to establish new funds. Prime brokers such as Morgan Stanley, Goldman Sachs and Salomon Smith Barney play an important role in the industry; not only do they finance transactions, they also compare, match, process, and settle trades for hedge funds that trade at more than one securities firm. Stephen McMenamin noted in his essay on technology's impact on hedge fund investing:

> Prime brokers have helped lower the barriers to partnership formation in offering "hedge funds in a box" solutions. A number of firms facilitate the process of setting up and running a hedge fund by offering office space, infrastructure, partnership documents, information tools and easy payment in the form of soft dollars.

He adds:

> Prime brokers have responded to the industry's rapid growth by developing expertise in reconciling exotic instruments, such as derivatives, swaps and private placements, and in offering custom-made reporting services that reflect a hedge fund's unique strategy.

A LOW PROFILE

While hedge funds now number in the thousands, as of the end of 1999 only 10 hedge fund managers had more than $2 billion of assets under management. Thus, most hedge funds are relatively small compared to mutual funds. According to Cerulli Associates, the average hedge fund had $58 million in assets at the middle of 1999, which was an all-time record. Cerulli further reports that more than 84 percent of all hedge funds had less than $100 million in unleveraged assets. And only 2.5 percent of U.S. hedge funds had more than $500 million under management.

Given the small size of most hedge funds, it is not surprising that even sophisticated investors are often hard-pressed to name even one hedge fund manager beyond the handful who've been most prominent in the press, notably George Soros, Julian Robertson, and Michael Steinhardt. There's Jeff Vinik, who's known largely because he managed Fidelity's giant Magellan Fund before he left to start his own hedge fund. And there's John W. Meriwether, the former Salomon Brothers bond-trading wizard who headed Long-Term Capital Management.

But by and large, hedge funds are run by little-known, albeit highly skilled and experienced managers investing relatively small asset pools. Moreover, hedge fund organizations are unlikely to be prominent local employers, as the Vanguard mutual fund organization is in Valley Forge, Pennsylvania, nor big enough to be widely recognized and cheered on by their hometown, as the Janus mutual funds are in Denver. The typical hedge fund is just a handful of upper-middle-class men and women sitting in an unimposing suite of offices somewhere with a small, often generic-looking sign on the door ("Walnut Partners, LLP"). There are unlikely to be any neon signs, Little League sponsorships, or United Way chairmanships. These are organizations geared toward one thing: generating consistent, attractive returns for their limited partners and their own portfolios.

ALTERNATIVE VERSUS NONTRADITIONAL

A question that often comes up is: What's the difference between "alternative" investing and another frequently used term, "nontraditional" investing? Many sources use the terms "nontraditional" and "alternative" investments interchangeably. To me, nontraditional investment management is not simply anything that isn't traditional. Rather, it is a specific set of investment management ideas associated with alternative investments.

As Lookout Mountain Capital, an investment firm based near Chattanooga, Tennessee, explained in a 1999 report, "There are two basic schools of investment management," traditional and nontraditional, and these two "have evolved alongside one another with distinctly different fundamental assumptions, goals and structures." As detailed in Chapter 2, traditional money management is based on Modern Portfolio Theory (MPT), with its relative performance goal, its assumption that markets are efficient, and its premise that consistently beating the market over time is impossible without inordinate risk to capital. Traditional money management is also characterized by a fee structure based on the amount of assets under management.

By contrast, the Lookout Mountain report notes:

Nontraditional money management is not a subset of traditional money management, but rather a separate discipline based on the antithesis of MPT. It presumes that markets are saturated with inefficiencies, creating opportunity for increased investment performance *without increased risk to capital*. The principal goal of nontraditional money management is superior performance, and fees are usually weighted towards performance. Another significant difference is that the nontraditional money manager generally has the bulk of his personal assets at risk alongside his client's assets.

SUMMING UP

Given the structure and inherent flexibility of hedge funds, it's easy to see why they've attracted many of the best and brightest professional money managers—the very top echelon of investment talent in the world. Investing through hedge funds, they gain the freedom to manage money their own way plus the potential to be richly rewarded for their success. They aren't straitjacketed by the regulatory constraints and public relations requirements that can hobble mutual fund managers. And if they do well for their clients, there is no question that they will do very well for themselves.

The most important point for investors to understand is that hedge funds are fundamentally different from traditional money management firms. It's not just that hedge fund managers use different strategies and methods; they operate with a completely different mind-set. And the contrasts are dramatic. (See Table 4.2.)

Here are a few of the most important differences from traditional firms that the majority of hedge funds have in common. As a rule, they:

- *Strive to achieve high absolute returns.* They have both the motivation and the freedom to achieve that goal. This is almost the polar opposite of traditional managers who use prescribed tools and techniques to pursue a relative performance, beat-the-market objective.
- *Reject the notion that securities markets are highly efficient.* They do not accept the idea that achieving a small incremental return over the market averages is the best one can hope to do.

Table 4.2 **The Crucial Differences**

Traditional Investment Managers	Nontraditional Investment Managers
Relative performance objective: beat the market	Absolute return objective: achieve positive annual returns regardless of market direction
Success determined by market direction (long-only strategies are directionally dependent)	Success determined by manager skill (short selling can produce positive returns in down markets)
Invest in stocks, bonds, cash	Virtually unlimited investment options
Manage to a benchmark	Manage opportunistically
Equity managers tend to be 100% invested at all times ("Beat the market or you're fired!")	No pressure to be fully invested ("Whatever you do, don't lose my money!")
Asset-based fees (typically 50 to 75 basis points, but with heavy discounting)	Performance-based fees ("1 and 20" fee structure subject to a high-water mark; no discounts)
SEC prohibits managers from directly buying same stock as clients	General partners always invest alongside limited partners
Portfolio tailored to meet client needs, objectives, and guidelines	"My way or the highway"
Team approach	Star system
Clients hire a style	Clients hire a strategy
Stick to one's style disciplines no matter what; penalties for "style drift"	Do whatever it takes to make money; flexibility a plus
Investment process clearly spelled out	Investment process often hard to define ("Trust me")
Performance is style-driven (tends to cluster by style)	Manager skill drives performance (big gap between top and bottom performers)
Performance highly correlated with the market	Performance often has a low correlation with the market
Diversification is stressed (may produce closet indexing)	Positions often concentrated in sectors or industries
Easy to hire, easy to fire	Limited opportunities to enter partnership; liquidity varies, one-year lock-up often required
Slow to take profits and losses	Quick to pull the trigger
Work hard at good communications, seek media exposure	Limited communications, avoid the media

Rather, they believe the market offers abundant opportunities for creating wealth by perceiving what others do not. They might focus on emerging technologies, invest in themes that cut across traditional industry definitions, or capitalize on other investors' fears or misperceptions.

- **Have a different attitude toward risk.** Traditional managers get paid to invest with the mainstream, trying to *avoid* risk while participating in the long-term growth of the market. But hedge fund managers don't necessarily see risk as the enemy. Rather than trying to avoid risk, they work to *manage* it and even turn it to their advantage. In fact, the ability to take calculated risks on pockets of opportunity they perceive is one of the prime reasons hedge fund managers have the potential to earn superior returns.

- **Succeed by achieving outstanding returns.** Hedge fund managers get most of their financial rewards from performance fees and returns on their own personal investments in the funds they manage. In the traditional money management system, fees are driven by the amount of assets under management, regardless of performance. As Goldman Sachs put it in a 1995 report, *The Continuing Evolution of the Mutual Fund Industry*, "Managing money is not the true business of the money management industry. Rather, it is gathering and retaining assets.

- **Use a flexible, opportunistic investment style.** Traditional managers must maintain rigidly defined style disciplines at the insistence of institutional clients and consultants. To meet their absolute return objectives, hedge fund managers constantly adapt their strategies to the shifting realities of the marketplace.

- **Focus on avoiding losses above all.** To a traditional manager, the biggest worry is "benchmark risk"—that is, underperforming his or her benchmark. The primary concern of hedge fund managers is not losing money.

For all these reasons, conservative high-net-worth investors—those who don't want to bet their entire portfolios on the stock market's direction—may find that hedge fund investing is a great deal more attractive than it may initially seem.

Chapter 5

A Look at Hedge Fund Performance

All this talk about exploiting inefficiencies and generating absolute returns is fine, you might say, but where's the beef? How have hedge funds performed? What is it that they bring to a traditional, long-only portfolio? What about the risks? And just what is it that hedge funds actually *do*?

With 6,100 hedge funds that invest in a wide variety of instruments using a wide variety of strategies and markets, the answers to those questions aren't simple or clear-cut. But research does offer some perspective on the characteristics of hedge funds in the aggregate. For investors who want to know what kind of performance and what sorts of strategies might be available, this kind of overview is a good place to start, as long as you understand the limitations on what can be concluded from any such research. I'll give you some data first, and then we'll consider the caveats.

A BIG-PICTURE VIEW OF PERFORMANCE

Let's go back to the fundamental rationale for investing in hedge funds: It's a way to earn superior absolute returns that are not captive to trends in the capital markets. A wide variety of studies have been conducted to evaluate hedge fund performance, and their results suggest that the rationale holds up. I can't emphasize enough that each hedge fund strategy has

73

its own distinct risk/return characteristics. But if you're looking at this investment vehicle in the broadest possible terms, research generally confirms its appeal from a performance standpoint.

For instance, Professor Bing Liang of Case Western Reserve University recently conducted a study comparing hedge fund and mutual fund performance. Published in the July/August 1999 issue of the *Financial Analysts Journal* in an article titled "On the Performance of Hedge Funds," Professor Liang's analysis showed that:

> On a risk-adjusted basis, the average hedge fund outperformed the average mutual fund in the period January 1992 through December 1996; this performance difference cannot be explained by survivorship bias. Compared with mutual funds as a whole, hedge funds offer higher Sharpe ratios and better manager skills.

Professor Liang went on to conclude that "The performance superiority of hedge funds is probably attributable to effective incentive schemes, dynamic and flexible trading strategies, and the variety of financial instruments used by hedge funds."

A longer-term perspective is provided by Lee Hennessee, of the Hennessee Group in New York, who has been monitoring hedge fund investment results for a number of years. As shown in Figure 5.1, her Hennessee Hedge Fund Index has outperformed the S&P 500, an index of equity mutual funds, and the Russell 2000 over the 13-year period ended December 31, 1999.

Meanwhile, the International Monetary Fund also examined hedge funds in the late 1990s, based on concerns, after the LTCM "problem," that collectively hedge funds might have a deleterious impact on global financial systems. What the IMF found was attractive investment results. In its "Occasional Paper" titled "Hedge Funds and Financial Market Dynamics," the IMF concluded that "Over the 1990s, the average annual compound returns of the majority of hedge fund investments styles" have "handily exceeded those on the mature equity markets as measured by the Standard & Poor's 500 index and on the bond markets."

Sometimes the most useful studies are those which review and evaluate a number of existing analyses. One such review was conducted by Rama Rao, president of RR Capital Management Corp., and Jerry J. Szi-

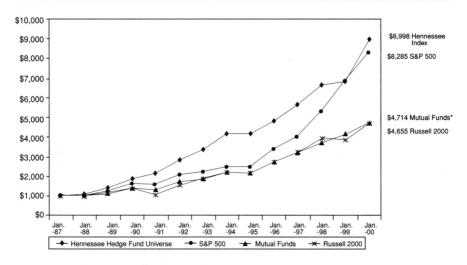

Figure 5.1   Hennessee Hedge Fund Index, S&P 500, Mutual Funds and Russell 2000 Comparative Performance Analysis: Growth of $1,000, January 1, 1987 through December 31, 1999

Source: Hennessee Group LLC.

*Mutual Funds: The average total return for all equity mutual funds according to Lipper Analytical Securities Corp. and Morningstar. No deduction has been made for sales loads or redemption charges.

lagyi, who at the time the study was written was director of financial services at KPMG Consulting. Their report, "The Coming Evolution of the Hedge Fund Industry," published by RRCM in March 1998, raises some questions on the way to its conclusion, as the following passage shows:

> Generally speaking, the studies conclude that hedge funds as a group do provide higher and superior returns on average compared to the S&P 500 and mutual funds. However, there are some concerns regarding the validity of each study. A central question relates to the makeup of the sample, size of the funds, the survivorship effect, and the self-selection bias of the funds reporting results.

The authors add that "Reporting of the data on hedge funds is voluntary and therefore, no one source is comprehensive." But on a more reassuring note, they also point out that more and more hedge funds are providing data for researchers, and as a result, "the differences between different studies also seem to be getting smaller over time which increases the significance of the results." Their ultimate conclusion: "Based on the studies available, the long-term average performance of hedge funds as a group can be estimated to be in the range of 17 to 20%, several percentage points higher than traditional equity returns."

A slightly different approach to assessing returns on hedge funds was undertaken by Leah Modigliani, an investment analyst at Morgan Stanley Dean Witter. In the December 12, 1997 edition of her firm's *Investment Strategy* newsletter, Modigliani analyzed the risk-adjusted returns of hedge funds used in varying combinations with a portfolio composed of the S&P 500 stock index. Modigliani—who, by the way, is the granddaughter of, and occasional collaborator with, Nobel prizewinning economist Franco Modigliani—looked at the risk-adjusted performance of 10 hedge funds "optimized" by combining them with various weightings of the S&P 500.

She found that "In almost every case that we examined, when a hedge fund was optimized for the most favorable combination with the S&P 500, it beat the index on a risk-adjusted basis." Significantly, she adds, "This analysis demonstrates that when held in combination with the S&P 500, the hedge funds add real value."

One subject on which the analysts uniformly agree is the diversification that hedge funds can bring to portfolios, a characteristic that to many investors is just as important as return. As the IMF report notes:

> Because of the differences in strategies of hedge fund investments with traditional long portfolios of stocks and bonds, and the resulting lack of systematic correlation with returns from these traditional sources, investments in hedge funds provide a powerful tool for portfolio diversification. The low correlation of hedge fund returns by investments styles with returns in bond and equity markets reveal the tremendous advantage of portfolio diversification—raising returns without increasing risk—available to a bond or equity only investor by allocating a proportion of his portfolio to hedge funds.

The IMF study also found that while volatility "varies greatly as a function of the strategy pursued," a subject discussed later in this chapter, "the data indicates that a long-term standard deviation of a diversified pool of hedge funds as a group is very similar to the standard deviation of the stock market as measured by the S&P 500 index."

RETURNS AT WHAT PRICE?

Of course, hedge fund performance is only half the equation. The crucial question is what level of risk investors must assume to achieve the relatively high returns and the diversification that hedge funds can bring to a portfolio. Some of the studies cited did look at risk-adjusted returns, which is the most meaningful way to view performance. But especially in light of hedge funds' reputation as high-risk investment vehicles, the subject of risk deserves added scrutiny.

While broad risk assessments are of limited value, given the diverse nature of hedge fund strategies, some generalizations are both important and useful to keep in mind. For instance, as observed in this chapter and the previous chapter, one big advantage of hedge funds over traditional investment vehicles is that they can employ techniques for lowering market risk, such as short selling. But while hedge fund investing can mean lower market risk, it may introduce another type of risk: manager risk.

Remember that in the world of traditional money management, clients and consultants insist that managers follow very precisely defined investment styles. Investment processes are meticulously spelled out, and decisions are usually made by committee or, at the very least, with constant oversight from a committee or supervisory hierarchy. Even when a mutual fund has a renowned star performer at the helm, there is always someone higher up with the power to rein in or fire the manager should things go wrong.

Hedge funds couldn't be more different. Investment decisions are typically made by one individual—the general partner—or a small team. And whoever makes the decisions usually does so with virtually full autonomy. Of course, it's from that freedom and flexibility that hedge fund managers gain their potential for superior performance, but manager risk is the other side of that coin. No matter how brilliant a manager might be or how impressive the track record, there's always the possibility that he or she might lose that golden touch or, worse still, go off the deep end. That's one reason why *transparency* is such an important issue for hedge fund investors; the manager risk factor looms even larger when you have no idea what a manager is doing.

Liquidity risks are also inherently greater with hedge funds. Their structure limits liquidity to begin with—investors can get in and out only at prescribed intervals, typically once a quarter. Beyond that, some hedge funds may invest in private placements or thinly traded securities, which are relatively illiquid. Getting in and out of these securities can be difficult or costly, especially on short notice. Thus, a hedge fund with a concentrated investor base may face problems if one or more major investors decide to redeem sizable portions of their holdings, forcing the fund to raise substantial amounts of cash. If the fund is invested in illiquid instruments, it might have to liquidate them on unfavorable terms.

Of course, hedge funds also pose the same risks that would be associated with any kind of investment. There are the usual systemic risks: A global economic downturn or some other major shock to the markets will almost inevitably have some impact on a hedge fund portfolio. Any or all of the specific instruments purchased may not perform as expected. And then there are operational or infrastructure risks: The hedge fund may run into problems in its own back office, or be affected by the administrative problems of those it deals with. Such problems can tie up money, hamper transactions, and ultimately impose opportunity costs besides dampening returns. Hedge funds aren't immune to any of the problems that might beset a mutual fund or any other kind of managed investment.

DIFFERENT STRATEGIES, DIFFERENT RISKS

Once aware of the risks endemic to all or most hedge funds, investors must be equally vigilant in evaluating risks associated with particular investment strategies and methods. Both the level and the nature of these risks vary widely from fund to fund.

Some strategies, even when successful, impose the risks that are inherent in what the fund is investing in. For instance, some managers may make huge bets—unhedged, of course—on anticipated shifts in commodities, currencies, and interest rates.

Likewise, added risks may be associated with some of the specific tools and techniques hedge fund managers may use, such as leverage. Leverage means paying for an investment partly with borrowed money, either actually borrowed or implicitly borrowed, as when a manager buys futures or options that have more underlying value than the fund's net assets. When a hedge fund's investment strategy is working, leverage makes it work even better; the use of borrowed money amplifies the returns. But at times when the strategy doesn't pan out, leverage can put a fund that much deeper in the hole. When things go wrong for highly leveraged funds, the results can be frightening. The words "Long-Term Capital Management" alone should be enough to make that case.

Fortunately, hedge fund investors don't necessarily have to take on the risks of using leverage if they don't want to. Cerulli Associates reported that at the end of June 1999, only 36 percent of the hedge funds they surveyed were employing any leverage at all. Cerulli also found that even among those funds that do use leverage, 85 percent do so only up to a two-to-one ratio. Thus, use of leverage by hedge funds is neither as pervasive nor as freewheeling as one might imagine.

Short selling is another technique that presents special risks. As hedge fund manager Lee Ainslie of Maverick Capital points out in his essay entitled "Hedged Equity Investing," (which appears in *Evaluating and Implementing Hedge Fund Strategies*, edited by Ronald A. Lake), "The first and most apparent disadvantage of short selling is the fact that over time you are fighting the natural upward trend of the market." As he notes, during the 14-year period from the middle of 1968 to the middle of 1983, the S&P 500 appreciated by less than 1 percent per year. But over the past seven decades or so, the stock market has been going up a majority of the time, so the odds have been against short sellers. Ainslie goes on to observe:

> The old saying "unlimited downside, limited upside" is quite true in short selling and has some unfortunate consequences. It is impossible to make more than 100 percent on a short sale, and even that event is exceedingly rare. Yet it is quite possible, and not altogether uncommon, to lose a multiple of the original investment in a short.

He adds:

> With short investments, poor selections are naturally "pressed." When a short investment is not working, and a stock appreciates, the size of the position also increases. As a short works,

and declines in price, the size of the position becomes smaller. As a result, poor short investments are increased, and the strong investments are decreased. Of course this trend works in the opposite way on the long side.

These are among the reasons why short selling is so risky when used as an exclusive strategy. When short selling is used to mitigate the market risk of a fully invested long portfolio, of course, many of the associated risks are offset, reducing risk levels overall.

THE WORST-CASE SCENARIO

By far the greatest fear of hedge fund investors is that a fund may take such a dramatically wrong turn that it blows up and investors lose everything. It does happen, though rarely. There have been a small number of well-publicized failures of hedge funds over the years, LTCM being the first to spring to mind. Before the LTCM meltdown in 1998, there was the problem of "the three Davids" in 1994: Hedge funds run by David Askin, David Wells, and David Gerstenhaber each lost substantial amounts as a result of complex investment strategies that unraveled.

Then there are the cases of alleged fraud. In the early 1990s, there was a hedge fund that closed down amid allegations that the manager was using money from new investors to pay returns to earlier investors, in classic Ponzi-scheme style. And in January 2000, the manager of the Manhattan Investment Fund was accused by the SEC of perpetrating a "massive fraud" on his investors to hide substantial losses incurred by betting against Internet stocks. The fund sent what the SEC described as fictitious statements to its 280 investors.

But the fact is that hedge funds have not had a high failure rate. Indeed, Hedge Fund Research estimates that in any given year during the 1994–1997 period, the highest percentage of hedge funds that closed down was 7 percent. Van Hedge Fund Advisors estimated that over the course of the 1990s, 10 percent of the funds in its sample had become defunct.

I should point out that funds have often closed down for reasons unrelated to performance. In some cases, partnerships were restructured or merged into existing partnerships. In others, a fund closed when its general partners retired or left the fund to start a new one. As stated in the International Monetary Fund report cited earlier, "There are, in fact, limited examples of hedge funds closing after incurring large losses."

WHAT DOES IT ALL *REALLY* MEAN?

Now, having given you an overview of hedge fund performance, I'm going to make this chapter's most important point. These numbers may help you decide whether hedge funds, as a group, are an investment possibility worth exploring. But when it comes to evaluating any particular hedge fund, they are virtually meaningless.

To illustrate why, I'll borrow a sports metaphor from Ted Caldwell, a hedge fund expert whose article on "Unified Hedge Fund Classification" appeared in the third quarter 1996 edition of the *Lookout Mountain Hedge Fund Review*. Caldwell begins his article on hedge funds with this passage:

> During the Summer Olympics of 1996, the U.S. track team produced eight gold medals with an average winning time of precisely 69.14 seconds. Of course the media didn't report this average time, because even sports novices would recognize it as an utterly useless statistic. Track events, like all athletics, are segregated into appropriate peer groups. Statistics for each separate group tell us the relative achievements of the participants and provide useful averages, rankings, and comparative performance. But applying the same measures across distinctly different groups provides us with meaningless statistics.

Caldwell accompanies this with the following data:

Category	Time (Seconds)
Women's 100 meter	10.94
Women's 4 × 100 relay	41.95
Women's 4 × 400 relay	200.91
Men's 4 × 400 relay	175.99
Men's 110m hurdles	12.95
Men's 400m hurdles	47.54
Men's 200 meter	19.32
Men's 400 meter	43.49
Average Winning Time (seconds)	69.14

What does this table of sports statistics have to do with hedge funds? It points out the fallacy of drawing conclusions about individual sets of performance statistics based on an aggregate number. Caldwell concludes, "The major classes and sub-classes of hedge funds, properly defined, are just as different from one another as the 100-meter sprint is from the 400-meter hurdles, and investors need to understand the differences before they enter the race."

Of course, it would be virtually impossible to track and evaluate all 6,100 hedge funds. So you have to make some judgments about which kinds of hedge fund strategies you want to consider, and which you should eliminate from the outset. The only way to do that is to break them down into categories.

COMPETING CLASSIFICATIONS

The trouble is that no standard system of classifying hedge funds has yet emerged. Information on hedge funds is hard enough to come by. But the confusion is compounded by the fact that almost every industry database and research source comes with its own proprietary classification scheme. And for a variety of reasons, including the lack of a centralized information source within the industry, no one system has become dominant.

Let's start with the MAR/Hedge database, which is maintained by Managed Account Reports and is one of the primary sources of research on the hedge fund industry. The MAR/Hedge system divides hedge funds into eight broad categories:

1. *Event-Driven funds* seek to capitalize on corporate events and "special situations." For example, they might focus on distressed securities, meaning those of companies in bankruptcy or reorganization. Also in this category are risk-arbitrage funds that take positions based on the expectation of an announced merger or acquisition by simultaneously buying shares in a company being acquired and selling the shares of the acquiring company.

2. *Global funds* take positions on directional moves in particular markets, as the macro funds do, but these tend to be more bottom-up oriented in that they pick stocks in individual markets they favor. They also tend to use index derivatives much less than the macro funds.

3. *Global Macro funds* take positions on changes in global economic conditions as reflected in equity prices, currencies, and interest rates. These funds can and do invest in anything anywhere— shares in Malaysia, bonds in France, buildings in Argentina, and derivatives in Chicago.

4. *Long-Only Leveraged funds* invest in equities and may resemble traditional investment management approaches in terms of their investment strategies, but they are structured as hedge funds, complete with incentive fees and leverage. Unlike some hedge funds, however, they don't use short selling.

5. *Market Neutral funds* attempt to reduce market risk by taking offsetting long and short positions. In contrast to the Jones model, market-neutral funds don't vary the proportion of assets that are long and short in response to the manager's market outlook. Rather, the goal is to precisely balance long and short positions to avoid any directional bet on the market. This label once applied only to funds that take offsetting positions in common stocks within the same industries—they might buy Schlumberger and short Halliburton, for example. However, this category has expanded to encompass funds that invest in a wide variety of instruments, including convertible arbitrage funds that take offsetting positions in convertible securities and the underlying equity, those that arbitrage stocks and index futures, and those that take positions on yield curves in bond markets.

6. *Sector funds* focus on a given industry or sector of the economy, such as health care, financial services, food and beverages, media and communications, natural resources, oil and gas, real estate, technology, transportation, and utilities.

7. *Short-Seller funds* are those that sell short as an exclusive strategy. Such funds attract investors wishing to hedge traditional long-only portfolios, or those wishing to take a position that a market is likely to decline.

8. *Fund of Funds* are hedge funds that invest in other hedge funds, sometimes using leverage.

That's one system. But Hedge Fund Research, another prime research source on the industry, developed its own system based on 15 different types of hedge fund strategies. In the mid-1990s, HFR expanded its classification system to include 28 categories, as a way of accommodating recent developments in the hedge fund industry. The result is a lengthy and decidedly complicated set of categories, as shown in Table 5.1.

On closer examination, it's clear that these 28 categories aren't parallel; they've been defined using differing criteria. Some are based on strategies, others on the kinds of investments chosen, and in other cases, the defining attribute is a type of financial instrument or a geographic

Table 5.1   **Hedge Fund Research: Hedge Fund Classifications**

Convertible Arbitrage
Distressed Securities
Emerging Markets: Asia
Emerging Markets: Eastern Europe/CIS
Emerging Markets: Global
Emerging Markets: Latin America
Equity Hedge
Equity Market Neutral
Equity Non-Hedge
Event-Driven
Fixed Income: Arbitrage
Fixed Income: Convertible Bonds
Fixed Income: Diversified
Fixed Income: High Yield
Fixed Income: Mortgage-Backed
Macro
Market Timing
Merger Arbitrage
Regulation D
Relative Value Arbitrage
Sector: Energy
Sector: Financial
Sector: Health Care/Biotechnology
Sector: Metals/Mining
Sector: Real Estate
Sector: Technology
Short Selling
Statistical Arbitrage

Source: Hedge Fund Research, Inc.

area. The categories include funds that invest in emerging markets around the world and those that invest in just one emerging market, such as Latin America. There are funds that invest in specific sectors of the economy, such as energy or technology, and funds that invest by timing the markets. And there are funds of funds, which invest in other hedge funds.

Rao and Szilagyi offer yet another classification in the report discussed earlier in this chapter. They used MAR/Hedge data to define the following 11 hedge fund investment styles:

Investment Style	Definition
Market neutral	50 percent long, 50 percent short
Convertible arbitrage	Long convertible securities; short underlying equity
Global macro	Focus on global macroeconomic changes
Growth	Look for growth potential in revenues and earnings
Value	Look for undervalued assets
Sector	Focus on a particular economic or industrial sector
Distressed securities	Invest in firms undergoing bankruptcy or reorganization
Emerging markets	Invest in developing-country equity and debt markets
Opportunistic	Trading oriented, capitalizing on market trends and events
Leverage bonds	Use leverage to invest in fixed income instruments
Short only	Take short positions

HUGE DIFFERENCES IN RETURN AND RISK

Categorization schemes aren't limited to these three, of course; there are plenty more classification systems out there, and new ones seem to keep cropping up with each major new study. But as you can see from a quick comparison of the three systems shown, each one is slicing and dicing the same list of funds in similar, but slightly different ways. And no one system seems to fit all hedge funds neatly. Each one is an after-the-fact categorization effort that tries to create enough boxes so every fund has a natural place. But the more success a categorization system has in easily fitting every hedge fund into a pigeonhole, the more pigeonholes it has, and the more complicated everything becomes.

In my opinion, it doesn't really matter which categorization system you rely on. Whichever one you choose, the important thing is to recog-

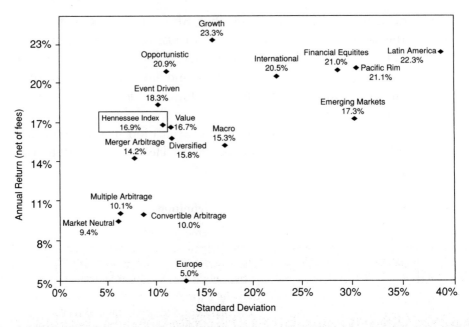

Figure 5.2   Hennessee Hedge Fund Universe Performance, January 1, 1990 through December 31, 1999

Source: Hennessee Group LLC.

nize how dramatically categories may differ in terms of both return and risk characteristics. Spend some time with Figure 5.2, which illustrates return and standard deviation data for various strategies from 1990 to 1999, as reported by the Hennessee Group.

Note that returns of individual strategies covered a broad spectrum, ranging from 5 percent to over 23 percent, while the Hennessee Hedge Fund Index return was 16.9 percent. Similarly, individual standard deviations varied widely—from 6 to 38 percent—while the standard deviation of the Index was around 11 percent. This clearly demonstrates why I maintain that aggregate hedge fund return and risk data is of little real use to investors, except to confirm that hedge funds as an investment category are worth exploring. Why care about the averages when performance varies so much by type of fund? And, of course, within each category there's also considerable variance among individual funds.

WHERE'S THE MONEY?

To understand the dynamics of the hedge fund industry, it's worth taking a quick look at how the total number of funds and assets break down among various fund categories, starting with information from MAR/Hedge. (Please note that the MAR/Hedge database consisted of 905 funds as of the end of 1999.) As Tables 5.2 and 5.3 show, global funds represent approximately 40 percent of the total hedge fund market, in terms of both the number of funds and assets in the strategy. Next in line is market-neutral, with approximately one-quarter of funds and 22 percent of assets.

Tables 5.2 and 5.3 also reveal the growing importance of the fund of funds category. There were none in 1980, 32 in 1990, and 265 in 1999. While total hedge fund assets have grown enormously in recent years, assets of funds of funds have also climbed rapidly, up over 85 percent since 1995. As a result, throughout most of the past decade they consistently accounted for roughly 15 percent of total industry assets.

In 1990, global macro funds represented 65 percent of the hedge fund industry's assets and held on to their leading position throughout the first half of the decade. However, during the latter part of the 1990s, they experienced a decline, ending the century with a 22 percent market share. It's interesting to note that global macro funds were the only category to show a drop in assets in 1999.

Table 5.2   **Hedge Funds: Number of Funds by Strategy, 1980–1999**

	1980	1985	1990	1995	1996	1997	1998	1999
Event-Driven	0	2	17	73	95	120	123	106
Global	1	9	40	248	334	404	337	364
Global Macro	0	2	13	40	50	61	57	58
Long-Only Leveraged	0	0	0	7	11	15	20	25
Market Neutral	0	5	18	123	159	201	171	231
Sector	0	0	1	16	23	40	77	104
Short-Sellers	0	0	6	10	11	12	16	17
Total	1	18	95	517	683	853	801	905
Fund of Funds	0	4	32	181	221	262	210	265
Total (including Fund of Funds)	1	22	127	698	904	1,115	1,011	1,170

Source: MAR/Hedge.

Table 5.3   **Hedge Funds: Assets under Management by Strategy,
1980–1999 (Millions of Dollars)**

	1980	1985	1990	1995	1996	1997	1998	1999
Event-Driven	0	29	379	3,827	5,574	8,602	9,838	13,118
Global	193	517	1,288	14,931	20,401	30,862	27,369	44,688
Global Macro	0	0	4,700	18,807	25,510	29,759	38,152	24,943
Long-Only Leveraged	0	0	0	85	180	376	311	646
Market Neutral	0	78	638	5,707	10,317	17,970	16,318	25,595
Sector	0	0	2	187	691	1,752	2,101	4,629
Short-Sellers	0	0	187	432	488	538	745	917
Total	193	624	7,193	43,976	63,162	89,859	94,834	114,536
Fund of Funds	0	190	1,339	9,416	13,163	19,717	17,324	17,592
Total (including Fund of Funds)	193	814	8,532	53,392	76,325	109,576	112,158	132,128

Source: MAR/Hedge.

Data from Hedge Fund Research also illustrates the decrease in macro funds as a percentage of industry assets over the last ten years. As shown in Figure 5.3, in contrast to Equity Hedge and Equity Non-Hedge strategies which picked up significant market share, macro funds' piece of the pie shrank dramatically. I expect that when this data is updated at the end of 2000, global macro funds will have given up even more ground due to outflows from funds overseen by Julian Robertson and George Soros.

Even though macros funds recently ranked fifth in terms of number of funds and, depending on the source, second or third in terms of assets, they claimed the top prize for average size of fund. As shown in Figure 5.4, macro funds in the Hedge Fund Research database averaged some $330 million in assets under management. By contrast, the funds in the category with the second-largest average size—event-driven funds—had average assets of only $170 million. Most categories were characterized by funds with less than $100 million under management.

THE WRAP-UP

The conventional wisdom about hedge funds is contradicted by the facts. A 1999 report called "The Case for Hedge Funds," issued by Tremont

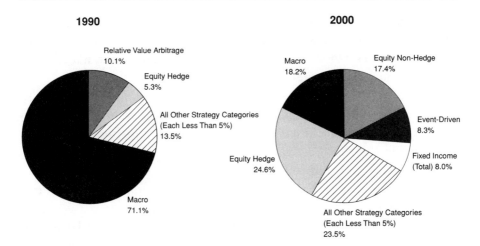

1990

Relative Value Arbitrage
10.1%

Equity Hedge
5.3%

All Other Strategy Categories
(Each Less Than 5%)
13.5%

Macro
71.1%

2000

Macro
18.2%

Equity Non-Hedge
17.4%

Event-Driven
8.3%

Fixed Income
(Total) 8.0%

All Other Strategy Categories
(Each Less Than 5%)
23.5%

Equity Hedge
24.6%

Figure 5.3   **Percentage of Hedge Fund Assets by Strategy, 1990 and 2000**
Source: Hedge Fund Research, Inc. 1990 data as of December 31; 2000 data as of
March 31.

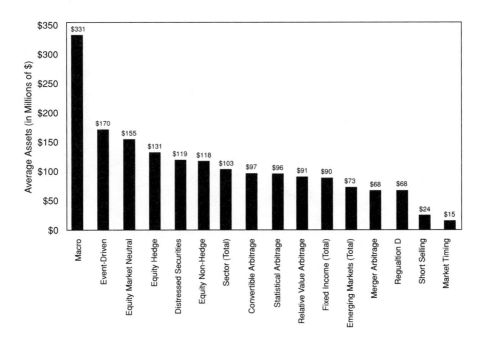

Figure 5.4   **Average Hedge Fund Size By Strategy, 1999**
Source: Hedge Fund Research, Inc.

Advisers and its United Kingdom subsidiary, TASS Investment Research, sums it up well: "There is a general perception that hedge funds are dangerously high-risk vehicles designed only for the elite. The majority of statistical and intellectual evidence suggests otherwise."

Once you get past the headlines to take a closer look at hedge funds, you can see that this is a highly adaptable investment vehicle—one that makes it possible to deploy cash in a diverse variety of instruments using a seemingly limitless array of strategies. In essence, hedge funds are a kind of parallel universe existing alongside traditional investment management, encompassing any kind of investment a traditional manager can make and a host of different ones as well.

Several analysts have found that hedge funds as a group have performed better than the markets, and therefore better than the majority of traditional investment managers. These findings suggest that as an investment vehicle, hedge funds may suit the needs of performance-minded, high-net-worth investors very well.

But it's critical for investors to realize that they can't draw any conclusions about the performance of individual hedge funds from this overview data; the world of hedge funds is simply too diverse. Hedge fund strategies can be very conservative or highly speculative, completely domestic or thoroughly international, aggressively traded or held for the long term. Almost any kind of investment strategy can be employed through a hedge fund, and whenever new strategies emerge, new hedge funds emerge to employ them.

Chapter 6

Narrowing the Field: "The Big Four" Strategies

As we've seen, hedge fund analysts and consultants have identified more than two dozen different "categories" of hedge funds. This laundry list of classifications is both good news and bad news for the investor who is put off by traditional investment management and intrigued by the prospect of capturing superior absolute returns.

The good news is that you can pursue a host of investment strategies using hedge funds. Whatever your views on market trends and opportunities, you can find a suitable approach. The bad news is that you have to sort through a maze of choices to find the best-fitting fund or funds for you. But in this chapter and the next, I'm going to try to help simplify that process.

In this chapter, we're going to look at four major strategies: global macro, event-driven, arbitrage, and balanced long/short. I call them "The Big Four." My goal here is not only to illuminate how these strategies operate, but to give you a better idea of what hedge funds in general can offer an investor. Finally, by giving you my own views on these strategies, I'll highlight some of the criteria I apply in evaluating hedge funds. I hope this will provide a starting point for your own reflections on which criteria are important to you.

GLOBAL MACRO: HIGH RISKS, HIGH REWARDS

Global macro funds are the poster children of hedge funds. These are the funds the media talk about when they say "hedge funds" are doing this or that. And when people think about hedge funds, these are the ones that come to mind. Yet in reality, only a small percentage of hedge funds—just over 6 percent—are actually global macro funds.

The reason that global macro funds are so well known isn't just because they are among the largest funds in terms of assets under management. It's also because they're often run by swashbuckling managers with celebrity-like status—people like George Soros, for example. How many other investment managers have made the cover of *Time* magazine?

These "Masters of the Universe" personalities make very large and often very audacious investments in a wide range of public and private markets around the world. They take big positions—unhedged, of course—because they believe in concentrated bets. Because global macro managers play their cards close to the vest, their dealings have an aura of mystery. However, once sophisticated speculators get wind of what they're up to, they quickly jump on the same bandwagon. As a result, the investments made by global macro managers often rise quickly in price, making the original bet a self-fulfilling prophecy.

Global macro managers seek to generate returns by identifying disparities in the relationship between price and underlying value across a wide range of markets. They look at stocks, bonds, currencies, commodities, and real estate. They may take both long and short positions in securities, futures, forwards, and options, amplifying their bets with massive amounts of leverage. Global macro funds, as their name implies, invest on a global basis. They can and do go anywhere in the world to seek opportunity.

Have Assets, Will Travel

As the name also implies, global macro funds take a macro view of investing. They look at the big picture, the sweeping trends that shape the course of markets around the world. They typically use a top-down approach, forecasting important trends and events in economies and nations around the globe, and analyzing how these developments will affect the valuation of various markets and financial instruments. Rather than poring over the financial statements of individual companies, delving deeply into P/E ratios, ROE, and debt capacity, global macro fund managers generate investment ideas with a much broader brush.

Like the CIA, they have legions of well-placed sources—analysts and researchers who roam the globe investigating ideas, kicking the tires, and counting the house. Is the cost of energy rising or falling? What are the implications for various emerging markets and companies? How will the moves of the world's central banks affect free-market financial activities? There's no telling where one might find the next big score. This is the realm of big thinkers, not green eyeshade types.

Win Big, Lose Big

Here's a real-life example. In 1998, global macro players were involved with a trade known as the "yen/dollar carry." Here's how it worked: First, you borrow Japanese yen at less than 1 percent. Then you invest the proceeds in U.S. Treasuries at 5.5 percent or emerging market debt at 10 to 12 percent, leveraging it all to the hilt. Sounds simple enough, right? And from January to August of 1998, global macro funds made it look easy to rack up annualized returns of 80 percent or more, seemingly with minimal risk.

But who can forget what happened in the fall of 1998? With the financial blowup in Russia, worries about Brazil, and, of course, the infamous Long-Term Capital Management debacle, investors lost their nerve and global markets were rocked by a massive flight to quality. Japanese banks began selling U.S. bonds to shore up their capital ratios. And global macro managers found themselves furiously buying yen to repay their Japanese loans. In just two short days, the yen rose 17 percent versus the dollar when, historically, the yen/dollar exchange rate would move only 5 percent in the course of a full year. Almost overnight, millions were lost, and the fortunes of these funds were reversed.

While others may seek to eke out a few basis points with countless small trades, global macro funds seek to catch the big waves. They often make very large, concentrated bets, employing derivative securities and leverage to magnify returns. As you might imagine, global macro strategies are extremely volatile—the ultimate in testosterone-driven investing. Yet risk is not without its reward, and maximum-performance-seeking global macro managers often achieve net annual returns of 25 to 30 percent or even higher.

George Soros, a true global macro legend, has compiled a record that can only be described as brilliant. Not only has he achieved annualized returns of 30 percent, he has done so over 30 years—an astonishing performance level no other manager in the *world* has matched. Born in Hungary, but now a U.S. citizen, Soros survived the Nazi terror in World War II by hiding in his family's attic. As head of the Quantum Funds, which he founded in 1969, Soros achieved folk-hero status by building phenomenal wealth for both his clients and himself, using a combination of intelligence, tenacity, and guts. In 1993, he became the first American to earn over $1 billion in *a single year*. Now a billionaire several times over, Soros apparently has a permanent slot on the *Forbes* list of the 400 richest Americans; he's been on it every year since 1986. He is also well-known for his philanthropy, annually donating several hundred million dollars of his own money to causes in Eastern Europe, the former Soviet Union, and the United States.

Profiting from Perceptions

So how does Soros do it? What is his investment philosophy? A main component is something he calls "reflexivity," a concept totally at odds with the tenets of traditional investment management and Modern Portfolio Theory. By reflexivity, he means that economic events are determined as much by perception as by reality, and that investors behave irrationally. Regardless of their level of financial sophistication and knowledge of the markets, they most often end up following the herd.

Soros capitalizes on this aspect of human nature by identifying the inflection point in economic trends, zeroing in on a bubble of irrational exuberance that is ready to burst. He seems to have an innate understanding of the cause-and-effect relationships at work in the world's economies, and an uncanny sense of when and how to take advantage of them. When he's confident that his perceptions are right, no position is too large. He's been quoted as saying, "If the stock goes up, you buy more. You don't care how big the position gets as part of your portfolio. If you get it right, then build."

And build he did in 1992, when he made world headlines after betting $10 billion—much of it borrowed—that Britain would devalue the pound. He was right, and over the course of a few weeks made a tidy $2 billion profit, $958 million of it literally overnight. The tabloids immediately dubbed him "The Man Who Broke the Bank of England."

Since then, of course, Soros has been in and out of stocks and bonds and real estate in countless countries. Sometimes he has bet wrong, as with his ill-fated attack on the Indonesian rupiah, but he always rebounds, ready to put millions to work in the next great idea.

Other global macro funds get less publicity but are no less wide-ranging. At any point in time, they are positioning themselves to profit from price movements they foresee in any number of different countries and markets.

Going for the Kill

By definition, global macro funds are highly aggressive vehicles. If they get it right, the returns are enormous; if they don't, the losses are staggering. Does the word "speculation" come to mind? Maybe that's a little too strong. "Aggressive" is probably a better characterization. Dion Friedland, chairman of Magnum Funds, likens global macro funds to the grizzly bears of the animal kingdom:

> Mammoth and quick, keen and powerful, these carnivores take no prisoners—not even human ones—when feeling threatened or hungry. They are sudden and aggressive; they go for the kill; they want it all, not content with only a mere morsel of their prey.

That description might seem a shade melodramatic, but upon reflection, it's really not so far off the mark.

Is the global macro world for you? It depends. For one thing, these funds are often difficult to access. The best-known funds may be closed to all but the A-list of the very wealthiest investors. And many have been set up as offshore funds that are off-limits to American investors. Unless you can make some arrangement through a Swiss bank or some corporation in the Cayman Islands, you can't invest alongside George Soros no matter how much money you have.

Logistics aside, here's the fundamental issue: Can your nervous system handle the inevitable ups and downs of these funds over the course of any given year? If so, you may do very well; many of these funds have generated extremely attractive long-term results. But remember, the risks can be just as outsized as the rewards. Global macro investing is not for the faint of heart, and thus not the strategy of choice for most conservative investors.

Some readers may be wondering how an investor could possibly justify assuming this level of risk. Well, try this on for size: Had you given $100,000 to George Soros 30 years ago, it would be worth over $260 million today. Was the return worth the risk? You decide.

EVENT-DRIVEN: A SPECIALIZED APPROACH

Event-driven funds are a totally different animal. Rather than riding major economic waves, they invest based on the expected outcome of significant events in the life of securities issuers—mergers and acquisitions, bankruptcies, spin-offs and divestitures, financial restructurings, lawsuits, and other assorted forms of corporate *sturm und drang*.

The opportunity lies in the uncertainty about how such events will unfold. Depending on whether a company succeeds in completing an acquisition, being taken over, or getting out of an antitrust suit with the federal government, its share price may move up or down significantly. Event-driven fund managers scour the marketplace for the corporate events they think will offer the best opportunities. Those who correctly anticipate the outcomes can profit handsomely from investing in the related securities.

Unlike traditional investment managers, event-driven specialists do not focus on the overall business prospects of the companies they track. Rather than being concerned with the enterprise's big picture, they have a much narrower interest: how the company will be affected by a particular event.

But don't think that they are like small-town firefighters, sitting around playing cards and polishing their truck until the fire alarm goes off. There are plenty of events unfolding at any point in time, so event-driven funds maintain a portfolio of companies. And not only do they attempt to foresee the *outcome* of events, they also anticipate the *onset*. Event-driven managers are constantly on the lookout for companies that are poised to make an acquisition, are likely to be put in play by an acquirer, or are about to be caught up in some other event. Thus, the results these funds achieve aren't limited by the frequency of events; corporate actions, dealings, and proceedings are always going on somewhere in the world.

The Crème de la Crème

What is critical is the event-driven manager's ability to foresee the course of events and the ways to profit from their outcomes. Because they so closely follow what's transpiring, managers of these funds are in a much better position than the average investor to anticipate what the future holds. Over time, they develop a keen sense of the various scenarios that can play out in unfriendly takeovers or product liability suits. And by tracking complex situations such as bankruptcy proceedings, they can spot the potential for agreements in one case to provide a precedent for the next.

Because event-driven situations are so intricate, the people who evaluate them are more often corporate finance types than portfolio managers. Many are MBAs, PhDs, or attorneys minted by the likes of Harvard, Stanford, and Wharton—a true financial elite. Only the anointed few have the blend of knowledge and acumen required to analyze the complex strategic, financial, and legal issues involved in event-driven investing. Many of them begin honing their skills at first-tier Wall Street investment banks and law firms, and then move on to specialized hedge fund boutiques. The opportunity to be independent while earning truly big bucks proves irresistible.

Those in this lofty echelon of the investment world spend most of their time and energy analyzing two major kinds of corporate events: mergers and acquisitions (M&A) and financial reversals so severe that investors brand the company's securities "distressed." These two types of events are so significant that they are often listed as separate hedge fund categories in their own right. Let's examine each, starting with merger arbitrage.

Profiting from M&A

Merger or risk arbitrage is not really arbitrage in the classic textbook sense of buying and selling the same item in different markets. Rather, it involves investing in the shares of companies involved in mergers, acquisitions, or leveraged buyouts. The goal is to correctly predict the outcome of the deal and transact accordingly in the shares of the companies involved. Predicting the outcome also incorporates elements of timing; it's important to anticipate how long it will take for the deal to close. If you get all these elements right, you profit from price movements in both the acquirer's and the target's stock.

When a company announces an acquisition, the stock price of the target almost always increases. However, it doesn't go up to the full offering price because there is always the risk that the deal won't go through. This creates an opportunity for the merger arbitrageur who believes the deal will close. He or she seeks to lock up the difference between the stock's price when the deal is publicly announced and its final offering price.

Because of the past decade's raging bull market, most companies are paying for their targets using an inflated currency—their own stock. So, to guarantee the arbitrage profit, a manager not only must buy shares in the company being acquired, but must also sell short the acquirer's stock as a hedge against any price decline.

In instances where the arbitrageur believes a recently announced acquisition won't go through, he or she can "Chinese the trade" and still make money. This involves simply reversing the positions, going long the stock of the acquiring company and shorting the target.

Merger arbitrage managers may boost returns with leverage as high as three to five times the amount of invested capital, making them much less leveraged than the global macro players. They might work on 25 to 30 deals at any one time, with returns as high as 25 percent annualized on a single transaction. And deal flow is excellent in both the United States and Europe. In 1999, there were over 10,000 mergers and acquisitions in the United States with a total dollar value of approximately $1.75 trillion. As deregulation and restructuring transform European commerce, deal volume there is expected to pick up substantially from 1999's already impressive $1.23 trillion.

Overall, merger arbitrage funds generally produce net returns in the low teens if unleveraged, or higher depending on the degree of leverage used. And because they are driven by discrete events, the returns have a low correlation with traditional stocks and bonds. But the strategy is not without risk. If, for instance, the stock market were to sustain something more than a major correction, falling 20 percent or more, the merger arbitrage market would take a beating since its trading currency—the acquiring company's stock—would be greatly devalued.

There is also the risk that a deal could fall apart unexpectedly and temporarily sour the whole merger market. This is exactly what happened in 1997 when the Federal Trade Commission nixed the Office Depot/Staples merger in a surprise decision. When one deal heads south, it creates a ripple effect, leaving the market nervous about the prospects for pending transactions. So don't be surprised if merger arbitrage funds show negative returns in years when an unusually large number of deals "break" or fall apart.

Dross into Gold

"Distressed securities" is the second major subcategory of event-driven hedge funds. Investing in securities that are distressed may not sound like a terrific moneymaker. But it can be an extremely smart play for hedge fund managers with the expertise to spot a diamond in the rough. Distressed securities are stocks or bonds of companies that are at or near the brink of bankruptcy—firms whose financial position is so precarious that their continued existence is a question mark. Their securities plummet in price as investors scramble for the exits, choosing to sell out at fire-sale prices rather than be left holding the bag. Many large public and private pension plans will automatically dump their securities in such instances, because they have no choice; investment policies and guidelines often prohibit them from owning any securities below a certain quality standard.

But as the saying goes, one man's trash is another man's treasure. Distressed security specialists are highly skilled investment bankers and bankruptcy attorneys who steep themselves in every aspect of a company's finances, including all terms and covenants of their securities. Once they know every detail and are convinced they're looking at a real opportunity, they'll make their move, paying, say, $30 for a bond that may have traded at $70 or $80 only a few days earlier.

Then they'll set about steering the company back to financial health. As large-stake investors, they become influential in the company's turnaround, either as an official member of the credit committee or unofficially as a vocal activist. If all goes according to plan, they may reap profits of up to 50 percent, usually within three years or less, as their positions gain back their lost value and, they hope, then some. Managers investing in distressed securities are often called "vulture investors" because they swoop in and pick over the carcasses of financially devastated corporations. But in truth, they provide the final rung on the ladder of liquidity for sellers who may otherwise have nowhere to turn.

Despite the rosy U.S. economic environment of the 1990s, there are still many companies in distressed situations, both domestically and abroad. And the right turn of events can dramatically accelerate the rags-to-riches cycle. In just four months, Credit Suisse First Boston's distressed-debt trading team made a staggering $130 million of pure profit by betting on the marked-down bonds of paging companies. When the IPO market for wireless Internet software companies heated up in early 2000, paging companies were suddenly back in vogue, boosting the value of the formerly distressed debt. Outside U.S. borders, Japanese banks have an estimated $600 *billion* of nonperforming loans on their books. In short, investment opportunities abound.

Because distressed securities funds perform rigorous due diligence, their hit rate is high. Most of the deals they invest in do very well, so you're unlikely to see any large negative returns here. And, unlike conventional stock and bond investments, what Alan Greenspan says on any given day isn't likely to have much impact on the issuer's turnaround.

Both major categories of event-driven hedge funds—merger arbitrage and distressed securities—generate very respectable returns ranging from 12 to 15 percent annually. Because of their strong performance throughout the 1990s, there has been steady growth in both the number of event-driven funds and their total assets under management.

ARBITRAGE: A MONEY MACHINE

As I noted earlier, arbitrage is the simultaneous purchase and sale of like securities in order to profit from pricing discrepancies between markets. Originally, arbitrage involved buying and selling the exact same security in different geographic markets, taking advantage of, for example, price disparities between exchanges in New York and Tokyo that might last only a few moments. But increasingly, the definition of arbitrage has been expanded to include trading in securities that are similar in some fashion, but not precisely the same. For example, an arbitrageur might buy an undervalued convertible bond and sell short the underlying common stock.

While most hedge funds typically limit their arbitrage activities to a narrow range of securities, collectively these kinds of funds invest in every type of security and derivative instrument known to mankind. Individual transactions generate small gains, but with the large, highly leveraged positions they take and the volume of trading they do, most funds produce returns anywhere from 12 to 15 percent a year. These types of funds won't make you rich, but if you already are, they'll keep filet mignon on the table and Dom Perignon in the fridge.

Financial Wizards in Action

Arbitrageurs operate under the premise that there are long-term, equilibrium price relationships that exist between various securities. They believe that when these relationships are upset, the dislocation is only temporary and they will ultimately revert back to normal. Arbitrageurs also seek opportunity in bad investment decisions made by less sophisticated investors. They quietly watch while someone pays too much or sells for too little, then scoop up the mispriced securities and wait for the market to return to its equilibrium state. And investors frequently do make pricing mistakes—they fail to recognize the true value of some feature of a particular security, like a call option. Or they incorrectly assess the probability of some future occurrence.

One way or another, although markets behave fairly efficiently, there are still mispriced securities, and arbitrageurs are constantly scouring the financial landscape to locate them. Once a mispriced security is found, they're quick to pounce, benefiting when the rest of the market sees the error of its ways. Because mispricings are typically small amounts, sometimes merely a few basis points, arbitrageurs take large positions. They also use huge amounts of leverage—up to 100 times their invested capital—to amplify the minute pricing anomaly they're trying to capture.

Many arbitrageurs are top-of-their-class MBAs. Others are literally rocket scientists with advanced degrees in engineering and nuclear physics. Typically, these wizards are perched on the in-house, proprietary trading desk of one of the powerhouse Wall Street firms like Morgan Stanley and Goldman Sachs. They use their brains and the firm's extensive capital and computer systems to take advantage of temporary price inefficiencies.

In addition to being smart, these specialists are also creative, taking arbitrage concepts and applying them to a broad range of investment instruments. For example, fixed-income arb specialists hold offsetting long and short positions in related fixed-income securities and their derivatives. A fund might buy 30-year Treasury bonds and sell interest-rate futures or buy Japanese government bonds and short U.S Treasury notes. Because fixed-income prices are influenced by yield curves, volatility forecasts, cash flow estimates, credit ratings, and various other factors, arbitrageurs use sophisticated, computer-driven analytical models to isolate the price dislocations they seek.

A focal point for fixed-income arbitrage is the relationship between U.S. Treasury securities and other fixed-income securities. Because U.S. Treasuries are perceived as the world's safest securities, bond investors and traders from all walks of life use them as a pricing mechanism, a price benchmark if you will. They quote prices of corporate and foreign government bonds as a spread off a Treasury security with a comparable maturity. So, if the "WMT 6.875%s of '09" trade at 110 basis points off the 10-year Treasury note and the 10-year note is yielding 6.0 percent, the

Wal-Mart bonds are priced to yield 7.1 percent. The riskier the bond, the wider the spread.

These spread relationships are constantly expanding and contracting, reflecting a variety of market forces. Fixed-income arbitrageurs are continuously on the lookout for potential sales candidates that are expensive compared to Treasuries (narrow spreads) and possible buy opportunities that are cheap compared to Treasuries (wide spreads). They move in and out of various securities in hopes of correctly anticipating the changes in spreads and, therefore, the changes in the prices of various fixed-income securities.

In the case of convertible bond arbitrage, funds construct long portfolios of convertible bonds and hedge those positions by selling short the underlying stock. Convertible bonds are bonds that can be exchanged into a fixed number of shares of stock in the issuing company at a predetermined price. Because convertibles have features of a bond and a stock, their value reflects both types of instruments. Generally, in a declining market, the price of a convertible will fall less rapidly than the price of the underlying stock. But when stock prices are rising, the convertible's price closely tracks the stock price. By shorting the stock and buying the convertible bond, arbitrageurs earn the coupon on the bond (net of dividend payments on the short position), the risk-free rate on the short sale proceeds, and arbitrage profits from trading the volatility of the hedge they've put on. This strategy is so popular that it accounts for 50 to 60 percent of all secondary convertible bond market activity.

One Principle, Many Applications

There are many different flavors of arbitrage—for example, mortgage-backed securities, index, and closed-end fund arbitrage. But whether it's fixed income or double chocolate chip arbitrage, the investment principles remain the same: develop an understanding of normal pricing relationships, look for dislocations, and then make investments that will profit when pricing relationships return to normal. This kind of investing can generate large numbers of small gains with limited risks. It works nicely unless or until there is a paradigm shift in a particular market that renders historical pricing relationships invalid. It's lucky for arbitrage hedge fund managers and their clients that these paradigm shifts don't happen every day.

Arbitrage is a bit like building a ship in a bottle. Actually, it's more like building 40 ships in 40 bottles, all at the same time. It's close work, dependent on finding tiny discrepancies in pricing relationships and rushing in to invest before they evaporate (i.e., before they are "arbitraged away"). There's no shortage of disparities, just as there's no shortage of events, actions, and proceedings. On the other hand, there is a shortage of investors skillful enough to perfectly price their each and every trade. The mistakes they make give arbitrageurs the ability to produce comfortable, if not spectacular, returns.

Arbitrage is about grinding out steady incremental gains of about 1 to 1.5 percent per month, and arbitrage hedge funds do this very nicely. They're well suited for preserving capital and generating consistent, positive returns. One word of caution. Every few years or so, there is some big blowup in the arbitrage market. Once again, the name Long-Term Capital Management comes to mind. Usually, it's after a flight to quality caused by a major shock to one or more of the world's economies. In times like these, investors sell out of lower-quality holdings and money floods into safe-haven Treasury securities, rapidly disrupting equilibrium prices.

Besides flight-to-quality risk, another problem investors face with arbitrage funds is that they have very high turnover and are constantly realizing gains and losses. Most of the time, these gains and losses are very short-term in nature. Since a hedge fund's tax consequences typically flow through to its investors, arbitrage funds are not the most tax-efficient investments going. These funds need to produce substantial profits in order to provide an after-tax return that is competitive with funds generating a much higher percentage of long-term capital gains.

Finally, there's the issue of access. The most successful practitioners of this strategy work on the proprietary trading desks of big investment banks such as Morgan Stanley or Goldman Sachs. It's not unheard-of for such managers to generate 40 percent annual returns—but that's on the firm's own money, and they're not about to let outsiders in on the deal. That's not to say it's impossible to find a good arbitrage fund. But the star managers are too busy making money for themselves, their partners, and a few ultrawealthy clients to worry about anyone else.

BALANCED LONG/SHORT: THE PARADIGM HEDGE

One of the first questions novice investors ask about hedge funds is, "Where's the hedging?" As we've already seen, many hedge fund strategies don't hedge at all. But for balanced long/short strategies, also known as "equity market neutral," "equity relative value," or "equity statistical arbitrage" (stat arb) strategies, hedging is the centerpiece of the approach. Balanced long/short managers seek the perfect hedge to help insulate their stock portfolios from market movements. Instead of being at the whim of the market's direction, they aim to capitalize purely on their ability to pick winning and losing stocks.

At any given time, investors may comment that the market is going up or the market is going down. But, of course, the market is simply an aggregation of thousands of individual securities. And while the market as a whole may be going up, many individual stocks are, in fact, going down. And when the market is falling, not every stock is declining, and even among those that are, some will inevitably drop at a faster or slower rate than others.

Wouldn't it be nice to get "the market" out of the picture—especially if you're nervous about how long a bull market is going to last—and just select the stocks that will do the best (or worst, in the case of shorting) regardless of the overall direction of things? This is precisely what long/short managers do: They attempt to take the market out of the investment equation. They create a portfolio in which long positions—stocks you own—are completely balanced by short positions—stocks you've sold. In an ideal world, if stocks go up, your longs are worth more, and your short positions are worth less. Similarly, if stocks go down, your longs are worth less, but your short positions increase in value. In theory, everything is hedged, balanced, and neutral, and market movements should have no impact on returns.

It's All in the Spread

The symmetry is all very impressive, you say, but how do you make any money? Balanced long/short managers make money by going long *under-valued* stocks and shorting an equal dollar amount of *overvalued* stocks. The idea is to pocket the positive performance (the "spread") between the longs and the shorts as well as the interest earned on the short-sale proceeds (roughly the Treasury bill rate). In a rising market, the long and short positions may both appreciate, but if the manager is a good stock picker, the long positions outperform the shorts. In a falling market, both sides of the portfolio may go down, but here the short side should go down even more. With market-neutral investing, you lock in the T-bill rate and the manager's alpha, for a total return of about 8 to 10 percent.

By alpha, I simply mean excess return—the amount by which a stock or portfolio outperforms some benchmark, usually the T-bill rate in the case of balanced long/short. Creating alpha means you've done better than some aggregate measure of the market, that you've added value above and beyond your performance bogey.

With market-neutral strategies, an outstanding stock picker can direct his or her alpha toward any benchmark an investor may choose— "portable" alpha, so to speak. In the hands of a skillful manager, "equitizing" a long/short portfolio can add a premium of 3 to 4 percentage points over the S&P 500. With an equitized portfolio, you invest the short-sale proceeds in S&P 500 futures instead of T-bills, gaining broad U.S. equity exposure. Equitizing takes an absolute return approach—market neutral—and turns it into a beat-the-market strategy, but with *twice* your manager's expected excess return.

A Quantitative Bent

In theory, market-neutral managers want to buy the best stock in an industry, and sell the worst stock in that same industry. They do this with matched pairs. If managers buy shares of AIG, they might sell shares of Aetna or another insurance company that they view as less attractive than AIG. Similarly, a manager might buy Gateway and short IBM— same sector, same industry, but different performance expectations for the two companies. Of course, there are a limited number of clear-cut, easily identifiable pairs. As a result, long/short managers match any number of companies sharing offsetting risk characteristics, even though they might not all be in precisely the same industry—buy GM and short Goodyear, for example. Most long/short funds hold about 80 pairs. Some pairs are one long and one short, while others are one long and three shorts, or two longs and one short. The pairs don't have to match up one for one, as long as in aggregate they neutralize market risk.

At the core of most long/short strategies is a quantitative model that evaluates a stock's risk characteristics along a number of factors: industry, sector, market capitalization, growth or value tilt, and so forth. Using various statistical techniques such as value-based regression analysis, these models sift through the exact characteristics they're looking for, providing managers with combinations of possible pairs.

Theory versus Practice

Because they are fully hedged, market-neutral strategies are the most conservative of "The Big Four." They won't get you rich, but they'll help you *stay* rich with 8 to 10 percent annualized returns (3 to 5 percentage points above T-bill rates) and volatility closer to that of a bond index than a stock index. For investors seeking to preserve wealth, this is a solid, conservative strategy. But for those of you aggressively seeking higher returns, you probably can't get there from here.

Are long/short strategies so conservative that nothing ever goes wrong? No, unfortunately, things can and do go wrong, and you can sink into a hole that's hard to climb out of. Problems arise if the stocks sold don't go down as hoped, and long positions don't go up enough to absorb the losses. As one veteran investor ruefully observed, "In my experience, more often than not, one side of such trades works well while the other side does very little or even suffers negative returns."

Charles Gradante, president of the Hennessee Group, a major hedge fund advisory firm, believes that a long/short strategy "is flawed" in the current investment environment. In the March 2000 edition of *Bloomberg* magazine, he notes that market-neutral managers essentially bet on a reversion or regression to the mean. But he argues that this strategy is failing in the present momentum market, where historical relationships no longer hold up. In an era when high-tech stocks with no earnings have dramatically outperformed solid blue-chip issues, he says, "We're in a conceptual market as opposed to a market of earnings," which has skewed the traditional relationship between stocks.

Proving his point, many model-driven market-neutral managers have been battered and bruised from going long value and short growth during a time when growth stocks have outperformed value issues by an unprecedented margin. According to the Frank Russell Company, an investment consulting firm, in 1999 the average market-neutral fund lost close to 6 percent. However, a few equity long/short managers had outstanding results in 1999, achieving double-digit returns.

One other sticking point: Long/short strategies aren't very tax efficient. As with arbitrage hedge strategies, fund turnover is very high. Positions get bought and sold every week or every month, generating short-term capital gains and losses.

THE BOTTOM LINE

Should you invest in any of "The Big Four"? That's a personal decision that should take many factors into account—your investment objectives, the size of your portfolio, the proportion put into alternative investments, your attitude toward risk, your level of financial sophistication, and so on. But here's how these four strategies stack up from my point of view.

Global macro funds offer access to big-name investment managers who roam the world seeking unique opportunities. They take a "swing for the fences" approach to doing things. Great returns, but risky! From the investors' standpoint, it's all too easy to be seduced by the siren song of outsized returns. They go into a fund because it was up 72 percent last year, forgetting that, as new investors, they don't benefit from last year's performance, which may not be repeatable this year. Worse, investors don't stop to ask how the manager achieved those results or what the risks were. Personally, I'm also bothered by some of the terms that the more successful global macro funds impose on new investors. Conditions such as protracted lock-up periods, big up-front placement fees, and so on really stack the deck too much in the manager's favor.

Having said that, I only wish I had invested a million dollars with George Soros 20 years ago. If I had, I'd be sitting on a yacht somewhere in the Mediterranean and certainly not writing this book. The real question is: How do you discover the *next* George Soros? If anybody knows, please call me!

Event-driven and arbitrage hedge fund strategies are fascinating investments. They are very complex, very intricate, and managed by some of the best financial minds in the world. Yet they are just a little too exotic for me. And if you've only got $1 million to invest, I cannot recommend putting all of your eggs in the one basket of distressed Japanese bank loans. To me, it doesn't make a lot of sense to invest in these strategies on a stand-alone basis, given what most conservative investors are trying to do. And remember, some of these funds can be risky.

Yet I would not rule them out entirely; in my opinion, there is a place for them in a diversified portfolio. But the best way to invest in these esoteric strategies is not by giving all of your money to one arbitrageur. The best way is to use a "fund of funds" approach, a subject I'll go into in chapter 9.

Balanced long/short strategies are also intriguing. And after the kind of record-setting stock market returns we've experienced, I must say there is something innately appealing about being market neutral. Who knows when the eventual top will come? You'd certainly be better prepared if you complemented a long-only portfolio with a matched pairs strategy. The trouble with long/short approaches is that they just don't produce the 15 percent annual returns I'm after, although it might be interesting to explore the possibility of boosting their returns with moderate leverage. And being conservative by nature, I'm just not comfortable with any kind of quantitative black-box strategy. Plus, I'd hate to get burned and have to dig myself out of a big hole while earning only 8 to 10 percent a year. As we saw in Chapter 1, losses are hard to make up. And then there's the tax issue. But equity market-neutral strategies *do* make a lot of sense for tax-exempt foundations and endowments that don't care about taxes and can use them as a substitute for bonds.

If you decide to go the balanced long/short route, I recommend you diversify manager risk by spreading your money across three or four carefully selected managers. Combined with other defensive strategies, a lineup of several market-neutral managers should provide attractive risk and return characteristics.

In summary, although you might want to invest in one or more of "The Big Four" strategies through a diversified fund of funds, to my mind none of them works as a stand-alone strategy for the conservative high-net-worth investor. But while these approaches don't exactly fit the bill, there is one that does. I've identified one time-tested strategy that I can get really excited about. In the next chapter, I'll tell you all about it.

Chapter 7

Is There a Hedge Fund Strategy for All Seasons?

When I first began exploring hedge funds some years ago, in search of alternatives to the outdated traditional investment approach, I faced the same dilemma as prospective investors today: How can one possibly sort out so many different kinds of funds to make a well-reasoned choice? If anything, the job has become tougher and the sense of urgency greater. As Elizabeth R. Hilpman observed in the March/April 1998 issue of *Investment Policy* in her article, "Hedge Funds Are Here for the Long Haul":

> The extraordinary returns achieved in the last generation raise the ante for finding strategies and talented individuals to, at the very least, preserve the wealth created in these markets. The talent pool in the hedge fund industry is getting deeper and stronger, allowing for greater choice by the investor. However, the proliferation of funds also makes it more difficult to identify winners and weed out losers.

Luckily, I found a way to simplify the process. My solution was to use my own investment objectives as both a starting point and a filter for considering candidate hedge fund strategies. Given the market's annualized returns of approximately 11 percent over the past 75 years or so and my overriding concern with capital preservation, I concluded that I would be very satisfied to earn a pretax return of 15 percent a year. If I could do that consistently, I would double my money in five years.

But I also sought something more. Besides attractive returns, I wanted a strategy designed to meet the goal of "no down calendar years," regardless of what might be occurring in the market. I wanted an approach that, if implemented properly, would insulate me from the trauma of a major market downturn, however imminent or distant it may be.

THE GOAL OF ABSOLUTE RETURN

Only later did I come upon a label to describe just what I was looking for. It turned out that Yale University was going down a similar path, seeking what it called "absolute return investments [that] provide returns largely independent of overall market moves." In fact, the Yale Investment Office lays claim to the distinction of having coined the term "absolute return" in 1989, when it established a formal asset allocation for strategies fitting that definition.

Now I had a name for what I was seeking: hedge fund managers who shared my absolute return philosophy. But where to go from there? I knew that absolute return investing wasn't a recognized, established investment style like value or growth; nor is it a strategy outlined in textbooks, or an investment process, or even a discipline. Rather, it is a philosophy that embodies a set of investment principles designed to produce consistent, attractive returns year in and year out.

In simplest terms, what I wanted was a hedge fund strategy for all seasons—a goal that many conservative investors share. Looking through this prism, the process of weeding out hedge funds became much more straightforward. Many strategies I was able to eliminate from the outset as being too risky, too "black box," too "one off," or too difficult to understand. That meant I could give closer scrutiny to the strategies remaining.

After a few minor detours along the way, I found that ultimately all roads led me back to Alfred Winslow Jones, the inventor of the hedge fund and the creator of the Jones model for investing—an enduring approach that dovetails neatly with my goals of 15 percent annual returns, with no down calendar years.

RIGHT FOR THE TIMES

You could say that I was going back to the future, for when Jones invented the hedge fund in 1949, he created a model that eloquently addresses the needs of twenty-first-century investors. During the 1990s, when "everybody" was making 25 percent a year in the stock market, it was hard to make a case for getting only a 15 or 20 percent return, albeit on a consistent basis. As acknowledged in the article "Putting the Hedge Back into Hedge Funds," by James Picerno, in the May/June 1997 issue of *Dow Jones Asset Management*, "Risk control is a tough sell during bull markets. Perhaps that's why many of today's hedge funds pursue high-risk strategies over conservative hedging systems of the type pioneered by Jones."

But if the high returns of the 1990s don't continue indefinitely, the ideas Jones put forward will be more valid than ever. And even if these kinds of returns do continue for some time to come, the risk-management aspects of the Jones approach make eminently good sense for any investor who believes that "trees don't grow to the sky." I'm as big a believer in the New Economy as anyone, but I'm not willing to tie most of my net worth to the belief that we'll never see another bear market. Nor do I want to watch months or even years of bull-market returns evaporate in downdrafts of volatility.

The Jones approach, remember, combines long investing and short selling to create a hedged exposure to the equities market. In this way, Jones made returns much less dependent on market direction, and much more reliant on manager skill. Unlike many of the strategies that are lumped together under the term "hedge fund," Jones's approach is a *true hedging strategy*—a distinction that's vital to conservative investors, yet one that, oddly enough, hedge fund databases and categorization schemes almost universally ignore.

You'll never find a Jones-model manager relying on complex formulas or black boxes. This approach centers on keen market insights combined with exceptional all-around stock-picking skills. In fact, it is one of the purest examples of skill-based investing, as distinct from the market-based investing of traditional managers.

Nor will you encounter the use of techniques that are fundamentally speculative. Managers seeking sky-high returns may feel pressure to invest in exotic derivatives, currencies, or commodities and make use of maximum leverage to meet their limited partners' ambitious performance goals.

But Jones-model managers who have set reasonable absolute return objectives don't have to take the inordinate (and inescapable) risks these methods entail. They make their money by investing in liquid, publicly traded stocks, applying only moderate leverage.

And while Jones-style managers are *opportunistic*, looking for market inefficiencies across industry sectors and capitalization ranges, they are also *systematic*. By definition, a Jones manager will generally, but not always, maintain hedged positions, though the relative proportion of long and short investments may vary dramatically with the manager's market outlook, as reflected in the fund's month-to-month net equity exposure.

A WORKHORSE STRATEGY

It is by adhering to these key defining principles that Jones-style managers gain the ability to deliver consistent, attractive returns—a characteristic giving this approach a level of utility that many other hedge fund strategies don't offer.

For instance, the Jones model's focus on absolute return and capital preservation makes it an appropriate vehicle for deploying significant portions of an investor's wealth. If you're a conservative investor, you may want to earmark a small portion of your portfolio for interesting, potentially high-reward strategies; there's nothing wrong with taking some extra risks with an amount of money you can afford to lose. But, these sorts of investments belong at the edges of your portfolio.

What belongs at the core, financial advisers universally agree, are liquid, relatively conservative investments in the major capital markets. The Jones model is just such an approach—one that can be the centerpiece of a portfolio's liquid equity investments. Going back to the example of Yale University, which invests with a longer time horizon than most high-net-worth individuals but probably has similar objectives otherwise, we find an investment policy that allocates 90 percent of Yale's assets to equities (both public and private), including 22 percent to absolute return strategies. While you may or may not want those same proportions, this is not a bad scheme for individual investors to ponder as a starting point.

Because Jones-model funds invest in liquid, publicly traded stocks using familiar fundamental research methods, they're also excellent starter funds—an ideal way for those new to hedge fund investing to begin testing the waters.

ADVANTAGES OF A LONG/SHORT APPROACH

While I'm explaining why I believe Jones's approach is particularly well suited to the needs of conservative high-net-worth investors, I want to emphasize a key point that even experienced investors may overlook: Any form of investment hedging involves a trade-off. When you build portfolios to limit downside risk, you always give up something on the upside. In a booming market, a hedged portfolio will not yield as high a return as a fully invested, long-only strategy. That's the price you pay for hedging.

But what you gain in return is a large measure of protection when markets are choppy or declining. A hedged equity portfolio has an anchor to windward no matter which way the market is moving: If stocks are falling, the short portfolio will offset some of the losses being suffered by the long portfolio. And, of course, in rising markets, the reverse is true, though a skillful manager may be able to profit from some short picks even when the market averages are trending upward. "Hedging," Jones liked to say, "is a speculative tool used to conservative ends." It's important to note that Jones-style managers can also raise cash as a defensive maneuver when the market seems shaky; they don't have the pressure to stay fully invested that traditional managers do.

The Jones model has other advantages, too. For instance, it essentially doubles the universe of investment possibilities and allows managers to capitalize on their full range of insights. A manager running a long-only fund selects those securities perceived to have strong appreciation potential; no matter how astute the manager's perceptions about weakening sectors or overvalued companies, there's no way to profit from them. If you think about it, a long-only manager is like a boxer who steps into the ring with one arm tied behind his back. Jones perceived that skilled managers who buy long and also sell short can apply the full sum of their insights and experience.

Another important consequence of short selling is that it frees managers to be more aggressive on the long side. Before Jones came along, shorting stocks, when it was done at all, was a sporadic, piecemeal tactic. Jones made it a consistent and essential part of his investment process. In one of his rare interviews, in 1968 Jones told *New York* magazine, "The logic of the idea was very clear." By going short, he said, "You can buy more good stocks without taking as much risk as someone who merely buys." But Jones actually took this idea one step further, recognizing that with the added dimension of risk control he gained from hedging his equity exposure, he could be bolder in pursuing stocks with strong appreciation potential.

In the seminal April 1966 *Fortune* article that put Jones in the spotlight, author Carol J. Loomis explained Jones's rationale by comparing his approach with that of a conventional investor. Say that both investors start with $100,000. The conventional investor might invest $80,000 in stocks and the rest in "safe" bonds. This gives the investor an equity exposure of 80 percent.

Jones, in contrast, would use the $100,000 to borrow and invest more money, perhaps another $50,000. Then Loomis says, "Of the $150,000 total, Jones might put $110,000 in stocks he likes and sell short $40,000 worth of stocks he thinks are overvalued." Thus, Jones ends up with $40,000 of his long position hedged—offset by a short position—and the remaining $70,000 fully exposed.

In this example, Jones's *net* equity exposure is 70 percent—even less than that of the conventional investor. Yet Jones's market opportunities total $150,000—nearly double those of his long-only counterpart. "The main advantage of the hedge concept, then," Loomis concludes, "is that the investor's short position enables him to operate on the long side with maximum aggressiveness."

Jones also believed that managers experienced at short selling gained market insights that enhanced their performance on the long side. He felt that even when short picks turned out to be unprofitable, the process of analyzing and making them often yielded useful kernels of understanding. In his 1968 interview, Jones put it simply: "Men who learn to sell short seem to have better judgment on what stocks to buy."

TWO SOURCES OF PROFIT

The Jones-style portfolio's blend of long and short investments produces what's commonly referred to as a "market-neutral component." In the example just given, this component would comprise the $40,000 in short sales plus $40,000 in offsetting long positions, also known as the portion "within the hedge." But don't let the term "market-neutral" confuse you; even knowledgeable investors often use it—mistakenly—as a classifying label for Jones-style strategies.

Those strategies the hedge fund industry classifies as "market-neutral" are decidedly different from Jones's approach, in that their long and short positions are intended to be directly offsetting. For instance, a market-neutral manager might buy shares in Ford and short GM, in hopes of neutralizing both directional and sector risk while capitalizing on a belief that Ford will outperform GM. This is certainly a valid approach—but one that's more conservative and yields lower returns than the one Jones designed, as noted in the previous chapter's discussion of the balanced long/short strategy.

The Jones model takes a different tack in that there is no one-to-one relationship between individual long and short positions. The hedged portion of the portfolio is constructed from the very best long picks and the very best short picks, regardless of industry or sector. And significantly, the short positions aren't there merely to serve as a hedge against the long positions; they're expected to make their own contribution to the portfolio's returns.

Ted Caldwell clarifies this point in his article "Jones Model Funds" in the fourth quarter 1995 *Lookout Mountain Hedge Fund Review*:

> The original true hedge fund, Alfred Jones's model, creates an arbitrage between a basket of long positions and a basket of short equity positions. Although managers seek to profit from short positions, it is not necessary for them to do so, to profit within the hedge! All that is necessary to profit within the hedge is to generate a positive spread from the arbitrage, with short positions rising less than long positions, or long positions declining less than short positions.

SPECULATIVE TOOLS, CONSERVATIVE ENDS

As an alternative to taking short positions in individual stocks, hedged equity funds may achieve the same effect by using derivative instruments such as put or call options or index options. However, it's important to distinguish between funds that make aggressive, highly leveraged, directional bets using derivative instruments and those that use derivatives primarily to hedge their downside risk.

Leverage is another speculative tool that the Jones model applies to conservative ends. Use of moderate leverage enabled Jones to invest more assets in what he saw as his best stock picks, thus reaping greater rewards from his insights, but also risking larger losses if his judgment was wrong. Just as the risk control he gained from hedging freed Jones to be more aggressive on the long side, it also allowed him to amplify profits through use of moderate leverage.

Alex Porter, who once worked for Jones and went on to manage his own hedge fund, in 1998 described Jones's leveraging technique to James Grant of *Grant's Interest Rate Observer*:

> Assume that you have $100 in equity capital and that you're long $80. Assume next that you buy another $50. This margin-assisted increment brings your total long exposure to $130. How to protect yourself against a downturn? By selling short $50 against the $50 of incremental longs. Thus, your net long exposure is reduced to $80.

Porter added:

> That's the way it started. . . . shorting against the increment. He figured if we can just pick stocks, let's leverage that, but not let the leverage kill us. Let's go short against the increment. Let's go short against the leverage.

But as the ratio in this example suggests, Jones kept a tight rein on his use of leverage. As with derivatives, the degree of leverage applied is part of what separates a conservative hedging strategy from a far more speculative one.

DEPENDENCE ON MANAGER SKILL

To fully understand Jones's approach, it's essential to recognize that he didn't seek to completely eliminate marketing timing from the picture—and this is another way his approach differs from market-neutral strategies. Whether a Jones-model portfolio is net long or net short overall depends on whether the manager is bullish or bearish on the market. The higher the net long exposure, for example, the greater the manager's confidence that the market will rise. In contrast, a balanced long/short approach maintains an equal dollar weighting of related long and short positions at all times, just as its "balanced" label implies, regardless of what's occurring (or expected to occur) in the market.

The bottom line—and this is a critical point for prospective hedge investors to highlight and underscore—is that unlike the traditional investment arena, where market direction is the single biggest factor in performance, the success of a Jones-model approach depends first and foremost on manager skill, particularly skill in individual stock selection. As Carol J. Loomis observed in her 1966 *Fortune* profile, "Jones's record in forecasting the direction of the market seems to have been only fair." But she added, "Despite these miscalculations about the direction of the market, Jones's selections of individual stocks have generally been brilliant." Given the stellar returns that Jones's funds achieved over a period of many years, it seems that his being a brilliant stock picker was good enough.

The beauty of Jones's hedging concept isn't what led so many money managers to follow in his footsteps; it was the amazing performance record he compiled. His fund began with $100,000 in 1949. By the mid-1960s, his fund had more than $100 million and had left the nation's top-performing mutual funds in the dust in terms of performance over the preceding 5- and 10-year periods.

KEEPING UP WITH THE JONESES

For today's investors, the more relevant issue is whether Jones's intellectual progeny have come anywhere close to matching his prodigious performance. But as is often the case where hedge fund statistics are concerned, it's not so easy to come up with a straightforward answer. For whatever reason, the industry doesn't break out Jones-model funds as a distinct category, so there's no easy way to track performance of Jones-model managers as a group. Many research sources do track the "balanced long/short" category, but for the reasons noted earlier, that is not a valid proxy; balanced long/short strategies are much more rigid than Jones-model strategies and have very different performance characteristics, with considerably lower expected returns.

The closest substitute researchers currently offer is the "hedged equity" category, and here some overall performance data is available. According to Hedge Fund Research, one of the industry's primary data sources, "Equity Hedge" funds registered an average annualized return of 23.7 percent from January 1990 to December 1999, with an annualized

standard deviation of 8.7 percent. Compared with the S&P 500's performance over the same period, these funds yielded higher returns, but also
much lower volatility: 8.7 percent versus 13.4 percent for the S&P.

It's instructive to note that the trade-off inherent in a hedged investment approach—the giving up of some upside return in exchange for
some downside protection—is reflected in the year-by-year performance of
these funds. As shown in Figure 7.1, returns from hedged equity funds
somewhat lagged the market in the boom years of 1995 through 1998. But
their performance shone in the falling market of 1990.

Attractive as these returns are, there is another dimension to hedged
equity performance that may be equally appealing to many investors: The
hedged equities portfolios offered more *consistency* in their returns than
did the S&P 500, as illustrated in Figure 7.2. In fact, the standard deviation of returns for the hedged equity portfolios was lower than the comparable measure for the S&P 500 in one, three, five, and ten-year periods
ending December 31, 1999, according to data provided by Hedge Fund
Research. That's not surprising. The point of hedging is not just to en-

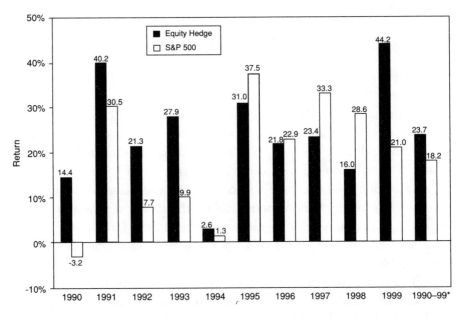

Figure 7.1   Equity Hedge versus S&P 500: Annual Returns, 1990–1999
Source: Hedge Fund Research, Inc.; Standard & Poor's.
*Annualized.

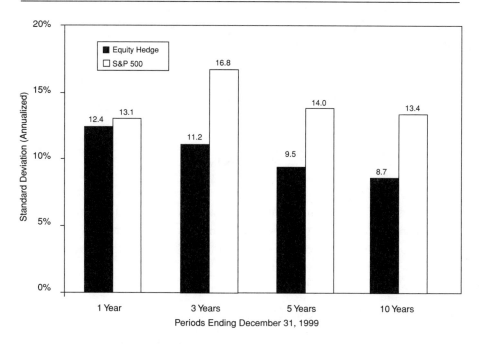

Figure 7.2 **Equity Hedge versus S&P 500: Annualized Standard Deviation of Monthly Returns, 1990–1999**

Source: Hedge Fund Research, Inc.; Standard & Poor's.

hance returns, but to modulate the impact of stock price movements—and that's just what these funds did.

Table 7.1 summarizes how over the past 10 years hedged equity strategies have produced a higher return with lower risk, and, therefore, a better *risk-adjusted return* than the S&P 500. A better risk-adjusted return (as measured by a higher Sharpe ratio) means that hedged equity strategies generated more "dollar bang for the risk buck." In other words, investors were more highly compensated for the amount of risk taken with hedged equity strategies than they were owning an S&P 500 index fund. And that better risk-adjusted return was achieved with relatively low *correlation* to the market, a concept we'll elaborate on in the next chapter.

Of course, as I've said regarding broad-brush hedge fund statistics before, they should all be taken with a grain of salt, especially when terms and definitions are being loosely applied. You can be certain that not all hedged equity fund managers adhere to the principles of A. W. Jones. But for category-level performance measurements, "hedged equity" funds are

Table 7.1   **Equity Hedge Statistics versus the S&P 500, 1990 through 1999**

	Annualized Return	Annualized Standard Deviation	Sharpe Ratio	Correlation vs. S&P 500
Equity Hedge	23.7%	8.7%	2.15	0.64
S&P 500	18.2%	13.4%	0.99	1.00

Source: Hedge Fund Research, Inc.; Standard & Poor's.

the closest thing to the Jones model we've got. Their performance may be enough to encourage investors to look more closely at the methods and records of individual hedged equity managers—and in the final analysis, those are the statistics that matter most.

A TALE OF TWO MANAGERS

We already know that although A. W. Jones spawned the hedge fund industry, it wasn't in his own image. Ted Caldwell traced this evolution in his article, "Classifying Hedge Funds: What's in a Name?" in the March/April 1998 issue of *Investment Policy*:

> The proliferation of hedge funds didn't begin until 17 years [after Jones established his fund], in early 1966, when in the midst of a major bull market the financial media finally discovered Jones's operation. But the fact that Jones conceived a *conservative* investing system was lost on most of the imitation funds that were established in the following years. They appear to have been set up primarily to invest with leverage in a bull market, and to keep 20 percent of their investors' profits.

> Caldwell goes on to decry the industry's failure to distinguish between "funds that actually hedge and funds that don't," flatly stating that "the media and the investment world in general continue to miss the point. Funds structurally similar to Alfred Jones's have been called 'hedge funds' ever since—with complete indifference as to whether or not they hedge."

But what of the true inheritors of A. W. Jones? How have they carried on his legacy? A look at two of the best-known hedge fund managers today can give us some sense of where the poles of the spectrum, at least, might lie.

At one end is a manager who is far more often associated with the larger-than-life pyrotechnics of global macro investing than with any conservative hedging approach: Julian H. Robertson Jr., who is a perennial on the *Forbes* list of the 400 richest Americans and for years vied with George Soros for the distinction of running the world's biggest pool of hedge fund assets.

But what's seldom noted in recounting of the Robertson legend is that for a time he ran a substantial portion of the assets of A. W. Jones & Company on a contract basis. He was hired by Robert L. Burch III, Jones's son-in-law, shortly after he took over the company (which, by the way, is still in existence). As Burch himself recently told me, Robertson and Jones were philosophically "very close." What's more, Jones considered Robertson to be his "heir apparent."

The North Carolina native and former Kidder Peabody stockbroker established Tiger Fund Management in 1980, applying the hedged equity model to his $8 million in assets under management. It wasn't long before he had Wall Street sitting up to take notice; Tiger recorded a 24.3 percent gain in 1981, while the S&P 500 lost 5 percent.

Robertson went on to compile an extraordinary record over the next 18 years, averaging an annual return of 29 percent—the best performance of any manager through this time period—before faltering at the turn of the century. Still, even with its recent losses, one dollar invested in Tiger at its inception has grown to $82, after fees, today. Only George Soros can challenge Robertson for the throne; when performance is compared over an even longer time period, Soros rules.

But outstanding as it is, Robertson's record can't be claimed for the disciples of A. W. Jones. What happened to Robertson is telling to those seeking a hedged equity manager: He became so successful that he could no longer employ the strategy behind that success. Once the Tiger Funds passed the $3 billion or $4 billion mark, the hedged equity approach became untenable. If you're a pure stock picker working on both the long and short sides, it becomes increasingly difficult to find enough good ideas you can put to work. Sooner or later, you're forced to look at other ways of making money, such as currencies, commodities, or private placements.

This is exactly what happened to Robertson. He turned to the global macro style for which Tiger has become known, pushing stock picking into the background as he grew his set of funds to over $20 billion in assets as of 1998. But along the way, he helped launch the career of the manager who is arguably Jones's best-known disciple today. As A. W. Jones & Company begat Robertson, Robertson begat Ainslie.

THE NEW GENERATION

Lee Ainslie went straight from business school to Tiger Fund Management, where he managed portfolios using the Jones approach. In 1993, he was hired by the Texas entrepreneur Sam Wyly and some family members to manage a portion of their substantial wealth under the auspices of Maverick Capital, which Wyly had founded in 1990. By late 1993, the fund was opened to out-side investors, and by February 1995, Ainslie was sole manager of two Maver-ick hedge funds with some $2.5 billion under management.

While Ainslie may no longer be the purest example of Jones-style management—he, too, has branched out somewhat as his asset base has mushroomed—he is certainly among the most highly regarded. In 1997, *Lookout Mountain Hedge Fund Review* described him as "running the best conservative Jones model fund we know of, barring none!"

And for the most part, Ainslie has generally strayed little from the master's principles. In a July 15, 1996 *Barron's* article entitled "A Classic Approach," Ainslie summed up his philosophy in one sentence that could have come from Jones's lips: "A hedge fund manager wins big by picking stocks, not timing the market."

As Ainslie told *Barron's*,

> We are sort of the opposite of what some people consider hedge funds to be. We aren't trying to make market calls or make macro-economic bets or figure out which sector is going to be hot and which is not. We are working hard to take all of that out of the equation, making our success dependent purely upon our ability to pick longs and shorts.

Sound familiar? Ainslie gave credit where credit was due:

> The classic hedge-fund approach, which was started by A. W. Jones in 1949, combined the idea of using a little leverage with

investing in longs and shorts, to have net exposure to the market below your equity value. In other words, for every $100 invested the classic hedge fund may have $110 in long securities, $70 in short securities, for a net exposure to the market of only $40, or 40%. And actually, on a percentage basis, that would be a pretty fair characterization of Maverick.

Ainslie elaborated on the Jones legacy in an interview published in *Investing with the Hedge Fund Giants*, a 1998 Financial Times/Pitman Publishing book by Beverly Chandler. "We have simply refined Mr. Jones' original hedged approach," he said, "to include stronger risk control and to bring greater focus to our efforts on security selection."

He sounded a similar note in an interview with *Fortune*, observing, "Our expertise is in stock picking. We don't want to fool ourselves or our investors by pretending to do anything else." And like Jones, Ainslie believes that investment decisions should be driven by the kind of thorough, fundamental analysis—visiting companies, evaluating management, interviewing customers and suppliers—that fewer and fewer managers bother to do anymore.

If Ainslie has largely replicated Jones's methods, one wonders whether he's replicated Jones's performance, too. The 1996 *Barron's* piece observed that Ainslie had "outperformed the market indexes for every region where he's invested" since joining Maverick. An update came in a January 11, 1999, *Fortune* article which noted, "Over the past five years, Ainslie and his team are up 25.5 percent annually (that's net), vs. 19.9 percent for the S&P." But in this uncertain and volatile investment climate, Ainslie and Maverick Capital will undoubtedly have more chances to prove their mettle—particularly now that they're managing upwards of $4.5 billion.

A CHOSEN FEW

Of course, Robertson and Ainslie are just two of the descendants of A. W. Jones; my best guess is that there are in the neighborhood of 40 to 50 managers who would proclaim themselves to be followers of the Jones model. So in the context of the $355-plus billion hedge fund industry, their ranks are small. Given the success that Jones and others have had with his hedged equity approach, one may wonder why.

One answer can be found in the May/June 1997 *Dow Jones Asset Management* article cited earlier in this chapter:

> Conceptually, hedging is no better or worse than any other investment strategy. The brilliance—or the stupidity—of the approach depends on implementation. The Jones model is considered one of the more brilliant applications of hedging, thanks to its potential, if properly executed, for risk reduction without drastically neutralizing upside opportunity.

The key phrase in that passage is "if properly executed." Remember, Jones was revered as a brilliant stock picker—and it's not easy to be brilliant. A traditional manager may do well for years, simply by riding the market's currents. But for a Jones-model manager to do well, he or she must elevate stock picking to a refined art, selectively identifying stocks expected to rise and others expected to decline. And if the results are lackluster, it can't be blamed on the market.

As Jones himself explained it, his approach required skill in maintaining two kinds of balance: one between "boldness and caution," the other a balancing of "gullibility and skepticism." He emphasized that "a money manager doesn't dream up ideas. He gathers ideas from other sources." In Jones's mind, the trick was to be enthused by ideas while also maintaining a healthy level of skepticism. "I've seen both extremes and the ultra-gullible is the worst because he can be led up the garden path," he said. "But being too skeptical is not very good either."

Perhaps the biggest obstacle for would-be Jones-style managers is the difficulty of short selling, which seems to be something of a God-given talent for those who do it successfully. Of all the investment disciplines, shorting may be the most difficult to master. In essence, it takes what most investment managers have been trained and disciplined to do and turns it upside down. Rather than uncovering companies with prospects for growth, short sellers must be early (but not too early) in identifying those headed for a fall—the has-beens, rather than the up-and-comers, the companies more likely to stumble than surge ahead.

This is harder than it may seem. Most of Wall Street's idea-generating apparatus is geared to going long, not short. These days, analysts may issue 50 or 100 buy recommendations for every sell—and remember, when they say "sell," that's typically a cue to dispose of existing holdings, which isn't the same as a short recommendation; it may only mean the stock isn't expected to rise as fast as some others.

But beyond that, shorting demands a different mind-set—the ability to see a cloud in every silver lining. As Jones told *Institutional Investor* in 1968, "Some people are not congenitally equipped to sell short. It goes against their psychological makeup." For Jones-model managers, the challenge is even greater: They must be able to operate in the short-sell mind-set and the growth-oriented long investment mind-set at the same time.

This is truly skill-based investing—and with the Jones model, the key to success is the skills of the manager making the decisions. As *Institutional Investor* said of the Jones approach in its 1968 article, "Perhaps more than most kinds of investment management it depends on the brain power of the men who run the show." Thirty years later, *Grant's Interest Rate Observer* said pretty much the same thing in its October 9, 1998 issue: "The genius of the Jones partnership lay not in a foolproof system but in the talent and prudence of the people who managed it." Any investor who's interested in exploring Jones-model funds should keep these words in mind.

DEFINING CHARACTERISTICS

Given all the confusion over hedge fund classifications and labels, it's worth taking a moment to make sure you'll know a Jones-model fund (or a pretender) when you see it. Managers may vary some elements of the original Jones model, but here are some of the essential characteristics that these funds share. A Jones-model fund is one that:

- Invests for absolute return, rather than trying to beat the market or meet some arbitrary benchmark. A well-run Jones-model fund should be able to target annual returns in the neighborhood of 15 percent without use of leverage, or somewhat more if leverage is used. If the target return is more than 20 percent, that's a red flag that may indicate use of a high degree of leverage or some other potentially risky techniques.
- Strives for "no down years." Clearly the emphasis is on avoiding losses above all.

- Generally, but not always, maintains hedged positions. The proportion of long and short investments will vary (sometimes dramatically) with the manager's outlook on the market.
- Raises and lowers cash levels according to perceptions of the market's overall risk/reward characteristics.
- Is flexible, not limiting investments to a certain style, sector, or capitalization range; may blend both growth and value, for instance.
- Invests opportunistically, capitalizing on market inefficiencies.
- Views stock picking as the primary source of return.
- Makes decisions in an entrepreneurial fashion. Decisions are usually made by just one or two senior people and not by a committee.
- May make concentrated investments. While some level of diversification is essential, Jones-model managers tend to focus on those themes, sectors, or companies in which conviction is highest.
- Tends to be small in size. Jones-style managers typically run between $50 million and $500 million. More than that, and they may have trouble generating enough good ideas to put all their assets to work.
- Stays away from inherently speculative strategies or techniques. While they may make moderate use of leverage or derivatives, as described above, a Jones-model manager with reasonable return objectives shouldn't have to engage in risky business. When it comes to exotic derivatives, currency trading, commodities, excessive leverage, or private placements, a true follower of Jones will just say "No."

IS IT FOR YOU?

The pluses and minuses of the Jones approach are evident: If your goal is to win some performance derby, the Jones model is the wrong horse to bet on. On the other hand, if your goal is to achieve returns that are consistent as well as attractive—well, there's something about that Jones boy.

Of course, *every* investment strategy has its pluses and minuses. The fact is, no strategy can produce superior *relative* returns in a bull market and also produce superior *absolute* returns in a bear market. No one has yet figured out how to square that circle. But in this investment climate, one thing seems clear: The higher the market goes, the more critical it is to insulate portfolios from volatility and the risk of a major decline. And that's exactly what the Jones model is designed to do.

I must point out, though, that if you're convinced the stock market will continue to provide the lofty returns it rang up in the 1990s, then this hedged equity approach is definitely not for you. You should stick with a traditional approach that focuses on relative performance—preferably through index funds, since most traditional money managers have not been able to outperform a rising market.

But if you're a conservative investor who believes that the stock market is still a two-way street, you may want some protection against market risk while profiting from the market's upside potential. In this case, the Jones approach to investing can be a valuable addition to your investment portfolio—and not just as a sideline, but front and center as a cornerstone of your equity investments.

Implicit in the Jones model is the belief that formulas, models, and "black boxes" cannot be counted on to provide the consistency conservative investors want. Only skilled and dedicated managers can do that. This may not be an altogether satisfying notion in this era of computerized neural networks and artificial intelligence. We would like to think that with enough advanced technology we can take the unpredictability out of investing. But, thus far, even our most sophisticated systems have fallen short. There is still no substitute for seasoned market experience and judgment.

What Gerald Loeb said more than three decades ago is still true today. A veteran Wall Street investor and commentator and author of the investing classic, *The Battle for Investment Survival*, Loeb concluded that "The priceless ingredient in a hedge fund is its management." And he warned that a hedge fund "in anything but the most capable hands" has the potential to "produce more than average difficulties."

The Jones model recognizes this, just as it recognizes other realities of the investment marketplace. It is grounded in the belief that good managers can, in fact, succeed in identifying stocks with a higher-than-average probability of going up or going down. But these managers cannot forecast which direction the overall market is going, at least not with any certainty or consistency; nor can anyone else. Since markets fluctuations are inevitable, it makes sense that an approach combining exposure to the market's upside with a measure of downside protection has the best chance of delivering consistently attractive returns.

You can sample an assortment of other complicated and exotic strategies, and find that many of them earn good returns for a little while, sometimes for longer periods. But if you care about achieving consistent returns, look to the heirs of Alfred Winslow Jones.

PART III

MAKING HEDGE FUND INVESTMENTS

Chapter 8

Investing in Hedge Funds— How Much?

I hope by now I've convinced you that hedge funds can be extremely attractive vehicles for high-net-worth investors seeking superior risk-adjusted returns, year in and year out. But some interim steps are needed before you can put a good idea into practice. The first question is, how much of your money should you invest? Should it be a major share of your investable assets, or a small, token percentage?

The answer probably lies somewhere in between. But settling on a precise figure isn't easy. As with any investment, it takes thoughtful consideration and analysis. With hedge funds, this is especially true since you can't get in the game simply by emptying out your piggy bank or petty cash drawer. Unlike mutual funds, where the price of entry can be $500, in the world of hedge funds you typically need to commit serious money— at least $250,000, and perhaps more like $500,000 or even $1 million.

Whatever size check you mail off to a hedge fund, it's likely to be a pretty large one. So, before you take out your pen and start writing, you need to know how a hedge fund investment fits into the broader context of your total financial picture. Only then can you know the appropriate number of "000s" to fill in the blank.

THE ASSET ALLOCATION CONCEPT

In recent years there has been a significant shift in the way people think about selecting investments for a portfolio. In earlier times, if you were a

131

savvy investor you would ponder trends and events from your particular corner of the universe, assessing any and all investment opportunities you might spy. After careful consideration, you might decide to invest in one of those opportunities—buy a certain stock, or put money into a specific fund, or buy a particular building. And then another opportunity would come along, which you would then investigate, deciding whether to jump on it or let it pass by. Your investment portfolio became a collection of your very best ideas. The better each of those ideas was, it was assumed, the better the total portfolio.

But with the advent of Modern Portfolio Theory in the 1950s came the view that this seat-of-the-pants approach wasn't good enough. While each investment idea might very well be attractive on its own merits, it didn't necessarily follow that collectively they made for a well-constructed portfolio. The aggregate collection of "best idea" investments was likely to be too heavily weighted in one direction or another, exposing an investor to sizable, unintended risks. In other words, the "best ideas" portfolio wasn't well diversified.

Then in 1986, an investment manager named Gary Brinson and two of his colleagues wrote a landmark article in the *Financial Analysts Journal* concluding that asset allocation explains over 90 percent of portfolio performance. According to their research, selecting the best individual securities within a given market—the most attractive stocks or the most attractive bonds—didn't matter nearly as much as the percentage of assets committed to the stock or bond markets as a whole. Their analysis suggested that all that huffing and puffing to choose just the right security wasn't worth the effort. What really counted was being in the right asset class.

Rusty Olson, Director of Pension Investments Worldwide for Eastman Kodak, explains in his book, *The Independent Fiduciary* (John Wiley & Sons, 1999), why asset allocation matters:

> Investment results within an asset class are so dominated by the wind behind that asset class, *any* manager's results will be highly impacted by that wind. If large U.S. stocks achieve high returns, so will nearly all managers of large U.S. stocks; and those managers will not be able to escape the slaughter if large U.S. stocks should crash.

Olson defines "the wind" as "all the things that tend to affect the returns of *all* investments in any particular asset class at any given time."

This revolutionary way of thinking caught on quickly, and soon it was widely accepted that the best way to build an investment portfolio was to begin with a big-picture assessment of the proper asset allocation. Only then should an investor begin looking at individual securities. This concept had intrinsic appeal because it embodied the principle that diversification is important to successful investing. And everyone knows you shouldn't put all your eggs in one basket.

The trouble is, no one agrees on how many baskets you should have or what those baskets should be. In addition, asset allocation decisions are a double-edged sword. If you put a lot of money into an asset class that does well, you make more money than if you'd invested only a little. But if you limit your exposure and that asset class performs poorly, you're better off because of those limits. The ex post facto principles of asset allocation are clear: You should put as much as possible into the winners and as little as possible into the losers. Unfortunately, investments don't come with tags that say "winner" or "loser." As a result, we need some rules of thumb to guide us through the asset allocation process.

HOW THE PROS DO IT

If you studied finance in college or graduate school in the past 30 years or so, you are probably familiar with Modern Portfolio Theory's "efficient frontier," a mathematical method of determining the ideal asset allocation scheme to fit your particular objectives. To plot the efficient frontier, an investment management consultant uses a computer model that crunches through every possible combination of asset classes. What's more, it identifies the precise asset mix expected to produce the optimal portfolio for any given risk or return objective.

As Yale Endowment manager David F. Swensen explains in his book, *Pioneering Portfolio Management*:

> An efficient portfolio dominates all others producing the same return or exhibiting the same risk. In other words, for given risk level, no other portfolio produces a higher return than the efficient portfolio. Similarly, for a given return level, no other portfolio exhibits lower risk than the efficient portfolio.

As graphically depicted in Figure 8.1, the efficient frontier is the line that connects all optimal portfolios across all levels of risk and return.

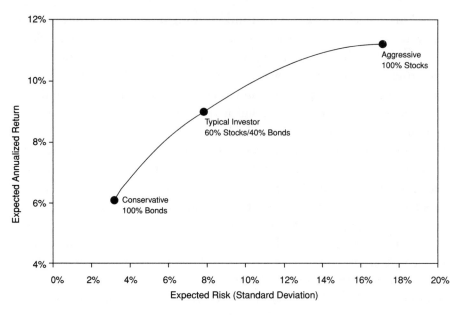

Figure 8.1   **Theoretical Efficient Frontier**

For example, the efficient frontier might show that if you are willing to tolerate annual swings of plus or minus 9 percent around your expected rate of return, to reap the largest gains you should put 60 percent of your money in stocks and 40 percent in bonds. If you ignored the efficient frontier and instead divided your money equally between stocks and bonds, your portfolio wouldn't be expected to perform as well—it would be suboptimal. Any combination of asset classes other than the efficient frontier's 60/40 split would have a lower expected return at your chosen level of acceptable risk, or a higher level of risk at your targeted level of return.

The concept of the efficient frontier has transformed the way institutional investors carve up their assets. It is widely recognized as the theoretically rigorous way to construct an investment portfolio. But practically speaking, how does it work? And, more importantly, how *well* does it work?

To figure out how to apportion assets according to the efficient frontier, institutional investors start by drawing up a list of acceptable asset classes—stocks, bonds, cash, and so forth. Then, they quantitatively describe each asset class using three inputs: expected return, expected risk, and expected correlation with other asset classes. This is all well and good. But here's the question: Where do they get their numbers?

The answer is that most institutions use historical information as a basis for estimating expected return. They get that data from sources such as Ibbotson Associates, a leading consulting firm that compiles annualized performance data for most of the leading asset classes going back as far as 1926. But institutional investors don't necessarily take the historical return data at face value. Although they find it useful to look at past returns, they know that history may not repeat itself. So, many institutional investors massage the historical data, incorporating their own views about the future or the forecasts of one of Wall Street's reigning gurus. They may eliminate or discount prior outlier years that are deemed extreme and nonrepresentative of an asset class's performance. Or they may pick their return estimate based on a conviction that the future is likely to replicate the past only since a given time period.

Institutional investors equate risk with volatility, and their volatility measure of choice is the standard deviation of returns. Standard deviation quantifies the dispersion of any given period's returns around the period's average return. If stock prices are moving around a lot, they have a high standard deviation or relatively high volatility. If bond prices follow a smoother and steadier course, that's low standard deviation, or relatively low risk. As Gary Brinson has said, standard deviation "just measures the degree of bumpiness in the road." Like return data, historical standard deviations for most major asset classes are widely available. But here again, the past isn't always a reliable predictor of the future, and institutions adjust these measures to reflect their own unique outlooks.

The third input into the efficient frontier is expected correlation or covariance. A major goal of the asset allocation process is to find asset classes that have low or even negative correlations with each other and combine them in ways that smooth out investment returns. In other words, if stocks zig, you want to mix them with an asset class that zags—perhaps bonds or real estate. From a purely mathematical standpoint, combining assets that don't move in tandem reduces portfolio volatility without lowering expected return. Institutions develop an appropriate assumption of how asset classes move in relation to each other based on correlation statistics that are widely available for most major categories of securities.

With these three factors, investors have most of the information needed to plot their efficient frontier—estimates of return, risk, and correlation for each asset class they are considering. But as these assumptions are input, it's also essential to enter certain constraints, which can apply to any single asset class or combination of asset classes. Without these constraints, the optimizer might tell us, for instance, that the most efficient portfolio consists of only emerging market debt and small-cap growth stocks! Thus, investors should establish their broad asset allocation guidelines at the outset. For example, you might stipulate that no more than a certain percentage of the portfolio should be in international stocks.

All the assumptions and constraints are entered into an efficient frontier optimizer, which is simply the computer software that develops the range of optimal portfolios. The software generates a graph like the one shown in Figure 8.1. That's the efficient frontier, and it shows you the precise mix of assets that will maximize your return per unit of risk.

HOW HEDGE FUNDS FIT IN

Figure 8.2 shows an efficient frontier analysis that incorporates hedge funds. This chart paints a clear picture why institutional investors are clambering on board the hedge fund bandwagon. They recognize that hedge funds have the potential to increase their plan's expected return, and, *at the same time*, reduce its risk. Because hedge funds present so substantial an opportunity for diversification, what investment committee member wouldn't want to consider introducing them into the mix?

In a 1998 study, Rama Rao, head of RR Capital Management Corp. and Jerry J. Szilagyi, who at the time the study was written was director of financial services for KPMG Consulting, confirmed the diversification benefits of hedge funds:

> In summary, hedge funds as a group seem to offer higher returns with average volatility and have a low correlation with traditional investments. Based on Modern Portfolio Theory, it is possible for investors to boost returns while simultaneously lowering volatility by including hedge funds in their optimum portfolio versus a portfolio constructed exclusively with traditional instruments like stocks and bonds. It is our view that as investors become more and more sophisticated and become aware of these performance characteristics, they will allocate a larger portion of their investment assets to hedge funds.

Among their evidence, Rao and Szilagyi cited an analysis by Dr. Matthias Bekier and his group at the University of St. Gallen, which found

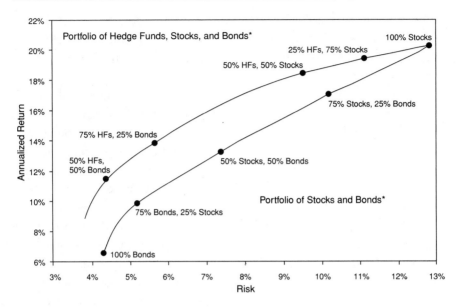

Figure 8.2   **Hedge Fund Efficient Frontier**
Source: Hennessee Group LLC.
*Hedge fund portfolio: Hennessee Hedge Fund Index from January 1973 to December 1999; stock portfolio: S&P 500 Stock Index; bond portfolio: Lehman Brothers Government/Corporate Bond Index.

that "more than 70 percent of hedge funds have correlation coefficients with the S&P 500 and Lehman bond indexes below 0.3, which is considered to be a statistically insignificant correlation. An r-squared of 1.0 represents perfect correlation, while an r-squared of 0.0 represents no correlation."

As Leah Modigliani concluded in her analysis of hedge funds published in 1997 by Morgan Stanley Dean Witter, "While a particular portfolio may not perform well when evaluated independently, that portfolio may still be a wonderfully advantageous addition to a larger portfolio." And she added, "Our work shows that this maxim is especially relevant to hedge funds."

A SKEPTIC'S VIEW

Just like large institutions investing billions of dollars, wealthy individual investors must also make decisions about how to allocate their assets. And after seeing how the big boys do things, you may be ready to start compiling return, risk, and covariance data. Big-money investors have relied upon this approach for years, so there must be something to it, right? But slow down and take a deep breath. The institutional approach has some limitations you should be aware of.

First, there are its theoretical drawbacks. For example, the old saying "garbage in, garbage out" never rang more true. Efficient frontier models are driven entirely by the numbers you input, and their outcomes vary wildly depending on the input assumptions you make. If you rely solely on historical data, you're assuming that returns, standard deviations, and correlations will remain unchanged. And if you incorporate any given pundit's forecast, you're betting that particular seer is right. So, unfortunately, asset allocation still involves a strong element of luck; I'd argue that the odds are against producing an outcome that will prove to be on target.

In his book *Hazardous to Your Wealth: Extraordinary Popular Delusions and the Madness of Mutual Fund Experts*, investment manager Robert Markman commented: "The major flaw in the efficient frontier model is the assumption that it is possible to determine the future correlations between various equity asset classes. I maintain that is simply impossible." Markman complains that this effort is built on shifting sands because the relationships between the returns on various types of securities are constantly evolving.

David F. Swensen notes that:

> The way in which asset classes relate to each other may not be stable. Most investors rely heavily on historical experience in estimating quantitive inputs, yet continuous structural evolution would be sufficient to cause historical correlations to be of questionable use in building portfolio allocations. Even more disturbing, market crises tend to cause otherwise distinct markets to behave in a similar fashion. . . the behavior of markets in the period immediately surrounding the 1987 crash caused many investors to wonder what happened to the hoped-for diversification.

The limitations of the institutional approach aren't merely theoretical; investor experiences bear out the suspicion that asset allocation may not always work that well. In the late 1990s, when large U.S. growth stocks, particularly technology stocks, began to dominate the market, investors who stuck to their prescribed asset allocations were left behind.

Up against the wall, the financial consultants protested en masse: Nobody could have predicted that large-cap U.S. growth stocks would rack up the best five back-to-back years in their history; that's not what asset allocation models are supposed to do. But the bottom line is that after all the intellectual heavy lifting required to construct portfolios scientifically, the end result is often mediocrity—that is, the same level of performance that could have been achieved with a random allocation to index funds.

Beyond these general limitations, there are caveats that apply specifically to individual investors. One relates to the stark contrast between institutional and individual time horizons. Institutions invest with horizons of 25 years or more. They can afford to wait out periods of volatility or underperformance when a particular asset class leaves them hanging for an extended period of time. But try to find a high-net-worth investor who is willing to wait for rewards through long years of lackluster performance. The young ones don't have the patience, and the older ones don't have the time.

It's also intriguing to observe the institutional mind-set. Plan sponsors find safety in numbers. And why wouldn't they stick with a systematic and almost universally sanctioned approach? A plan sponsor in charge of a $10 billion fund was once heard to remark, "I'd much rather lose a billion dollars by sticking to my formal asset allocation policy than lose ten million by straying from the path. I could defend the billion-dollar loss to the investment committee. All I'd have to do is say, 'Don't blame me: The market was down ten percent, and everybody lost money!' But I'd sure be in hot water over the ten-million-dollar-loss."

For institutional investors, clinging to a tightly prescribed scientific asset allocation policy is a pragmatic way to gain a measure of job security. But individual investors face no such pressures; they're free to use whatever approach they think will work best.

When individual investors start looking into hedge funds, the institutional asset allocation approach becomes even more problematic. In general, it is difficult to insert nontraditional investments into a traditional asset allocation framework using Modern Portfolio Theory.

David F. Swensen has this to say about the problem:

Nontraditional asset classes provide interesting challenges. Unlike traditional marketable securities, alternative assets exist outside established markets. No benchmark returns provide guidance to investors seeking to model asset characteristics.

Past data, limited in scope, generally describe active manager returns, with results inflated by substantial survivorship bias.

When it comes to hedge funds, efficient frontier analysis has added limitations. The most fundamental problem is that, in my judgment, hedge funds do *not* constitute an asset class. They are *nontraditional investment strategies* with risk/return profiles ranging from church-mouse conservative to junkyard-dog aggressive. As explained in earlier chapters, it is impossible to generalize about the characteristics of hedge funds. So it would be unwise to take too literally the results of any efficient frontier optimizer incorporating such generalized inputs.

Even if it were possible to come up with valid average data for hedge funds, a statistician would object; there simply isn't enough hedge fund data to make efficient frontier results statistically significant. While data on stocks and bonds go back to 1926, hedge funds have nowhere near that lengthy a history. Although the idea has been around for over 50 years, most hedge funds are of relatively recent vintage. We have little more than a decade's worth of solid hedge fund data at best.

AVOID THE TRAP

The efficient frontier approach is certainly conceptually tidy and mathematically elegant. At first glance, it seems like a foolproof, scientifically engineered asset allocation machine. You come up with your estimates, plug them into the right software, and presto—out comes the magic formula for apportioning your money. Looking through the rearview mirror, it's all nice and neat and scientific.

But investors—particularly individuals investing in hedge funds—run into big problems when they view the efficient frontier method as infallible and its outcomes as fact. So, please, don't allow yourself to be trapped by its precise, scientific appeal. As soon as someone starts talking about "mean-variance optimization" in the same breath as hedge funds, your antenna should go up. Remember, it's Modern Portfolio *Theory*, not Modern Portfolio *Law*. And watch out for anyone telling you different—they're probably trying to sell you something.

This is not to say that I don't believe there's a place for asset allocation methodologies. While hedge funds don't fit neatly into a mathematical asset allocation framework, they *do* fit beautifully with its underlying principles. Hedge funds can be a sound addition to a portfolio because they contribute a distinct set of characteristics—a different rhythm—to the asset mix. With their focus on absolute returns and unique, proprietary strategies, hedge funds provide something that is not offered by traditional stocks and bonds, by investments in real estate, or by holdings in a family business.

SOME REAL-LIFE EXAMPLES

Our task in this chapter is to examine practical, commonsense ways of determining an appropriate allocation for hedge funds. The issues are still the same: You need to diversify enough to avoid excessive financial pain should a particular investment or market suffer a sharp decline. But you don't want too much diversification—you need to put sufficient money into an investment to enable it to have a meaningful impact on your portfolio's overall results.

Frank Helsom, executive vice president of Bessemer Trust Company in Florida, suggests an interesting approach. He asks his clients to think about dividing their assets into two separate pools. The money in the first pool is for maintaining their high standard of living. It is invested in a wide range of conservative stocks and bonds, including tax-free municipals. The second pool is not needed for day-to-day financial well-being and, therefore, can be invested more aggressively. In advising a particular client on composition of that second pool, Helsom recommended an asset mix that, in addition to conventional stocks and bonds, included 20 percent in alternative investments like hedge funds.

For another perspective let's turn to the Institute for Private Investors, a group of more than 200 high-net-worth families, most overseeing assets of $50 million or more. According to a 1997 survey conducted by Charlotte Beyer, the founding principal of the Institute, these ultra-affluent families allocate anywhere from 10 to 80 percent of their portfolios to alternative investments. And the 1999 update of this survey showed hedge funds continuing to dominate that category. Specifically, hedge fund commitments were more than double those of any other type of nontraditional investment, including private equity and venture capital.

In a 1997 article written for the Investment Management Consultants Association (IMCA), Ms. Beyer described some of the varying approaches the Institute's members have used to make their asset allocation decisions. One went through all the rigors of efficient frontier modeling and optimization, and followed the resulting prescription to the letter—

unfortunately, with very disappointing results. Trapped in the science, he underweighted U.S. equities in the face of a raging bull market. Another very wealthy member did just the opposite, completely abandoning the set of asset allocation rules he had set for himself. He watched the equity portion of his portfolio rise to unprecedented heights . . . and did absolutely nothing about it. He was afraid to trim back his positions because of the tax implications of huge unrealized gains. Although he is happy with his extraordinary returns, he feels "paralyzed" by them, now that he can no longer play by his original set of asset allocation rules.

A third member ignored all the conventional wisdom—and he's the guy that I can relate to. He has close to 70 percent of his assets in hedge funds and believes that the smartest money managers are either hedge fund managers already or soon will be, after they leave their mutual-fund jobs to start up their own funds. This investor has a return bogey he expects every one of his managers to meet or exceed over a several-year period. And his asset mix is unlike any you're likely to get from a traditional investment management consultant. He has 50 percent of his money in what he calls "core" investments; the other 50 percent is in "specialty" investments—for example, a high-yield international fund and a biotech partnership. His results have been excellent. Equally important, he has stayed true to his highly personal asset allocation principles.

DRUM ROLL, PLEASE

These investors' experiences provide some useful insight into the challenge of allocating your money across the spectrum of investment choices. But here's another anecdote I find particularly illuminating. According to Ms. Beyer, one member of the Institute listened to an adviser's asset allocation presentation, with all its formulas, graphs, and pie charts. He then quietly but shrewdly observed, "This task of allocating assets and selecting managers for my family is not just about charts and dots. I need to have more of my own intellect and intuition involved in the process." Bingo.

Like this investor, who was dissatisfied with formulaic, cut-and-dried allocation methods, I too believe that the process for high-net-worth investors must be a blend of theory and good old-fashioned common sense. How much to invest in hedge funds depends on a number of factors that are unique to each individual and family. There's simply no off-the-shelf, one-size-fits-all solution.

So, I can't honestly offer broad, general advice for allocating assets to hedge funds. But I did promise you some rules of thumb. The best guidelines I've seen come from two blue-chip advisers to ultrahigh-net-worth individuals, Graystone Partners in Chicago and Rockefeller & Co. in New York. (You've probably already guessed that the latter started out managing the considerable wealth of the Rockefeller family.)

When asked to generalize, these two firms recommend putting a minimum of 10 percent of your assets into hedge funds. Why? Less than that, and your hedge fund allocation won't have a meaningful impact on your portfolio's performance. And that would be pretty disappointing, since it takes some time and effort to select and monitor them.

These experts also advise that you continue to add to your hedge fund holdings over time (assuming, of course, they have performed up to expectations), eventually upping the ante to an allocation of approximately 25 percent of your total investment portfolio. This approach reminds me of the global macro legend, George Soros, who advocates testing the investment waters and then building on your winning positions.

Some investors, depending on their own unique circumstances and comfort level with nontraditional investing, will put a substantially higher percentage of total assets into hedge funds. But they are the minority, and for most investors, 25 percent appears to be a reasonable target.

YOUR FINANCIAL FUTURE

One or two other aspects of your personal financial picture should factor into your asset allocation decisions—future cash flows, for instance. Are you continuing to add meaningful amounts to your wealth? Or is what you've got pretty much what you're going to have?

Of course you never know for sure—you could win the lottery tomorrow. But if you're 35 years old, made a bundle on stock options, and are still working, chances are you're going to make a lot more money over the next 30 years. If, however, you're 58 and have just sold your business and are planning to take it easy from here on out, the money you have now is likely to be your nest egg for the future. And if you've inherited a sizable sum from your dearly departed Great Aunt Agnes, you probably have a pretty good idea if you're going to inherit more money from some other relative.

Your outlook for future income affects your investment decisions in two ways. If you expect to continue earning more, you can take bigger risks in your investments. Your future earnings are a way of replenishing your inventory of funds. With money continuing to pour in, you can probably afford to take a sequential view of your asset allocation—next month I'll add this, and next year I'll do that. Conversely, if you're retired or not generating any meaningful income, then you need to make sure your existing investments will meet your needs. If the lid is already on your pot of money, make sure that your current asset allocation recipe is just right.

DON'T FORGET THE IRS

The last important variable that enters into your asset allocation decision concerns the tax collector. As you go about the process of determining how much money to put into hedge funds, you need to consider the variety of tax consequences associated with these investments. Remember that different kinds of hedge funds generate different kinds of tax liabilities.

In addition, many investors have the choice of placing an investment in a taxable portfolio or in a retirement plan, trust, or other tax-advantaged account. Don't assume you're always better off not paying taxes. In many cases, these taxes are simply being deferred. And while paying taxes later is usually better than paying them now, that's not always the case. So, you need to evaluate which investments are best for a taxable portfolio and which are better suited for a tax-advantaged portfolio.

Before you decide how much to put into hedge funds, consider the potential tax liabilities versus those generated by other types of investments. And don't overlook the tax liabilities you might incur if you liquidate other investments to buy hedge funds. Should you sell something to raise hedge fund investment cash, it could be a taxable event. There may be nothing wrong with doing that; the point is to consider the consequences ahead of time. And of course, you'll want to make sure that you leave yourself with enough cash to pay any taxes due. New hedge fund investments are often subject to an initial lock-up period, and tax collectors aren't known for their patience.

Of course, these calculations can become quite complicated, and everybody's tax situation is different. So, it's always a smart idea to check with your tax attorney or CPA before making any final asset allocation decisions.

Chapter 9

Tapping into the
Wealth of Resources

Remember the Arlo Guthrie song, "Alice's Restaurant"? Even if you weren't a fan of folk music, you might still know the refrain, "You can get anything you want at Alice's Restaurant." Well, hedge funds are the same way. You can invest in any kind of strategy you could ever want or imagine.

You also have a lot of choices in deciding what role you want to play in researching, evaluating, and selecting hedge fund investments. Perhaps you're the do-it-yourself type—someone who would be comfortable sorting through candidates, poring over partnership agreements, and making decisions all on your own. But you could also choose to operate with expert guidance from a consultant or adviser. Or you could decide to delegate the task, keeping your personal involvement to a minimum. In that case, you could turn your money over to a fund-of-funds manager who makes decisions on your behalf.

Which approach is best? It all depends on your time, priorities, and proclivities. You can buy a chicken in the butcher shop, take it home, baste it, and roast it for dinner. Or you can go to the supermarket and get a rotisserie chicken that's ready to eat. Or you can have your chicken served with an exquisite sauce by a waiter who'll cater to your every whim. These are all perfectly fine ways of eating chicken; the best way is strictly a matter of personal preference. Similarly, when it comes to investing in hedge funds, only you can decide how hands-on you want the process to be.

Regardless of whether you go it alone, seek advice, or delegate to a third party, plenty of resources are available if you know where to look. But there's more to it than simply responding to an ad, filling out some forms, and mailing in your check. While investing in a mutual fund can be almost that simple, investing in hedge funds requires a bit more work.

You may already be asking yourself, "Why bother with all this when other investments are so easy?" But the very fact that you're reading this book suggests that traditional investments aren't meeting all your needs. And if you're a candidate for investing in hedge funds, that means you have substantially more at stake than the typical mutual fund investor. So, don't be put off just because hedge funds take a little more time and energy. As you'll soon see, the effort will be worth your while.

This chapter will give you some help in getting started, no matter how much or how little hands-on involvement you want to have. First we'll survey some information sources that are useful to any prospective hedge fund investor, and essential for the do-it-yourselfer. I'll also name the sources I'd personally recommend to those seeking expert guidance and advice. Finally, we'll take a closer look at the benefits and costs of investing through a fund of funds.

FOR STUDENTS OF THE INDUSTRY

If you decide to do all or much of your own research, it's probably because you're the kind of investor who gets a charge from discovering hot growth companies, picking stocks, and matching wits with the professionals. For anyone who thrives on intellectual challenge and the thrill of the chase, there's real excitement in hedge fund investing. The pulse quickens as you begin to zero-in on which strategies, managers, and funds are just right for you.

Even if I've convinced you that the Jones model is an ideal approach for a conservative high-net-worth investor, you'll still need to choose among the many funds offering hedged equities. But as I've noted, selecting a hedge fund is inherently more challenging than picking a mutual fund or hiring a traditional investment manager. Here's why.

First, objective information on hedge funds isn't that widely available. Remember, hedge funds are prohibited from advertising or broadly marketing their investments. In this regard, they couldn't be more unlike mutual funds, which are relentlessly promoted and continually evaluated, ranked, and rated by the likes of Morningstar and Lipper. The headlines blare from every newsstand, as *Money*, *SmartMoney*, *Bloomberg Personal Finance*, and *Worth*—not to mention *Forbes*, *Fortune*, and *Business Week*—all tell you precisely which mutual funds to buy. Of course, one might ask why, if they've really identified the all-time greatest funds this month, they will inevitably recommend a different batch of funds next month. The advice may be contradictory, but at least there's no shortage of it.

Likewise, there is a steady stream of information available on traditional money managers. Investment management consultants such as the Frank Russell Company, Wilshire Associates, and Callan Associates, among many others, thoroughly cover the waterfront, evaluating and comparing each manager's philosophy, process, style, and, of course, performance. One can also turn to the array of trade publications covering the traditional money management industry, including *Pensions & Investments*, *Institutional Investor*, *Plan Sponsor* magazine, and *Money Management Letter*, to name just a few.

In contrast, hedge funds are much less scrutinized, and the prohibition on advertising is only part of the reason why. As I've noted, hedge fund managers are not exactly eager to disseminate information about themselves and their strategies. And because data on holdings and performance are more difficult to obtain, the media devote much less ink to hedge funds than they do to most other kinds of investments. When they do cover the industry, it's most often in the context of a certain global macro manager's extraordinary bravado or a certain fund's precipitous meltdown. It's all very entertaining, but not particularly enlightening.

There's also the fact that prospective hedge fund investors constitute an extremely limited market, given investment minimums of $250,000 and up. Recently I asked a columnist from the *Wall Street Journal* why the paper didn't write about hedge funds more often. "It doesn't make any business sense," he told me. In other words, since only a small fraction of the *Wall Street Journal*'s readers are accredited investors who can pony-up what it takes to get into hedge funds, why waste the space reporting on them?

Considering the paucity of data and the shortage of media attention, it's no surprise that researching hedge funds is a bit more involved than checking out some mutual fund ratings. But if you're willing to look a little deeper and toss your net a little wider, you can find a wealth of worthwhile information. Allow me to be your guide.

Reservoirs of Information

Even though hedge funds get little regular play in the mainstream financial press, valuable nuggets of information do occasionally surface. For example, every month or so *Barron's* publishes an interview with a respected hedge fund manager, exploring in depth the manager's strategy, holdings, and viewpoint on future investment opportunities. These are always recommended reading, because they provide a rare glimpse into the thinking and methods of these normally inaccessible managers. And I wouldn't stop at reading the latest edition of *Barron's*; I'd try to get hold of back issues as well. Every once in a while, *Fortune* or *Business Week* publishes an informative update on hedge funds, as do *Forbes*, *Worth*, and *Bloomberg Personal Finance*.

But for really comprehensive reporting on hedge funds, you need to look beyond your local newsstand. A good place to start is with the *Journal of Alternative Investments*. It's published quarterly by Institutional Investor, Inc., and, while scholarly in tone, contains interesting and useful articles. The annual subscription fee is $500, and you can sign up online at www.iijournals.com. I highly recommend it to anyone seriously interested in the subject.

For a less academic viewpoint, I'd consult *MAR/Hedge*, a monthly newsletter devoted exclusively to hedge funds. It's published by Managed Account Reports in New York, which also puts out the *MAR/Hedge Performance and Evaluation Directory*, a semiannual compilation of detailed statistical data and manager contact information on some 1,500 hedge funds and funds of funds. The monthly newsletter costs around $600 a year; the directory, around $750. If you want to test the waters before committing to a full year's subscription, Managed Account Reports will send you a single sample copy. You can subscribe or order a single copy online at www.marhedge.com.

Institutional Investor recently launched its own monthly newsletter, *Alternative Investment News*, complementing its more scholarly journal. The newsletter features breaking news, manager updates, and items picked up from other investment news sources. Subscribers also have access to real-time updates on the web. Charter one-year subscriptions are $1,595; you can subscribe at www.iialternatives.com.

Speaking of the web, it's become a gold mine of information on hedge funds. Do-it-yourself investors, in particular, should definitely check out the databases, analytics, news, and general hedge fund information that are available with just a few clicks of your mouse. Table 9.1 lists a few sites you might want to bookmark as a start.

Some of these provide information for free, while others have subscription fees. And, remember, web sites come and go. So follow any interesting-sounding links you find and use your search engine to keep current on whatever's available. Just be sure to keep in mind the same caveat I'd apply to any hedge fund database or news item: Consider the source. Don't assume it's reliable and objective unless you know who's behind the information, and never invest based on information from just one source.

On the Conference Circuit

Attending conferences is another great way to learn a lot about hedge funds. Conferences are a funny thing, though. In one sense, they're like the *National Enquirer*. You may not know a single person who'll admit to reading the tabloids, but somehow they sell like hotcakes. It's the same with investment conferences. Some folks in the industry put them down and, admittedly, some of the speakers are there largely to pitch their products, not always subtly. But you can still glean plenty of useful information despite the occasional commercial, and you'll also get to meet a lot of smart, interesting people.

Several of the hedge fund web sites I mentioned earlier post a calendar of upcoming events, offering a convenient way for you to stay current on who's hosting what, when, and where. About half a dozen

Table 9.1   **Hedge Fund Web Sites**

Web Address	Sponsor
www.altvest.com	Altvest, Inc.
www.hedgefund.net	Tuna Group, LLC
www.hedgefunds.net	Info-Web Technologies, Inc.
www.hedgescan.com	Lamp Technologies LLC
www.hedgeworld.com	HedgeWorld
www.plusfunds.com	PlusFunds.com
www.thehfa.org	Hedge Fund Association

organizations regularly sponsor hedge fund events. One of the largest is the Institute for International Research (IIR; www.iirny.com), a professional conference organizer that hosts a variety of events including the well-attended Annual Hedge Fund Forum each May. Our publishing friends at Managed Account Reports sponsor four or five conferences every year, some on alternative investing, some are dedicated specifically to hedge funds. *The Economist*, the highly regarded, London-based weekly publication, has begun holding its own annual Alternative Investment Forum; for information, visit www.economistconferences.com. Consulting firms and investment advisers that cater to a well-heeled clientele also host seminars from time to time. But these are usually by invitation only, and have broad agendas like "Wealth Management" or "Nontraditional Investing," with just a portion of airtime earmarked for hedge funds.

Most conferences last a day or two, and, in addition to their formal agendas, offer excellent networking opportunities over lunch, cocktails, and dinner. The price of admission ranges from zero to several thousand dollars. Free events mean that the sponsor—usually a financial advisory firm—hopes that in exchange for information, you'll hire the firm to manage your assets or build your portfolio of hedge funds.

Many conferences are held every year; you could attend one every week if you wanted to. But once you have a basic grounding on the issues, it's not too hard to narrow the field down to those sessions addressing your particular interests. Personally, I like to go to two or three conferences a year—especially those in Bermuda and Switzerland.

The Commercial-Free Channel

If you want to avoid any kind of sales pitch, you may be more interested in the Institute for Private Investors, one of the most objective and educational sources of hedge fund information I know. If you're someone who truly enjoys investing and wants to learn as much as you possibly can about the wonderful world of hedge funds, you're going to love the Institute. And no one is going to try to sell you anything—there's nothing commercial about it. You can just relax and take everything in.

Charlotte Beyer founded the Institute in 1992 and is still leading the charge. The Institute provides its members with information on investments, taxes, and estate planning. Currently, the membership includes over 450 individuals representing more than 200 families, roughly 80 percent of them having assets of $50 million or more.

At the core of the Institute are its educational events—forums, special briefings, seminars, and international field trips, all offered in a relaxed, noncommercial mode. The Institute's curriculum is shaped by its Leaders Council, a group of approximately 40 top-notch investment professionals representing leading money management, brokerage, banking, and consulting firms. The Leaders Council includes a lot of smart, motivated individuals who are often also great salespeople. But their sole role in the Institute is to inform and educate. If they tried to use that venue as a sales opportunity, I promise you, the Institute would show them to the nearest exit.

The Institute conducts three forums a year: one in San Francisco and two in New York, each lasting from one to two days. The forums cover a wide range of wealth management topics like "Hedge Funds and Tax Efficiency," "Value vs. Growth" investing, and "Asset Allocation Grill" and offer high-powered speakers such as Abbey Joseph Cohen of Goldman Sachs. Special briefings are "mini-forums" held once a month in major cities. They typically last a day or part of a day, and focus on a single topic such as "Selecting Managers," "Funds of Funds," and "Pretax Returns Look Nice, but It's the Money You Get to Keep."

If you're feeling particularly studious, you might be interested in attending the Institute's annual five-day intensive seminar at the Wharton School at the University of Pennsylvania where you'll learn about everything from the history of the stock market to Modern Portfolio Theory. And if you're up for adventure, the Institute's annual international destination program might be just the thing for you. Lasting a week or more, these are field trips to learn about global investing opportunities firsthand in places such as Argentina, Hong Kong, Morocco, and the United Kingdom. The itinerary usually includes meetings with high-level government officials, local fund managers, and prominent entrepreneurs.

Aside from all of these terrific educational forums, the Institute also has a "members only" web site that offers member survey results, a calendar of events, access to a library of educational materials, and ways for you to network with other members.

Let me assure you, what you don't find in articles, newsletters, and databases you will find at the Institute. You'll also get to meet fascinating people whose backgrounds and interests may dovetail with yours. Membership ranges from $2,000 to $5,000 per year, and if you join, you'll probably agree that it's money well spent. You can get information about the Institute for Private Investors by calling its offices in New York or by visiting its web site at www.memberlink.net.

GETTING ADVICE FROM THE EXPERTS

The do-it-yourself approach isn't for everybody. There are plenty of smart, well-informed investors who wouldn't dream of making a $250,000-plus commitment without getting expert input. And even if you become quite knowledgeable about hedge funds, it can still be helpful to get a second opinion. But which expert to consult? Easy as it is to find someone eager to give investment advice, it's a bit harder to find someone who can provide truly insightful, knowledgeable advice on a nonmainstream topic such as hedge funds.

Your first impulse may be to turn to a financial adviser you already know and trust, whether a financial planner, stockbroker, tax accountant, or lawyer. But understand that any generalist in the field is likely to have limited, if any, direct experience with hedge funds. If such an adviser ventures some opinions, you need to ask what I call the All-Important Question: "How much of your personal money is invested in hedge funds?" If the answer is "None," move on. No matter how convincing the self-described expert may be, if he or she doesn't personally invest in hedge funds, walk away. You may get an opinion, but it's not likely to be well founded.

In my experience, very few general financial advisers have personal experience with hedge fund investing, so I'm not surprised they aren't a good source of advice on the subject. But I've always wondered why senior investment management consultants aren't more knowledgeable about hedge funds. Even though they deal mainly with large corporations, foundations and endowments, and state and local governments, many of them also work with some very wealthy families. So why aren't they better versed in an investment category that attracts so many high-net-worth investors?

I can only surmise that most consultants derive the bulk of their fees from big institutional clients, so becoming a hedge fund expert isn't high on the typical consultant's priority list. Remember, institutional investors focus on relative performance, not absolute return. Since institutional investors don't generate much demand for hedge fund consulting, traditional investment consulting firms can't justify the cost of developing comprehensive hedge fund tracking and evaluation capabilities; it would simply be too expensive for them to assemble a skilled professional staff and the resources needed to be competitive with the more specialized consultants. As hedge funds are embraced by more and more investors, traditional investment management consultants may become more knowledgeable on the subject—but they're not there yet.

Turning to the Specialists

If a cardiac exam were to show that you needed bypass surgery, would you let your family physician wield the scalpel? Of course not. You'd go to the best cardiac surgeon you could find. This may not be the most light-hearted analogy I could offer, but it's a pertinent one. If you want real help in navigating the intricacies of hedge fund investing, I believe that only a specialist will do. But you won't find "Hedge Fund Consultants" listed in the Yellow Pages, so let me recommend several I'd class among the best.

Some of these experts can be found in surprising places. For instance, you might not think of major money center banks in connection with hedge fund specialists. But in fact, both Chase Manhattan and Citibank have private banking departments staffed with investment professionals who are extremely knowledgeable about hedge funds. Both these banks advise high-net-worth investors all around the globe, and you'll often see their senior representatives making the rounds of the various conferences. If you're not already a client of one of these two banks, the easiest way to learn what they can offer is by visiting their web sites at www.chase.com and www.citibank.com.

Several other institutions have well-deserved reputations for serving the needs of the very wealthiest families. Perhaps your great-great-grandfather founded some steel mills, or maybe you just completed a successful IPO. If you're in the ranks of the mega-rich, you can turn to institutions such as Morgan Guaranty Trust, Northern Trust, Wilmington Trust, and U.S. Trust for counsel on everything from money management to estate and tax planning to charitable giving. These organizations all do an exemplary job of helping the highest-net-worth investors with coordinated, full-spectrum wealth-management services, but their accent is on traditional money management; for the most part, they are relatively new to the realm of alternative investments.

But I can recommend at least two old-line, blue-chip New York institutions for solid advice on nontraditional investments—Rockefeller &

Co. (www.rockco.com) and Bessemer Trust (www.bessemer.com). Like the previously named trusts, these firms provide big-picture portfolio advice and a complete menu of services to those charged with stewardship of very large fortunes. But each one also has a long and successful record in the area of alternative investing. In fact, Rockefeller & Co. is known as a pioneer in nontraditional investments: Laurance Rockefeller, one of founder John D. Rockefeller's grandchildren, began targeting venture capital deals back in the late 1930s. Bessemer was founded in 1907 as the family office of Henry Phipps, a partner of Andrew Carnegie in the Carnegie Steel Company. Its purpose was to invest the $50 million Mr. Phipps received in the sale of the steel business to J. P. Morgan. In 1974, the family decided to take on outside clients.

Another of the world's foremost consultants to wealthy individuals and families is Graystone Partners out of Chicago. Compared to Rockefeller & Co. and Bessemer, Graystone is the new kid on the block. But in less than a decade, the firm has earned a stellar reputation and built a client base of 60 families, most of them with assets of $100 million or more. David B. Horn, who set up Northern Trust's Wealth Management Group, started the firm along with Louise Wasso-Jonikas, a former Goldman Sachs trader. Hedge funds are an integral part of the array of investments Graystone analyzes before recommending a portfolio mix to a client. In December 1999, Graystone was bought by Morgan Stanley Dean Witter to help serve its impressive roster of well-heeled clients.

And no list of venerable consulting firms would be complete without Boston-based Cambridge Associates, LLC (www.cambridgeassociates.com). Cambridge has been around for over 25 years, working with the crème de la crème of the foundation and endowment community as well as wealthy individuals and families. Cambridge consults with its clients on the full range of investments, both traditional and alternative, and advises more than 40 institutions and family clients specifically on hedge fund investing.

Expert and Accessible

If you're looking for an adviser that deals primarily with hedge funds, or if you're not quite up to the hefty minimums noted earlier, there are several excellent consulting firms to consider.

One very notable candidate is the Hennessee Group in New York (www.hennesseegroup.com). In fact, E. Lee Hennessee, the company's founder and chairman, is one of the best-known hedge fund consultants around. She constantly publishes articles, is quoted by financial publications like the *Wall Street Journal*, Barron's, and *Business Week*, gives keynote addresses at hedge fund conferences, makes television appearances, and so on. Her name is practically synonymous with hedge fund investing. Charles Gradante, the firm's president and CEO, is also widely known in hedge fund circles. Likewise a familiar figure in the business media, he has also testified before Congress as a hedge fund industry expert. In short, this is a first-rate group of people who focus solely on hedge funds and understand every aspect of investing in them. One thing I find particularly appealing is that the firm actively encourages dialogue between its clients and their hedge fund managers. You get to know your managers personally through face-to-face meetings and various educational programs the Hennessee Group puts on.

Another industry leader is Hedge Fund Research (HFR; www.hfr.com) out of Chicago, a hybrid research and consulting firm. Joseph G. Nicholas, HFR's chairman, is a familiar name in the hedge fund world, and has written two books, *Investing in Hedge Funds* (Bloomberg Press, 1999) and *Market Neutral Investing* (Bloomberg Press, 2000). Hedge Fund Research offers consulting services, databases, performance indexes, directories—you name it. And as this book went to press, the company was in the midst of launching the industry's first "hedge fund supermarket." Modeled after Charles Schwab's Mutual Fund OneSource, HFR's new service will let investors screen, review, and actually buy and sell hedge funds online. I'll let you know what I think about it in my next edition.

Tremont Advisers (www.tremontadvisers.com), a Rye, New York, consulting firm founded in 1984, also ranks high on any list of hedge fund consulting firms. Among other services, Tremont will create a custom pool of hedge fund strategies for those investing $20 million or more. If you're investing less than that amount, they will advise you in selecting from "off-the-shelf" fund-of-funds opportunities. In 1999, Tremont acquired London-based TASS Investment Research, which maintains a database of 2,000-plus hedge funds, giving Tremont excellent access to hedge fund data. Robert Schulman, president of Tremont, is one of the most knowledgeable and well-respected experts in the industry.

James R. Hedges IV, of Naples, Florida, oversees more than $2.5 billion in hedge fund capital for 50 wealthy clients through his LJH Alternative Investment Advisors. He also selects and monitors hedge funds for Miami's Dimension Capital, which represents wealthy Latin-American families.

Van Hedge Fund Advisors International (VAN; www.vanhedge.com) is another excellent source of research and data. VAN maintains one of the largest proprietary hedge fund databases in the world, covering over 3,400 funds, and produces monthly the Van Hedge Fund Index of U.S. and off-shore hedge fund performance.

Relatively new to the area of individual investor services is San Francisco–based Meritus Research, Inc. (www.meritusresearch.com), which previously focused solely on the institutional market. Meritus offers web-based access to analyses and rankings of some 200 hedge funds; it also assists investors in identifying and evaluating top managers within style categories.

Then there are advisers that look at the broader universe of alternative investments, such as Alternative Investment Strategies (AIS). The firm was founded in 1996 as a partnership between Joe S. Wade, the firm's president, and a wealthy Birmingham, Alabama, family. There are two AIS offices—one in Birmingham, the family seat, and one in Memphis, from which the firm's parent company (Consulting Services Group) provides traditional consulting services to institutional investors worldwide as well as high-net-worth families. Aside from its flagship family relationship, AIS also advises a growing number of outside clients.

Last but not least is Windermere Investment Associates out of Portland, Oregon, another adviser to high-net-worth individuals on both traditional and alternative investment strategies. Windermere can set you up with a custom portfolio of hedge fund managers, complete all of the necessary paperwork and documentation, and help you monitor the managers on an ongoing basis. The resumes of this group are extremely impressive, particularly that of Nancy Jacob, the firm's founder and president. Before founding Windermere in 1997, Ms. Jacob, who is a Ph.D., served as chairman and CEO of CTC Consulting, a Portland-based subsidiary of U.S. Trust, and was formerly a dean of the Graduate School of Business at the University of Washington in Seattle.

The Price of Good Advice

There's no magic in what these consultants do, nor is there any secret formula. The advice they provide is based on their accumulated industry knowledge and a great deal of diligent, ongoing research. They rigorously track and analyze performance of a broad array of hedge funds as well as the investment strategies pursued and the people behind it all.

If you think you want this kind of help, bear in mind that it doesn't come cheap: Hedge fund consultants typically charge a fee based on the amount of assets invested. This can range from as low as 10 basis points all the way up to a full percentage point, and in many cases there is a minimum annual fee of $100,000 or more. Some hedge fund consultants charge less, but make up for it by accepting payments from the hedge funds they recommend, an arrangement that should lead you to question whether you're getting unbiased advice. So if you hire a consultant, make sure that the firm's fee income comes from clients and clients alone.

Wall Street Gets in on the Act

Until recently, Wall Street's retail brokerage firms saw little reason to get involved with hedge funds, which lie outside their traditional scope of business. But they've finally awakened to the fact that there is a huge market segment of investors who are wealthy but may not be able to afford million-dollar minimums.

The big brokerage houses are quickly making up for lost time, pooling individual investments of as little as $100,000 and putting the money into select hedge funds or funds of funds. The trend was spearheaded in part by Don Marron, chairman and CEO of PaineWebber, who has personally been a very successful and sophisticated hedge fund investor.

Also prominent in this burgeoning sector are Donaldson, Lufkin & Jenrette; Merrill Lynch; and the Canadian Imperial Bank of Commerce's CIBC Oppenheimer. Some industry insiders are putting their money on Salomon Smith Barney and Ed Orazem, its head of alternative investments. Their reasoning: The firm has put substantial resources into creating a high-powered traditional consulting capability, smoothing its move into alternative investments.

Investors should know that this access does come at a price, since the brokerage firms layer their own asset-based fees, and sometimes a performance fee, on top of the hedge funds' own charges. But for those who want to get into the hedge fund game for less than the typical minimum, the brokerages are providing a way.

WHEN IN DOUBT, DELEGATE

We certainly operate in a service economy; today you can hire someone to take over virtually any chore, from walking your dog to bringing groceries to your door to waiting in line at the Department of Motor Vehicles. In the business world, too, outsourcing has become a key catchphrase. Many corporations have decided that it makes good financial sense to contract out whatever functions someone else could perform better or more efficiently, whether that be janitorial services or data processing.

You can apply the same rationale to hedge fund investing. Whether it's right at the outset or after doing some research yourself, you may elect to delegate most of the investment responsibility to someone else. You can do that by investing in a fund of funds—a limited partnership that doesn't make direct investments, but invests in other hedge funds. In this case, you're hiring the fund-of-funds manager to do the research, the evaluation, the fund selection, and the monitoring—in short, to make the hiring and firing decisions.

Here's how it works. The fund-of-funds manager takes your money and invests it in a number of different hedge funds—as few as five or six or as many as 20 or more. You're relieved of any need to weigh the merits of market-neutral managers or decide which merger arbitrage fellow looks good; with a fund of funds you get a turnkey solution. It's one-stop shopping, and you have a professional money manager minding the store. The manager's job doesn't end when your investment has been placed in a set of hedge funds; the funds and their performance are constantly monitored. If the manager's assessment of a fund changes, he or she replaces it with a more attractive choice.

Instant Diversification

The fund-of-funds approach offers a variety of advantages. First and, for many investors, foremost is accessibility. While the price of entry for an individual hedge fund is often a million dollars or more, you can usually buy into a fund-of-funds portfolio for far less. Minimums are often a relatively modest $250,000 to $500,000. Funds of funds pool investor contributions and buy partnership interests in hedge funds, enabling investors to access funds they might not be able to afford on their own.

Similarly, a fund of funds may be an established investor in a hedge fund that isn't otherwise accepting new clients. As I explained earlier, there are limits on the number of investors in any given hedge fund, and many managers want to keep their funds at a certain size. And the better the manager's record, the more likely it is that the fund is turning all new investors away. A fund of funds may be the only way to invest with one of the industry's stars.

Another big advantage is that through a fund of funds, you can sample strategies that are attractive but don't make sense as a stand-alone investment. Who wants to put their entire $10 million nest egg into a distressed Japanese debt strategy? It may be great as an addition to your hedge fund portfolio, but not as the mainstay. With a fund of funds you can invest in a smorgasbord of hedge fund strategies.

Which leads me to the main benefit of the fund-of-funds approach: diversification. With hedge funds, it's beneficial to spread your investments among several managers and strategies. If you've got a great deal of money, you can buy into a half-dozen different funds all at once, and, bang!—you're diversified. If you can't ante up enough for that, a fund of funds provides instant diversification in one relatively affordable package.

Hedge funds, like mutual funds, are already diversified investments, so it's less risky to invest in a single hedge fund than in a single stock or real estate asset. But hedge fund performance data reveals that while some strategies and funds produce remarkably consistent returns, others display significant volatility; moreover, their ups and downs can have varying degrees of correlation with broad market movements. Thus, when it comes to hedge funds, diversification is still a useful tool of risk control, and it can also increase upside potential by providing exposure to diverse opportunities.

Grosvenor Capital Management, a leading fund-of-funds manager based in Chicago, explains it this way:

> Because of the diversity of strategies, hedge funds offer a broad spectrum of expected risk and return and have a low correlation to one another. As a result, combining these strategies into a systematically diversified portfolio can result in superior, long-term results with less volatility.

Grosvenor also notes:

> Funds of funds offer valuable risk control through diversification. By investing in a multi-strategy, multi-manager fund of funds portfolio, investors can mitigate the unique risks associated with investing in any single strategy or manager.

Of course, the point isn't merely to spread assets across a number of funds. If you want risk protection, the funds must employ diverse strategies that have little or no correlation to the mainstream market and, equally important, to one another. Thus, whenever you're considering a fund of funds, you must always understand the particular strategies in which it invests. Like a master chef, a good fund-of-funds manager is intimately familiar with all the ingredients at one's disposal, and knows just how to combine them for the desired effect.

Lower Risk, Higher Rewards

When it comes to the risks and rewards of hedge fund investments, a knowledgeable consultant will tell you that a well-diversified fund of funds is capable of delivering the best of both worlds. Compared with investing in a single hedge fund, it can *increase return* while *decreasing risk*. Modern Portfolio Theory demonstrates how the right mix of asset classes can yield superior long-term results. In the same way, the right combination of hedge funds can outperform a single hedge fund investment on both the risk and reward sides of the equation.

Sounds impossible, right? It's like the thought that runs through a reluctant airline passenger's head right before takeoff: No way can this thing fly! But as counterintuitive as it sounds, this concept does fly. For the benefit of all you skeptics out there, let's look at some actual numbers. Once again, though, it's important to emphasize that this approach works well *only* when it combines truly diverse fund strategies. In the example in Table 9.2, Manager I uses short-term trading; Manager II, risk arbitrage; III, a distressed securities strategy; and IV, short selling. The fund of funds blends all four strategies.

As you can see, Managers I, II, III, and IV each had a five-year compound annual return of 20 percent, while the fund of funds blending these strategies returned 21 percent. But take a look at the standard deviations! Not only did the fund of funds deliver higher return, it did so with substantially less volatility—that is, *less risk*. This is a perfect illustration of the benefits of diversification: By combining dissimilar strategies, you get equally high or even higher returns, but with lower risk. As you mathematicians have already figured out, the superior performance of the fund of funds stems from the compounding effect of a less volatile, more stable return.

A compelling case can be made for including a fund of funds in a tra-

Table 9.2   Individual Hedge Fund Manager Returns versus Fund of Funds Returns

	Manager I	Manager II	Manager III	Manager IV	Fund of Funds
Year 1	35%	22%	7%	(8%)	14%
Year 2	27%	(2%)	29%	19%	18%
Year 3	(10%)	39%	35%	45%	27%
Year 4	19%	25%	35%	35%	28%
Year 5	36%	20%	(1%)	16%	18%
Five-year annual compound return	20%	20%	20%	20%	21%
Standard deviation	16.86	13.20	15.07	18.12	5.51

Source: August 8, 1993, *Barron's*; Martin Gross of Sandalwood Securities, Inc., Roseland, NJ.

ditional portfolio of stocks and bonds. Figure 9.1 shows how for the five years ending December 31, 1999, a fund of funds outperformed small U.S. stocks (Russell 2000) and international stocks in developed countries (EAFE) with a lower standard deviation. And although the S&P 500 and the Nasdaq Composite posted higher returns during the period, the fund of funds achieved better risk-adjusted performance.

Figure 9.2 illustrates how the fund of funds was also less sensitive to market movements as shown by its low beta.

A Fund-of-Funds Taxonomy

Just as hedge funds come in a variety of flavors, so do funds of funds. They, too, can be categorized according to their investment strategies and objectives. Martin Gross sees funds of funds falling into four categories, which he described in a chapter of *Hedge Funds*, a 1997 book edited by Jess Lederman and Robert A. Klein:

1. *Target return:* "The fund-of-funds manager allocates capital to hedge funds in an attempt to generate a target return usually in the 10 to 15 percent range."
2. *Maximum return:* "Under this option, fund-of-funds managers select those hedge funds whose investment strategies they believe

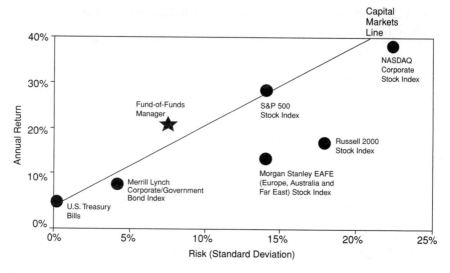

Figure 9.1   **Fund of Funds Return versus Risk (Standard Deviation), Five Years Ending December 31, 1999**

generate the highest return under current market conditions and are willing to accept greater volatility as a result."

3. *Dedicated strategy*: In this case, "the fund-of-fund manager selects hedge funds that invest in a particular asset class, such as emerging markets, or to event-driven strategies, such as distressed securities and merger arbitrage."

4. *Combination*: "Under this option the fund-of-funds manager mixes lower risk strategies with more aggressive ones to create a fund with a more balanced risk posture."

Gross added that many fund-of-funds managers, indeed "perhaps a majority" of them, "utilize diverse investment strategies along with many managers implementing each strategy." Indeed, some funds of funds use as many as 40 managers.

The Costs of Convenience

While funds of funds can offer genuine benefits, naturally there is a price to be paid. Funds of funds impose another layer of fees on top of those charged by the hedge funds themselves. Typically, that added fee

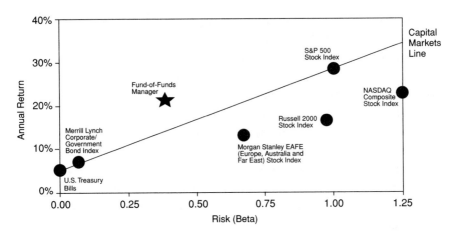

Figure 9.2   **Fund of Funds Return versus Risk (Beta), Five Years Ending December 31, 1999**

amounts to 1 percent of the assets under management, though it may run 1.5 percent or higher. In addition, funds of funds may also charge a performance fee based on a percentage of the investment returns they earn, often 5 or 10 percent of profits above some hurdle rate. Combine these charges with the fees you're already paying the hedge fund managers, and it's clear that you need a fund of funds with strong performance to come out ahead.

Another issue is liquidity constraints. Funds of funds typically impose limitations on withdrawals, and these are often based on the policies of the hedge funds in which they invest. In other words, you can get your money out of a fund of funds only when the fund can get its money out of the underlying hedge funds. You might be attracted to a fund that has more liberal withdrawal provisions—say, one that allows monthly withdrawals with a minimal notice requirement—but you could be making a trade-off without even being aware of it. If the fund of funds provides that liquidity by investing only in hedge funds that allow monthly withdrawals, you could be eliminating the best-performing funds from your universe. If you invest in a fund of funds, the safest course is to view it as a long-term, core holding.

Even if you opt for the hands-off approach you get with a fund of funds, it's vital to recognize that you can't abdicate all responsibility for your investments. The success of a fund of funds is heavily dependent on the experience of the fund manager. So it's essential that you assess the manager's experience and performance record, while also understanding exactly how the manager constructs and monitors the portfolio of funds. You should also be clear on all fees and terms, including restrictions on liquidity. And of course you need to understand the strategies employed by managers of the underlying hedge funds, including risk factors such as the degree of leverage applied.

If you're interested in a fund of funds, *Barron's* is a good place to begin your exploration. Every quarter, *Barron's* publishes performance data from Managed Account Reports on a universe of fund-of-funds managers, some of them brand-new, others going back several years. It should be noted that some firms offer fund-of-funds management as well as consulting services. That combination can be appealing, but it can also raise questions regarding conflicts of interest. So make sure to consider whether the firm's fee structure might bias its recommendations in any way.

THE BOTTOM LINE: HAVE FUN

In this chapter you've seen that you can take any number of approaches to selecting the hedge funds that are right for you. If you think you'd enjoy the process and you tend to prefer keeping a tight rein on your investments, by all means, do the job yourself. A wealth of resources are out there just waiting for you. And there's little point in turning the job over to a consultant or fund-of-funds manager if you're inclined to sit around second-guessing them.

If you'd like the convenience or the comfort level you'd get from some expert help, you can start with the list of specialized consultants I've provided. Finally, if you want the built-in diversification and professional management of a fund-of-funds approach, leaf through one of the special quarterly editions of *Barron's* for a list of managers you can contact.

Whichever approach you decide to take, I encourage you to get out, meet people, and enjoy the process as much possible. The realm of hedge funds is a fascinating place, filled with some of the most intelligent and cosmopolitan investors you'll ever know. They converse about intriguing financial opportunities, convene in exotic places, and come from some of the most interesting backgrounds and families on the planet. As the next chapter will explain, hedge fund investing is ultimately about people.

Chapter 10

Selecting a Hedge Fund That's Right for You

At first blush, selecting from a universe of more than 6,000 hedge funds worldwide appears to be an overwhelming task. It's like going out to dinner and being handed menus from every single restaurant in the city. Who can possibly track and evaluate all those choices? Given the sheer variety of hedge funds, each almost as individual as a manager's fingerprints, the task of settling on one seems as difficult as finding the needle in the proverbial haystack.

If you approach it the way the average investor selects mutual funds—deciding primarily on the basis of performance numbers—picking a hedge fund is a potentially perilous undertaking, too. A fund may have an exemplary record of producing attractive returns, but that's not the whole picture; in fact, it's only the barest outline. As Joe Nicholas observed in his book, *Investing in Hedge Funds*, "Relying entirely on statistical analysis often results in poor investment decisions, but it is a common practice because it is the easiest analysis to perform."

Why shouldn't you rely on past performance when choosing a hedge fund? Well, for starters, the databases make it virtually impossible to do meaningful comparisons. They don't tell you which funds use leverage or which ones invest in exotic derivatives. Some returns are shown net of fees; others, gross. And, typically, the numbers haven't been audited by an outside party.

It's not that the hedge fund managers and database providers aren't being aboveboard. It's just that unlike traditional investment management where performance is subject to the AIMR stamp of approval, the hedge fund industry doesn't have an accepted set of common performance presentation standards. There *is* no level playing field here. So when you're looking at performance of various hedge funds, you can forget apples-to-apples comparisons. The very best you'll get is apples to oranges to bananas to grapefruit to kiwi.

Another issue when trying to evaluate performance numbers is that it's unclear what time frame to look at. Should you focus on the last 12 months or the last 24? Or is it better to look at 5 or 10 years' worth of data? A unique challenge you face when picking hedge funds is that quite often hedge funds with attractive long-term records are closed to new money. At the same time, if a fund can have only 99 investors and after five years it still has a substantial number of slots available, you have to ask yourself, "What's wrong with this picture?"

Finally, performance numbers don't even begin to tell you what risks the manager incurred while pursuing those returns; nor do they illuminate the pitfalls an investor might encounter in the future. Until the day it blew up, Long-Term Capital Management had an excellent track record accompanied by a low standard deviation. Anyone focusing solely on investment performance would have eagerly handed money over to LTCM. It just goes to show you that while relying on the numbers may seem like the right and logical thing to do, it's a classic mistake—and one that can lead to serious trouble.

So, if it's not all about the numbers, what *do* you need to know? Well, you have to look at all the issues *behind* the numbers. The reasons why are summed up well in *Hedge Funds Demystified*, a 1998 report done for the Pension & Endowment Forum by Goldman Sachs and Financial Risk Management Ltd.:

> Among and within strategy sectors, managers differ substantially in their implementation. Most importantly, managers differ with regard to investment diversification, portfolio hedging, security hedging, the use of derivatives, the degree of leverage, and the amount of short sales. It is therefore imperative that investors look beyond the risk and return profiles of the sectors and more fully evaluate a potential manager's investment and risk management processes.

In other words, more important than the actual numbers themselves is understanding how the fund produced them. A fund may have a spectacular short-term record—but did it earn those numbers on assets of only one or two million dollars? Or did it get lucky with speculative investments such as commodities or currencies? Did the fund invest in liquid, publicly traded stocks, or in obscure, thinly traded securities and even private placements? Did the strategy target an area where opportunities constantly arise, or did it take advantage of an economic phenomenon unique to one moment in time? What role did IPOs play? Were the investments made without leverage, or was the fund leveraged to the hilt? Did the manager bet the farm, putting the lion's share of assets into just two or three hot-performing stocks? Until you delve into the players, techniques, and methods behind the performance numbers, you'll have no idea what you're getting into.

But don't let all these questions discourage you; I'm going to let you in on a little secret. As I learned after I first got involved with hedge funds some years back, selecting a hedge fund doesn't have to be a long, convoluted process. If you combine a systematic approach with your own judgment and common sense, selecting a hedge fund can be relatively straightforward. In fact, once you start relaxing enough to get interested in the strategies and the people, it actually becomes a lot of fun. And the real reward is the comfort level you gain from being confident you've chosen a fund that's right for you.

"Right for you"—those three words are really the key to the whole thing. Your own investment objectives and preferences should be both the starting point for the process and the driving factor in your thinking all the way through. When you know exactly what you want in a hedge fund, you have a sound basis for eliminating everything you don't want. Suddenly, the path becomes much clearer and easier, without all those unproductive dead ends.

This approach ties into my long-held belief that hedge funds should be bought, and not sold. Why let yourself be persuaded by a third party that one fund or another is a good investment? If you look at the most successful investors, whether in stocks or real estate, they have one thing in common: They all have their own unique criteria for what constitutes a great investment, and adhere to these criteria religiously. Each investor approaches things differently, and one way isn't necessarily better than another. It's just what works for that particular individual.

When your choices grow out of your own objectives and preferences, you can avoid being drawn into an investment that may be good for someone else, but isn't necessarily good for you. You can also circumvent the pitfalls of endlessly searching for the "best" hedge fund. The truth is, there is no one ideal investment. The critical thing is to arrive at your own personal set of criteria, and apply them in a logical manner. This chapter is intended to give you a framework for doing just that.

A STEP-BY-STEP APPROACH

Over the years, I've developed a systematic, step-by-step approach to selecting hedge funds. It starts with several top-down, broad-brush ways of eliminating large numbers of funds quickly and efficiently. Then it incorporates bottom-up, in-depth analysis of a short list of candidates, leading you to the one fund you'll want to include in your portfolio.

The obvious reason my methodology begins with big-picture, top-down screens is that there's no practical way for you to review comprehensively over 6,000 hedge funds, much less keep up with them. Some people try to do that, such as consultants and fund-of-funds managers, but that's their full-time career.

You, on the other hand, don't have to put yourself through this painstaking effort. You can follow my process and eliminate large slices of funds right off the bat, leaving yourself with a manageable list of finalists to put under the microscope. Personally, I can't imagine anything more tedious than sorting through a huge hedge fund universe. I've got more interesting things to do with my time than stay up all night poring over offering documents—especially when I know that I'll probably end up rejecting 99 percent of them. In short, you don't need to make a career out of selecting a hedge fund; nor do you have to become an expert on the subject. You simply need to know enough to be able to make a sensible decision so you can live with your choice and reap the benefits down the road.

STEP 1: START WITH SOME QUICK, EASY CUTS

Are you a U.S. citizen? If so, you can exclude 50 percent of all hedge funds from your decision set right off the bat. As a general rule, U.S. citizens cannot invest in offshore funds, and that rules out about half of the world's 6,100 hedge funds. There are some exceptions to this rule, especially if you've got a cousin in Liechtenstein. That makes almost anything possible. However, it's beyond the scope of this book to explore the intricacies of investing in off-shore funds. And even if I knew all of the loopholes, I wouldn't expose them here, since I'd have the IRS knocking at my door in a New York minute.

Unfortunately, the U.S.-citizen rule has kept most Americans out of some fabulous investments, such as George Soros's Quantum, Quasar, and Quota Funds. Even though Soros is a U.S. citizen conducting business out of New York City, his funds are domiciled in the Netherlands Antilles and the British Virgin Islands.

But don't worry; there are plenty of terrific choices based right here in the United States. And look at it this way: In one fell swoop, we've cut our hedge fund universe down to 3,000 candidates. What's more, we can easily lop off another 2,000 or so by applying four standards I'd recommend to any prudent investor: First, I'd eliminate any hedge fund that doesn't have a three-year operating record. Second, exclude start-up funds that haven't yet reached critical mass—that is, any fund that doesn't have at least $50 million in assets. Third, because of issues surrounding full disclosure, I would say no whenever the investment management organization behind a hedge fund is not registered with the SEC. Finally, cross out any funds that are just plain too large, which in my book means those with assets of over $1 billion. Funds that size are just too unwieldy to manage. On this point I agree with Jeffrey Tarrant, president of Arista Group Inc., who in his essay published in *Evaluating and Implementing Hedge Fund Strategies* opined that "At $1 billion under management, any specialty manager will have problems of excess capital."

By sticking to these four criteria, you're bound to miss at least one or two great investment opportunities. But so what? No screen you can apply will be perfect. If you're going to err, you want to do it on the side of being too selective, rather than not selective enough.

STEP 2: DECIDE ON A STRATEGY

At this point, you're already down to well under a thousand hedge funds. But before you begin looking at individual funds, you need to make one all-important decision. Before you can think about which fund is right for you, you must first determine which *strategy* you want to pursue. That doesn't call for exhaustive research on hedge fund strategies; what it does require is a clear idea of your own goals and objectives. You can't find the right hedge fund unless you know what you're seeking. And to paraphrase the well-known, pseudonymous financial commentator Adam Smith, "If you don't know who you are, hedge funds are a bad place to learn."

Getting Rich versus Staying Rich

By far the most important question is, Do you want a "getting rich" strategy or a "staying rich" strategy? What I call "staying rich" strategies are those *targeting* annualized returns of 10 to 15 percent going forward. "Getting rich" strategies *target* annualized returns of 15 to 20 percent or higher. What are the critical variables separating them? They lie in the manager's mind-set— that is, his or her performance expectations and the operating style used to try to fulfill them, particularly the level of risk he or she is willing to assume.

Realize, though, that the level of return the strategy actually achieves is a different matter. A "staying rich" manager may in fact earn returns of 30 percent, 40 percent, or even higher in a given year if conditions are especially favorable. The thing is, on January 1 of the following year, this manager will mentally reset the goal for the new year at 15 percent and, what's more, won't be tempted to change methods in an attempt to extend the winning streak.

On the other hand, when the "getting rich" manager is flush with success (and the performance fees earned), he or she will almost invariably swing for the fences all over again. When you investigate a hedge fund blowup, you'll almost always find that it's a "getting rich" manager to whom one of two things has happened: The manager has either kept the pedal to the metal too long, ignoring warning signs to slow down, or fallen behind his performance bogey and taken extraordinary risks in an effort to catch up.

Of course, who wouldn't want to earn annualized returns of 20 to 30 percent over the next decade? But that begs the critical question: Are you comfortable assuming the level of risk that inevitably accompanies returns of that magnitude? For instance, how do you feel about investing in speculative instruments such as commodities, currencies, or exotic derivatives? Are you comfortable having your money tied up in illiquid private placements? Or how about leveraging your investment to a ratio of one hundred to one? (That's essentially what Long-Term Capital Management did.)

Until someone repeals the laws of economics, there's no escaping the fact that higher returns are generally accompanied by higher risks. There are some rare exceptions, but none you'd want to count on. As Nobel-prizewinning economist William Sharpe once noted, "Most of academic finance is teaching that you can't earn forty percent a year without some risk of losing a lot of money."

Only you can answer these critical questions about risk and return. Of course, the experts have their opinions, but they're not the ones who will be living with the investment choices you make. I've already told you where I stand on these issues: While I'll be pleasantly astonished if the market continues providing the high returns we've enjoyed in recent years, I think it's more realistic to expect market averages to fall closer to the long-term norm of 10 to 11 percent annually. Historically, after a decade during which equity P/E ratios have averaged higher than 20, returns over the following decade have invariably been dismal. That's not being pessimistic; that's just looking clearly at the probabilities.

Personally, I'll be very satisfied if my hedge fund investments earn 15 percent annually, net of fees, with no down calendar years. That latter proviso is a critical one, since capital preservation is my first and foremost objective. Your situation and your views on the market may be somewhat different. But since you're reading a guide for prudent investors, I'll presume that you, too, are a high-net-worth investor of somewhat conservative stripe.

If you, like me, put yourself on the "staying rich" side of the fence, right off the bat you've eliminated the entire global macro category of funds, one of "The Big Four" strategies we talked about in Chapter 6. You've also eliminated the numerous specialty or niche strategies, which focus on selected industries or sectors. Unlike a fund that uses a true hedging strategy, these are usually long-only funds—which to my way of thinking makes them resemble a turbocharged mutual fund more than anything else. The difference is that they invest on margin and charge a 20 percent performance fee—a premium that I personally wouldn't pay for a long-only approach. That's not to say there isn't a place for these funds; they may be just the ticket for an aggressive investor's portfolio. But I wouldn't recommend them for a conservative investor.

Adding Your Own Criteria

So what's left to consider? Well, plenty of options. Still open to consideration are three of "The Big Four" strategies—event-driven, arbitrage, and balanced long/short—plus the Jones-model approach.

Table 10.1 shows how some of the major strategies we've discussed break out in terms of risk/return. Of course, this matrix doesn't take into

Table 10.1   **Matching Hedge Fund Strategies to Your Objectives**

Typical Targeted Return	Risk Level	Example Strategies	Risk Characteristics
		"Getting Rich" Strategies	
20–30%	Very high	Global macro—capitalizes on major global economic shifts; includes bets on currency, commodity, and interest-rate movements	Highly speculative; maximum use of leverage
15–20%	High	Specialty—seeks superior opportunities in a targeted industry or sector, such as technology or telecommunications	Most likely uses leverage to boost returns; primary risks are deterioration of secular trends and extreme volatility
		"Staying Rich" Strategies	
15%	Moderate	Jones model—profits from both winning and losing stocks through an opportunistic blend of long and short investments	May use moderate leverage; conservative, but less so than balanced long/short
12–15%	Varies based on strategy	Event driven—profits from effects of corporate events on the price of a company's securities Arbitrage—profits from price discrepancies among markets	Statistically low risk as a category but individual strategies may be quite risky; strategies are often complex and nearly impossible to understand
10%	Below average	Balanced long/short—seeks to neutralize market risk by equally balancing long and short investments	Fundamentally conservative; easy to understand

account all strategies, and some are too variable in performance for me to generalize about. But any individual fund can be put into a slot based on its target returns and risk level. Remember, this matrix is just one more tool to help you nail down the choices; it doesn't have to be overly rigid or formal, and a given strategy may straddle more than one group. Bear in mind that any strategy's performance can vary dramatically depending on how it is executed. So while one manager's event-driven strategy may suit you just fine, another manager's might be much too risky.

How do you now choose from the remaining possibilities? A prudent investor could make a case for investing in any of the "staying rich" strategies—or in any other strategy you might come across that appears to have a risk/reward balance fitting your profile. So this is where you should apply your own personal criteria. Spending some time mulling over what you want and, just as important, don't want will give you a much sharper picture of the kind of hedge fund strategy you're after. It will also solidify your conclusions about the risk and return level it's realistic to seek. In my case, I knew myself well enough to set my sights on a strategy that:

- **Is basically conservative.** As I said early on in this book, to me the pain of losing a hundred dollars is greater than the joy of winning a hundred dollars.
- **Is straightforward and easy to understand.** Even with all my years in the investment management business, I'm simply not comfortable with strategies that rest on complicated, arcane theoretical underpinnings.
- **Is focused on stocks.** To my mind, stocks are still the asset class of choice. While I believe the easy money has been made, the market still holds enormous opportunities for those who know how to uncover them.
- **Is an investment strategy.** A trading strategy with 500 percent annual turnover isn't for me, no matter how good the returns.
- **Is repeatable.** I want something with staying power, which means avoiding any strategy that capitalizes on fleeting economic circumstances or is rooted in a trend that has come and gone.
- **Incorporates short selling.** Because I'm concerned about lofty stock valuations and market volatility, I definitely want a true hedging approach.

Once I added up all my personal objectives and biases, it became evident that the Jones model is the ideal strategy for me. Your criteria and your conclusions may be quite different—there's no right or wrong here.

The important thing is that you go through the process of reflection and evaluation to settle on the strategy you're most comfortable with. The whole point of this exercise is to focus your attention on the critical factors, so you're on solid ground in deciding which strategies might interest you and which are definitely out of the question. For me, those decisions were clear-cut. Much as I'd love the chance to earn annualized returns of 20 to 30 percent in the future, I'm just not prepared to take on the risks that come with operating at those supercharged performance levels.

Bear in mind that our context here is the process of choosing a single hedge fund strategy for direct investment. If you find a strategy that appeals to you, but its returns are too volatile or its risk characteristics too varied across individual funds, you might consider investing through a fund of funds.

STEP 3: USE POSITIVE CRITERIA TO NARROW THE FIELD

Now that you've zeroed in on a strategy, you're ready to "shake the trees" and see what eye-catching funds within your chosen strategy fall to the ground. Here's where your personal network comes into play; word-of-mouth referrals remain one of the most common and effective methods of finding a hedge fund. You can also glean possibilities from some of the many research sources I outlined in the previous chapter, like newsletters and conferences. And at any point along the way, you may wish to get advice and feedback from a specialized consultant or some other expert adviser.

Up until now, we've been using a process of elimination to narrow our hedge fund universe. But once you've selected a strategy and compiled a list of prospective funds, it's time to draw up a list of *positive* criteria— those attributes that you *do* want in a hedge fund.

At the same time, you'll want to start doing some additional research. But that doesn't mean rushing out to gather exhaustive information about each fund. The best way to move systematically toward an ultimate decision is to think in terms of layers of information with progressively greater depth of detail. At one time or another, you'll need to cover all the bases—the fund's organization, its strategy and methods, its performance, and its people. But you should start with the information that's relatively easy to gather. You can look at more de-tailed information once you've narrowed the list down to a smaller number of firms.

So what now? Simply call each fund on your list to request a packet of informational materials. When you make the calls, be sure to let them know you're an accredited investor, and get the name of some-one who can answer any follow-up questions you might have. Then augment those packets with any pertinent information or comments you've already compiled from third-party sources; you'll want to com-pare input from all available sources to see how much consensus you get on individual funds.

As you go through these materials, start listing your personal fund-selection criteria. That's not as hard as it may seem; these are mostly a matter of common sense, and once again, there's no right or wrong. To give you a head start, Table 10.2 lists the criteria I personally used to eval-uate a field of Jones-model fund candidates. Your list of criteria should be shaped by the kind of strategy and fund *you* are seeking. So feel free to modify my list, or develop one of your own!

Once you have your criteria in hand, review them against informa-tion on the funds that have caught your attention. The materials you've collected may not answer all your questions. For instance, if you, like me, are looking for a true hedge fund, data on the fund's *net equity exposure*, month by month, is absolutely critical. Personally, I would never invest in a hedge fund that couldn't supply me with that information.

On the other hand, with some funds you may not need all the an-swers. One factor alone may be enough to place a fund on the reject list. For instance, you might unearth a fund that seems to be everything you're looking for, except that its investment minimum is way beyond your reach. At that point, you know it would be a waste of time to explore this fund any further, appealing as it may be.

If a fund seems to fit the right profile but you're missing some infor-mation, it's worth a follow-up call to the fund. At this stage, I'd recom-mend trying to limit the conversation to the specific points you want to fill in. Don't succumb to the temptation to gather more information than you really need at the moment. Comparing funds is easier if you have par-allel data on each, and if you keep the process well focused, you'll find that thumbs-up and thumbs-down decisions aren't so time-consuming or diffi-cult to make after all.

Table 10.2   **Jim Owen's Personal Fund-Selection Criteria**

(*Note that this list was developed with Jones-model funds in mind.*)

1. *Small, Independent, and Entrepreneurial*
2. *Absolute Return Philosophy*
   - Opportunistic investment style
   - Capital preservation a priority
3. *Disciplined Investment Approach*
   - Institutional-quality process
   - Blend of quantitative and qualitative factors
   - No "black boxes"
   - No derivatives or currency or commodity trading
   - No private placements
4. *Excellent Stock-Picking Skills*
   - Broad investment universe
   - Original research
   - Small-/mid-/large-cap and international capability
   - Strengths in both long and short investing
5. *Strong Risk Controls/Active Hedging Strategies*
6. *Moderate Use of Leverage*
7. *Impressive Track Record*
   - Superior risk-adjusted returns
   - No down calendar years
   - Reasonable tax efficiency
8. *Attractive Investment Terms*
   - Standard fees—"one and twenty" with a high-water mark
   - Monthly openings
   - No lock-up period
   - Full transparency
   - Account minimum low enough to allow a "toe in the water"
9. *Significant Co-Investment by General Partner(s)*
10. *Solid Operational and Client Service Infrastructure*

As in prior steps, the key is to be highly selective and look for any reason you might want to say "No thanks." And don't ever worry about missing a golden opportunity among the funds you've crossed off your list. Life is inevitably full of terrific opportunities that we let pass by, including all those we're never even aware of. But remember that there are always more good opportunities out there for the taking. Think of legendary investors such as Warren Buffett and Peter Lynch who've excelled by always keeping their eyes on the road ahead. They wouldn't dream of wasting a moment regretting the road not taken.

Clearly, performance will be one of the key criteria on *anyone's* list. We'll be talking more about performance later, but at this point all you'll need for each fund on your list is: (1) annual time-weighted total returns for at least a three-year period, and (2) annualized time-weighted total returns for the same period. Table 10.3 shows a common format for presenting this kind of information; note that the hedge fund numbers used are *strictly hypothetical*. As you review the numbers, make sure the fund is reporting performance both gross and net of fees. Also, confirm that the fund is giving you audited numbers. If any prospective fund declines to provide you with this basic level of performance data, take it off the list immediately.

Together with your other criteria, these performance figures should help you narrow your list of funds significantly. Remember, you're not looking for the fund with the best performance. At this stage, you simply want to flag those with performance that compares favorably with other funds pursuing the same strategy.

Table 10.3   **A Typical Format for Basic Performance Data**

Annual Time-Weighted Total Rates of Return (1/1/97–12/31/99)

	1999	1998	1997
Hedge fund—gross	90.00%	60.00%	20.00%
Hedge fund—net	71.00%	47.00%	15.00%
S&P 500	21.04%	28.57%	33.34%

Annualized Time-Weighted Total Rates of Return (1/1/97–12/31/99)

	One Year	Two Years	Three Years
Hedge Fund—gross	90.00%	74.36%	53.94%
Hedge Fund—net	71.00%	58.55%	42.45%
S&P 500	21.04%	24.75%	27.55%

STEP 4: FOCUS ON PERFORMANCE

By following the preceding steps, you've now pared the vast hedge fund universe down to a manageable number of candidates meriting closer inspection—somewhere between a half dozen and a dozen firms. Now's the time to take a hard, thorough look at performance data for each of those funds.

Given all my earlier exhortations about the dangers of picking a fund based on performance numbers, you may think I'm totally contradicting myself here. But I'm really not. When I say you can't pick a fund based on the numbers, I'm talking about *raw* performance statistics. As we've discussed, those numbers can be misleading. Performance can be reported in a variety of ways, and if the figures haven't been independently audited, you have no assurance of their validity. Even when the numbers are good, they'll tell you only one piece of the story.

Delving deeply into a fund's track record, on the other hand, can be revealing. When you look at performance the right way, you'll gain insight into a fund's strategy—and its execution of the strategy—that you simply couldn't get any other way.

So what do I mean by "the right way" to evaluate a fund's track record? Basically, you need to look at three kinds of measures—return statistics, risk statistics, and risk-adjusted return statistics. To get your hands on this data, simply go straight to each fund on your short list and ask for *monthly* performance data going back to the fund's inception. Remember, you'll need data covering at least 36 consecutive months for any analysis to be meaningful.

Let the fund know that you're a serious prospect conducting some basic due diligence, and give them an idea of how much money you are potentially prepared to invest. If you're a qualified investor, the fund should gladly provide you with the monthly data you're seeking. Most funds probably won't have the staff or the inclination to calculate all of the ratios described next. That's okay, except that you will need some assistance from someone practiced in number crunching to come up with these measures. Hedge fund consultants can do this sort of thing in their sleep, but you may know someone who can help you without charge—perhaps even a nephew or niece in business school. But you can't do any calculations without the monthly data. If the hedge fund won't provide that, once again, my advice is to cross it off your list.

Portfolio Analytics

Once all the number crunching has been done, put the information into a readable format. Tables 10.4, 10.5, and 10.6 show an example of portfolio analytics covering the period from January 1, 1997, through December 31, 1999. While the tables include the actual benchmark statistics for that period, all other figures are *hypothetical*.

You should note that if you depend on the funds themselves to give you these analytical measures, the odds are they will be based on *gross* returns, before fees and expenses have been deducted. Keep that in

Table 10.4   Return Statistics (1/1/97–12/31/99)

	Hedge Fund	S&P 500
Annualized return (gross)	53.94%	27.55%
Cumulative return (gross)	264.80%	107.51%
Excess return relative to S&P 500 (annualized)	26.39%	—
Excess return relative to T-bills (annualized)	48.94%	22.55%
Best month in period	21.00%	8.13%
Worst month in period	−16.00%	−14.44%
Best month in period (relative to S&P 500)	17.60%	—
Worst month in period (relative to S&P 500)	−15.20%	—

Table 10.5   Risk Statistics (1/1/97—12/31/99)

	Hedge Fund	S&P 500
Standard deviation (annualized)	29.50%	16.75%
Downside risk (semi-standard deviation, annualized)	13.24%	10.05%
Upside risk (semi-standard deviation, annualized)	30.90%	15.08%
Ratio upside risk to downside risk	2.33	1.50
Beta (versus S&P 500)	1.25	—
Correlation with S&P 500	0.60	—
R^2	0.36	—
Tracking error, relative to S&P 500 (annualized)	23.04%	—
Downside tracking error (semi-standard deviation, annualized)	12.75%	—
Upside tracking error (semi-standard deviation, annualized)	20.82%	—
Ratio upside tracking error to downside tracking error	1.63	—

Table 10.6   **Risk-Adjusted Return (1/1/97–12/31/99)**

	Hedge Fund	S&P 500
Jensen's alpha (annualized)	20.75%	—
Sharpe ratio	1.66	1.35
Sortino ratio	3.70	2.24
Treynor measure	0.39	0.23

mind, but don't let it bother you. Basing portfolio analytics on gross measures isn't an attempt to mislead investors. It's simply the clearest way of presenting a picture of portfolio characteristics, and that, ultimately, is what you really want to glean from this exercise.

As you review these performance statistics, keep in mind that there is no one precise number on which you can hang your hat. All the numbers are meaningful, and all contribute to an understanding of how the fund is run and what kind of performance to expect in the future.

Most of the measures in Table 10.4 (return statistics) are self-explanatory; pay special attention to three ratios: the excess return relative to the benchmark (annualized) and the best month/worst month (absolute) statistics. You may wonder why the S&P 500 and no-risk T-bills are being used as points of comparison. That doesn't necessarily mean that the manager is oriented to relative return; the benchmarks simply provide a yardstick against which investors can compare the fund's risk/return characteristics.

In Table 10.5 (risk statistics), the classic measure of risk, standard deviation, is far less relevant when you're analyzing a hedge fund. Why? Some volatility is desirable—that is, volatility on the upside. Downside risk is the kind of volatility to avoid. With this in mind, pay special attention to the ratio of upside risk to downside risk.

The correlation with benchmark measure is worth some attention, particularly if you're an investor seeking a true hedge against the equity market. The R^2 measure indicates how much of the fund's return can be attributed to the movements of the S&P 500.

As with standard deviation, tracking error (i.e., deviation from the benchmark) is far less important to hedge fund managers than to traditional managers who want, above all, to stay as close to their benchmarks as possible.

Hedge fund consultants and fund-of-funds managers will find the measures in Table 10.6 (risk-adjusted return) the most telling measures of all—especially the Sharpe ratio, which measures return per unit of risk as measured by standard deviation, and the Sortino ratio, which also measures return per unit of risk, but as measured by downside risk.

The Missing Number

I agree that risk-adjusted return really lies at the heart of the matter. But to be perfectly honest about it, I have never found the standard measures of risk-adjusted return to be completely satisfactory. None of them answers what I see as the critical question: Is the fund's level of volatility acceptable? In other words, are the returns high enough to compensate for the volatility? (This is particularly important if you're looking at "Getting Rich" strategies.) No single measure I've ever seen is up to the task—not even the Sharpe Ratio.

So I created a measure of my own, which I modestly named "The Owen Ratio" (trademark pending). The Owen Ratio is actually quite simple. I wouldn't put my money with *any* hedge fund where the ratio of annualized returns to the worst monthly decline isn't *at least* four to one. For example, if the fund's worst monthly decline is 15 percent and its annualized return, net of all of fees, isn't at least 60 percent, forget it.

I believe this one measure will enable you to quickly eliminate funds that may have fabulous track records, but whose volatility would surely keep you awake at night. It's also a measure you can apply to funds you already own, but aren't sure you're still comfortable with. On a personal note, this is the ratio that recently convinced me it was time to pull the plug on my investment in a fund that was doing extremely well, but made me incredibly nervous with its constant ups and downs. It was hard to let go when I was making so much money, but The Owens Ratio told me it was time to move on.

Getting Behind the Numbers

Here are some more questions to think about as you go through the data:

- *How has performance compared with the target returns for the strategy?* Are there major discrepancies? If so, why? This could be a red flag that a manager is straying from the strategy.

- *How many down months did the fund have, in comparison with the S&P 500?* How closely did those down periods track the S&P's?
- *How long did it take the fund to recover from bad performance?* What caused the rebound—a change in conditions or a change in strategy?
- *Has the fund's record been too good, relative to its strategy?* Strange as it may seem, you should be wary whenever you see a fund with performance that's substantially above the range typical for that fund category. I'd immediately try to discover whether this fund is using a high degree of leverage or some other risky technique to boost its returns.
- *Do the performance numbers cover a period of rising stock prices?* If so, I would take all risk measures with a grain of salt. They're sure to change in a falling market, and not for the better.
- *How do the fund's risk-adjusted returns compare with those of funds utilizing a similar strategy?* When it comes to measuring performance, this is the true bottom line.
- *Is the fund's record the result of skill or a bull market?* The easy answer is "a bit of both." The real question is, how much of each? If you can answer this question, you can be *my* consultant!

As you review performance statistics, there are several things to keep in mind. First and foremost, recognize that performance numbers reflect only one period in time, and nothing more. Don't make the mistake of extrapolating them into the future, because the numbers will always change, and the future may be quite different from the past 36 months. However impressive the fund's performance, it may be the result of market conditions that were unique to the time period covered, and may not be repeated—or may have already changed. A case in point is the hypothetical example shown in Tables 10.4, 10.5, and 10.6. Those numbers look fantastic. However, a closer look at what was happening during the time period covered (1/1/97 to 12/31/99) might raise some questions. That was a time when technology ruled in the marketplace, which should lead an investor to ask whether the fund achieved those spectacular numbers by making concentrated bets on technology stocks. If so, imagine what the same fund's numbers, including risk-adjusted return, might look like if technology were to fall out of bed.

Remember that you're not on a quest for the Holy Grail—the fund with flawless performance. There is no such animal, and if there were, the investment minimum would surely be $25 million and the fee somewhere north of "1 and 50."

Realize, too, that sooner or later every investment manager, nontraditional or traditional, is bound to hit a rough patch. It may last for weeks or even months. The numbers alone may not help you resolve the real issue, which is whether you have enough confidence to hang in there when the fund hits one of those inevitable bumps in the road. You can gain that kind of confidence only after you go through the next step in the process, personally interviewing your finalists.

STEP 5: INTERVIEW THE FINALISTS

A hedge fund's success depends more on the individual manager's skills than on any other single factor. When you invest with a traditional manager or mutual fund, you're buying the *process*. But when you invest in a hedge fund, you're buying the *people*. Plan on interviewing managers from each of your two or three final candidates. You can have your discussions on the phone or in person. Set up the interviews by calling the fund and requesting a 20- to 30-minute appointment for the purpose of completing your due diligence. Make sure that your interview will be with one of the principals.

Key Questions to Ask in an Interview

What should you be prepared to ask when the appointed time arrives? First, let me advise you what *not* to ask. Don't ask questions that are standard for interviews with traditional managers, such as, "How do you articulate your investment philosophy and process?" Or, "What is your stock-selection methodology?" These questions are so routine and tedious that they're bound to elicit a canned response. They're also unlikely to yield much information that's helpful in drawing conclusions.

Instead, ask a few thoughtful, open-ended questions designed to elicit real insight into the manager's thinking. If you don't get much of a response, that in itself will be a clue. If you do get a response, you're in for a real treat. Listening to top-notch hedge fund managers get excited about what they do is a terrific experience. Ask questions that will draw out that kind of response, such as:

- How did you end up running a hedge fund?
- How is managing a hedge fund different from running a traditional long-only portfolio?

- What's been your biggest challenge so far?
- Why do you think your particular strategy will be successful over the next three to five years?
- Where do your best stock ideas come from?
- How much of your research is done in-house?
- Have your methods for picking stocks changed within the past two to three years?
- What accounted for the fund's performance during its best year? Its worst year?
- What's been the maximum drawdown (the worst peak-to-trough decline which may occur intra-month and thus not show up in monthly performance data)?
- How big a bet will you make on a stock, industry, or sector if you have conviction?
- What is the maximum amount of leverage you will use?
- What techniques do you use to hedge your portfolio?
- What other tools do you use to control risk?
- Which is harder for you to do: sell your winners or your losers?
- What is your policy on taking cash up or down?
- How has your net equity exposure varied over the past 12 months?
- Under what conditions do you think an investor would be justified in pulling money from your fund?

Some Questions to Ask Yourself

After the interview, reflect on the following questions:

- *Do the manager's experience and skill sets fit the strategy?* If, for example, the strategy involves short selling, the manager should have demonstrated experience and skills in that specific area.
- *How would the manager's personality be characterized?* In my experience, successful hedge fund managers universally share certain personality traits. Almost without exception, the good ones are fiercely competitive, are mentally tough as nails, and have an insatiable drive to win. They're the Michael Jordans of the investment world: With 20 seconds left in the game and the team down by a point, these are the guys jumping up and down, begging for the ball.

- **What is the manager's attitude toward risk?** Is the manager the type who hates to lose money? Or so motivated by greed as to be willing to throw caution to the wind if that's what it takes to earn a big performance fee?
- **Is *performance repeatable*?** Or, was it caused by a one-time event or nonrecurring trend? For instance, hedge funds that were long in bank stocks did well during the period of brisk bank merger and acquisition activity. But when these transactions tapered off, so did returns.
- **Where does the manager gain an edge?** When it comes to evaluating the likelihood of superior performance in the *future*, this is the critical factor.

Then take some time to reflect upon your interaction with the people you just met. Here, any conclusions must turn on your own judgment. A manager may be demonstrably brilliant, with a sterling track record, but does that manager instill a feeling of confidence in you? Do you get a good sense of this person from your dialogue? And how comfortable would you be entrusting this person with your money?

Skill, experience, and integrity are critical factors in considering any investment manager—but doubly so when it comes to hedge funds. That's why, to me, the qualitative judgments concerning a hedge fund manager are far more important than the quantitative ones.

Once you've taken the time to talk with two or three fund managers and reflect on your interactions, some comparisons and contrasts will begin to emerge. It may not be obvious which one is the right choice, and if you've got two or three strong candidates to choose from, so much the better; that's not a bad problem to have. To make a final choice, you may need to spend more time weighing both objective and subjective factors. This isn't a decision to make on emotions alone; but neither should you make it purely on intellect. Apply both, and then trust your judgment.

How important are your own personal judgments about the people? They're nothing less than the key to the entire selection process. And personally, I would be willing to set aside any *single* objective criterion—including my insistence on a three-year operating record or on the fund having reached the critical mass of $50 million in assets—if I were to encounter a manager who inspired my full confidence and who seemed completely in sync with my own thinking. (In fact, I recently did put money with an emerging hedge fund manager with whom I felt so comfortable that I set aside my rule about not investing with start-ups.)

Ultimately, it comes down to this: Do you know and trust the people? Remember, the single biggest risk in hedge fund investing is "manager risk." No matter how superb a manager's record might be, if there were any inkling of a serious character flaw, such as an unwillingness to admit mistakes, or any question regarding the manager's basic integrity, I would just walk away.

In an essay published in *Evaluating and Implementing Hedge Fund Strategies*, hedge fund manager Lee Ainslie simply states, "Know the manager." He elaborates:

> No matter how intensive the due diligence process is or how frequently one communicates with a manager, an outside investor is never going to be in a position to understand every trade, every risk or mistake. At the end of the day, an outside investor is investing in an individual or team.

STEP 6: MAKE SURE THE TERMS ARE REASONABLE

After examining your finalists from every angle, you may conclude that all of them are equally deserving of your confidence. Or you may find one fund is a perfect fit. Either way, before you make your final decision there is one last step in the process.

The remaining, critical task is understanding the terms of the deal. And no matter how enthusiastic you may be about a fund and its managers, *never* commit to the investment until you have thoroughly reviewed the offering documents and made sure you're comfortable with all the terms. This final step is so important that it deserves a chapter all its own.

Chapter 11

Getting Comfortable with the Terms of the Deal

If you've found a strategy and a manager you like, but find you're still nervous about the prospect of writing that check (all those zeros!), it may be because of one word that constantly pops up in hedge fund literature and media coverage. The word is "unregulated." Everybody knows that hedge funds are unregulated, because that's how the *Wall Street Journal*, *Forbes*, and the *New York Times* describe them. The thing is, the conventional wisdom is wrong.

Here's the real story: It's accurate to say that as private limited partnerships, hedge funds are eligible for exemption from many of the rigorous requirements that apply to *publicly* offered investment vehicles such as mutual funds. Under the provisions of various federal laws, including the Securities Act of 1933, the Securities Exchange Act of 1934, the Investment Company Act of 1940, and the Investment Advisers Act of 1940, mutual funds must register with the SEC and comply with a maze of regulations that set standards for transparency; restrict holdings and strategies; put caps on fees and charges; limit use of leverage, short selling, and derivatives; establish liquidity requirements; and demand extensive, regular SEC filings, among other things.

For hedge funds, the ability to gain exemption from this body of regulations is crucial. The issue isn't so much that SEC filings are time-consuming and costly, though they certainly are both. What's more relevant is the flexibility hedge funds gain by not being limited to certain prescribed methods of investing; that's what frees them to be creative in seeking opportunities outside the mainstream.

What most observers overlook—even otherwise knowledgeable ones—is that hedge funds can win exemption only by adhering strictly to another whole set of requirements. For instance, hedge funds can accept money only from qualified investors who meet certain income/net worth tests; they may have no more than 99 limited partners in some cases, and no more than 499 in others; and their sales and marketing efforts are restricted, as are third-party solicitations on their behalf. If they trade in commodities or futures, they may be subject to requirements of the Commodity Futures Trading Commission (CFTC).

And remember, just because hedge funds are exempt from most requirements affecting mutual funds, they are still subject to the SEC's antifraud provisions. Furthermore, hedge funds must comply with the laws and regulations of each state in which they solicit participation. If you understand that hedge funds are indeed regulated, you know something that the vast majority of sophisticated investors don't.

So investing in a hedge fund doesn't mean you're venturing into wild and woolly territory where anything goes. But neither is it as straightforward as investing in a mutual fund, which has become a lot like buying any other kind of commodity: You simply browse the aisles of a fund supermarket, pick a flavor you like, check the price tag, and sign on the dotted line.

Getting into a hedge fund is much more like entering into a contract. In fact, that's exactly what you're doing. You are signing up to be a partner in a private limited partnership, and the partnership agreement is no less important or complex than one you'd need to invest in a private equity deal or co-own an apartment building.

Hedge funds spell out the terms of their partnership agreement and investment structure typically in three documents: the offering memorandum, the limited partnership agreement, and the subscription agreement. Mutual fund literature always warns against sending in your money without reading the prospectus first, and where hedge funds are concerned, this message should be underlined and printed in red:

Don't ever take the plunge until you fully understand and are completely comfortable with the terms of the deal.

That advice holds no matter how brilliant or well-known the manager. In fact, it's often the celebrity managers who impose the most onerous and unreasonable terms. Is it worth swallowing exorbitant fees and outrageous constraints on liquidity to invest with the fabulously rich and famous? That's a judgment only *you* can make.

Resign yourself to the fact that there's no shortcut to achieving a comfort level with a hedge fund's terms of investment. What the fund-of-funds managers and other professionals do—and what you should do as well—is systematically plow through the legalese, the warnings, and the boilerplate, paragraph by paragraph, ferreting out the crucial nuggets and nuances that shape the agreement.

Your task is to determine whether the specifics call for anything out of the ordinary, and if so, whether that's good or bad for you. You should not only evaluate the documents of the hedge fund you're considering, but also compare them with the terms of other funds. Once you've thoroughly reviewed the documents yourself, have your lawyer or accountant go through them as well. If your adviser isn't thoroughly familiar with the ins and outs of offering documents, find one who is.

THE KEY DOCUMENTS

None of these documents is exactly bedtime reading. They're written in language I can only describe as ugly. But just like filing your taxes or going to the dentist, doing this crucial part of your due diligence is one of those things you ultimately don't want to shirk. The purpose of this chapter is to take as much of the pain out of the process as I can. So any time you spend reading this will be an investment in making the whole thing easier.

Take some comfort, too, in the fact that all the fine print is there for a good reason. The objective isn't obfuscation, though it can certainly seem that the most important points are buried in a mountain of carefully couched, legalistic language. Realize that when hedge fund documents go into exhaustive detail, it's in the spirit of full disclosure. Should you ever be presented with a set of documents that appear sketchy or don't evidence a genuine effort to be fully disclosing, run the other way. This is one of those instances when less is definitely not more.

The Offering Memorandum

The offering memorandum (also known as the private placement memorandum) spells out the details of the hedge fund's investment structure. It is a hefty, densely written document that makes the typical mutual fund prospectus look like a Little Golden Book. Typically, it gets stamped "confidential" and assigned its own identification number so the general partners always know exactly how many copies exist and exactly who has them. That way they make sure they stay in compliance with certain state and federal solicitation rules.

Because hedge funds are exempt from the transparency requirements imposed on mutual funds, the offering memorandum is a prospective investor's primary source of information about a fund. It is also your principal source of protection. If at any point you think a fund isn't doing what it's supposed to be doing, reference to the offering memorandum is the only recourse you will have. So be sure to give it the same kind of focused, careful attention that Donald Trump would give a prenuptial agreement.

The Limited Partnership Agreement

The limited partnership agreement spells out the details of your contract with the fund, specifying the rights and obligations of general and limited partners alike. It also spells out the nuts and bolts of how the partnership will operate. One thing the agreement doesn't do is describe individual states' laws governing partnerships. Because regulations vary considerably from state to state, this clearly would be impractical. Among other things, such agreements generally stipulate that liability is limited to the amount an investor pays in (unless, of course, margin is used) and provide for pro rata allocation of all investments and expenses.

The Subscription Agreement

In essence, this is your application to be accepted by the hedge fund as a limited partner. The subscription agreement requests personal financial information confirming that you are qualified for inclusion in the partnership—in other words, that you qualify as an accredited investor. There's no ambiguity here, since the criteria are measured in black and white, dollars and cents. But the subscription agreement does have a subjective aspect, in that you are asked to make representations of your *suitability* for inclusion in the partnership. Remember, by law hedge fund investments are limited not just to affluent investors, but to *sophisticated* affluent investors. So the subscription agreement will ask questions designed to tell the general partners of the fund whether you have sufficient investment experience and knowledge to really understand what you're getting into. From a legal point of view, to protect the general partners, hedge funds can't do a mass solicitation. This means that the general partners must have some personal knowledge of the prospective investor's eligibility *before* they can send anything out.

If the general partners accept your agreement, you're in; you wire the amount of your investment to the custodial bank serving as a transfer agent, who in turn sends the funds on to the prime broker who actually holds the assets. Congratulations! You're now a bona fide limited partner. Shortly thereafter, you will receive a confirmation letter from the general partners and a complete set of all documents both you and the general partners have signed.

WHAT TO LOOK FOR—AND LOOK OUT FOR

To get to the substance of these documents, you have to get past the obligatory dire warnings and admonitions, wading through all the "thereons" and "hereafters." Only then do you get to the meat of what the fund is really offering you. Here's a typical paragraph describing a certain hedge fund:

> The Partnership is designed only for sophisticated persons who can afford a loss of all or a substantial part of their investment in the Partnership. There can be no assurances the Partnership will achieve its investment objective. An investment in the Partnership is subject to a number of risks described below in "Certain Risks."

It's enough to scare you away or drive you crazy. Needless to say, these documents are drafted by attorneys, usually ones that specialize in hedge funds. But don't be put off by the ominous tone. If you have any experience with legal documents, you understand that the alarmist language is just the lawyers' way of protecting their clients; no matter what happens, their response can be, "You can't say we didn't warn you." And remember, the lawyers are paid to look out for the general partners' interests, not yours.

Your Eligibility

Just as you scrutinize the details of any hedge fund you're seriously considering, the general partners are also going to take a close look at you. Before you get too deeply into the documents, first make sure you are eligible to invest in the fund. Here are the three questions you need to answer:

1. **Am I an accredited investor as defined by the SEC?** All hedge funds must apply one of two possible definitions. Under SEC rules, an "accredited investor" is either:
   - An individual who has earned $200,000 in annual income for the past two years ($300,000 if a spouse's income is included) and has a reasonable expectation of doing so in the future, *or* a net worth of $1 million (which may or may not include the value of your home equity and automobile, depending on interpretation). Funds employing this definition may have no more than 99 limited partners, and are exempt from SEC registration under Section 3(c)(1) of the Investment Company Act of 1940.

     OR
   - An individual holding at least $5 million in investments; a family company that owns not less than $5 million in investments; a person, acting for his or her own account or for the accounts of other qualified purchasers, who owns and invests on a discretionary basis at least $25 million in investments; or a company (regardless of the amount of such company's investments) if each beneficial owner of the company's securities is a qualified purchaser. Funds applying this definition may have up to 499 limited partners, and are exempt from SEC registration under Section 3(c)(7), a new exclusion created by the National Securities Markets Improvement Act of 1996.

     Hedge funds are universally scrupulous in applying these definitions, as the general partners assume a tremendous liability if they accept an unaccredited investor, even inadvertently. As a result, they will ask for complete documentation of your status as part of the subscription agreement.

2. **Even though I am an accredited investor, will the fund allocate me a slot?** If the fund's maximum size is 99 limited partners, you can be sure the general partners will manage the fund's available investor slots carefully, especially if the number of investors is close to the limit. And when slots are at a premium, it's usually the investor with the biggest check in hand who wins.

Along the same lines, you should determine the fund's situation regarding registration in your state. Depending on your state's registration requirements and whether the hedge fund has fulfilled them, it may or may not be prepared to accept any investors from your state. There may also be a limit on the number of residents it can accept from a given state before opening a big, bureaucratic Pandora's box of additional reporting requirements. This is another reason why a fund doesn't automatically accept a qualified investor.

3. **What percentage of the fund's assets consists of investments made by pension plans?** If you are a trustee of a qualified pension plan and your proposed investment would bring the fund's benefit plan assets up to 25 percent or more of the total, you may not be able to invest. Once a fund passes that 25 percent threshold, it becomes subject to ERISA standards and restrictions, and that's something the fund will undoubtedly want to avoid.

If you can't determine eligibility on your own, the fund will ideally have a compliance officer you can call. If there is no designated compliance officer, you may end up querying a general partner or an administrative person who will likely be well versed in compliance issues. Any questions that he or she can't answer will be referred to the fund's general counsel.

Fees

A two-tiered fee structure is one of the hallmarks of hedge funds. Managers are compensated in two ways: with a fixed percentage of the assets under management—the management fee—plus a portion of the returns achieved by the fund—the incentive or performance fee.

The annual management fee is straightforward, and is usually calculated as 1 to 2 percent of assets under management. Find out when these fees are paid and whether they are paid in advance or in arrears. Standard practice is to levy the management fee quarterly in advance.

As for the performance fee, the general partners typically get 20 percent of the fund's returns, with all the limited partners (i.e., you and all the other investors) dividing the remaining 80 percent. That may sound like a pretty large bite out of the fund's gains, but be assured that 20 percent is the industry standard. What's more, this fee is the manager's prime incentive to make you a great deal of money. Think of it this way: If you end up paying a huge performance fee, you ought to be delighted, because you'll be gaining four times that amount. So don't begrudge your prospective manager's cut unless the manager is asking for more than the usual share.

While the 20/80 split is standard, make sure that returns are calculated in ways that don't unduly favor the manager. The truly noteworthy stuff may all be in the fine print, so take the time to understand how returns are calculated. Find out, for example, whether the fund has the following:

- *Hurdle rate*: This is a minimum rate of return the manager must earn (typically the T-bill rate) before the performance fee kicks in.
- *High-water mark*: This is highly desirable, because it means that the general partners' incentive compensation doesn't kick in until after the fund shares have surpassed their previous high point ("look-back"). That way, if the fund's performance chart resembles a roller coaster, you won't keep paying your manager every time the fund climbs the same hill. In almost all cases, hedge funds that lose money in any given quarter or year must make up those losses before they can begin earning incentive fees the next quarter or year ("claw-back").

You'll also want to determine whether the performance fee is billed quarterly, semiannually, or annually. It may take a little bit of digging to figure out exactly what the fees will be. Here's what one offering memorandum had to say about the basic management fee:

> The General Partners collectively receive management fees (the "basic fee") from the Partnership, payable quarterly in advance within 10 Business Days after the first day of each calendar quarter (or the day the Partnership commences operations if other than the first day of a calendar quarter), calculated at the following annual rates (i) 1.00% of the net assets of the Partnership (the "Founder's fee") as of the first day of such quarter (or the day the Partnership commences operations, as the case may be) attributable to the General Partners and those Limited Partners who were Limited Partners as of December 31, 1999 (each a "Founding Partner," and collectively the

"Founding Partners"), and (ii) between 1.00% and 2.00% (inclusive) of the net assets of the Partnership (the "Nonfounders' Fee") attributable to the Limited Partners who are not Founding Partners (each a "Nonfounding Partner," and collectively, the "Nonfounding Partners"). The Nonfounders' Fee annual percentage rate applicable to the Partnership's net assets attributable to a specific Nonfounding Partner shall equal the sum of (a) 1.00% plus (b) the annual percentage finder's fee or placement commission, if any, payable by the General Partners to a financial intermediary with respect to such Nonfounding Partner's investment in the Partnership; provided, however, that in no event shall the percentage calculated pursuant to clause (b) above with respect to a specific Nonfounding Partner exceed 1.00% (i.e., in no event shall the Nonfounder's Fee annual percentage rate applicable to the Partnership's net assets attributable to a specific Nonfounding Partner exceed 2.00%). The basic fee will be deducted in determining the net profit or net loss of the Partnership, and will be prorated for periods less than a full calendar quarter.

Not exactly clear, is it? Beneath all the jargon, that passage simply says that investors pay a fee of 1 percent of assets under management, and must pay an additional fee that reimburses the fund for any finders' fees or commissions the fund paid to attract investors. However, the total fee can't be more than 2 percent. It's too bad they couldn't just put it that way.

Expenses

Management fees are not the only cost item associated with hedge funds; the general partners are also reimbursed for various expenses. Hedge funds can and do charge their investors for many of the costs incurred in making and valuing investments. Typically, an offering memorandum says something like the following:

The General Partner will be responsible for and will pay, or cause to be paid, certain "overhead expenses." Such "overhead expenses" will include the expenses of the Partnership of an ordinarily recurring nature such as office rents, supplies, secretarial services, charges for furniture and fixtures, compensation of administrative personnel, telephone expenses, and stationery. Such "overhead expenses" shall not include (i) legal, accounting or audit expenses, or (ii) investment expenses such as commissions, interests on margin accounts and other indebtedness, and custodial fees.

Although layering expenses on top of fees may seem a bit much—doesn't the manager pay for anything other than desk chairs and coffee cups out of his or her own pocket?—most hedge fund agreements specify that the fund reimburses the general partner for what lawyers call "usual and customary fees."

Would-be investors should be alert for any expense items that are not usual or customary, and for reimbursements that differ in type or amount from the industry norm. This isn't to say that there should never be deviations from industry standards; they may be warranted by the investment strategy or some other unique attribute of a fund. But the investor should always be aware of such departures and determine the rationale behind them.

Liquidity

Another vital issue is liquidity—specifically, understanding the rules for taking money out of the fund. That may not seem to be a high priority now, when you're focused on entering a relationship with a manager rather than terminating one. But it could be a concern down the road. Your financial situation could change, and you may find that you need to draw on the funds you've invested. Or you could be disappointed with the results and decide to redeploy your money. You can't know the future, but you should know the rules of the game right from the start.

The most immediate question is the fund's initial lock-up period, the interval during which you can't withdraw funds without paying a penalty fee. Although the lock-up period is typically one year, it can range from six months to five years. Whatever the constraint, the question is the same: Can you live with it?

The next question is what kind of liquidity you'll have once the lock-up period has ended. Most funds let you withdraw your money at quarterly intervals, as described in one fund's offering memorandum:

> Upon giving at least 30 days' prior written notice, any Limited Partner may withdraw all or any part of his Capital Account as of the last Business Day of each calendar quarter. Such notice must state the amount to be withdrawn or the basis on which such amount is to be determined.

With these kinds of stipulations, getting your money out of a hedge fund takes a bit more doing than simply calling a mutual fund's 800 number and telling them to wire funds to your checking account tomorrow. That may be okay with you, as long as you know in advance what's required. But don't assume that the only difference between withdrawing a hedge fund investment and selling stocks or mutual fund shares is a 30-day wait before you can collect your money. Here's a typical provision for a limited partner who wants to "retire," that is, withdraw all of his or her money from the fund:

> Not less than 90% of the estimate of such amount will be paid within 30 days after the date of such Partner's retirement or the last day of the fiscal year, as the case may be. Promptly after the General Partners have determined the Capital Accounts of the Partners as of such date and the Partnership's independent public accountants have completed their examination of the Partnership's financial statements, the Partnership will pay to such Partner or his representative the amount, if any, by which the amount to which such Partner is entitled exceeds the amount previously paid, or such Partner or his representative will be obligated to pay to the Partnership the amount, if any, by which the amount previously paid exceeds the amount to which such Partner is entitled, in each case together with interest thereon, to the extent permitted by applicable law, from the date of such Partner's retirement or the last day of the fiscal year, as the case may be, to the date of the payment of such amount at an annual rate equal to the brokers' call rate charged by the Partnership's principal broker from time to time.

Like the fund described in this passage, many funds have a holdover provision. This means that when you're cashing out of the fund entirely, the fund will initially return only 90 percent of your investment (usually within 5 to 10 days after the withdrawal date). The fund withholds the remaining 10 percent until its independent auditor has verified the fund's asset value (normally 45 days).

Here's another thing to watch out for: Many hedge fund agreements have an obscure clause saying the general partners reserve the right to return your investment "in kind" rather than in cash. This right is very seldom exercised, thank goodness, or no one would ever invest in hedge funds. But this language leaves open the possibility that funds could give you private placements or highly illiquid distressed debt securities instead of good old American greenbacks. That's one of the reasons why, as I told you earlier, I would never put my money in a fund that invests in private placements.

In short, getting money out of a hedge fund can seem to be a protracted process involving some period of uncertainty as to who owes what to whom. But in comparison to all other alternative investment vehicles such as venture capital or private equity funds, hedge funds are in fact highly liquid.

Use of Leverage

While there are no hard-and-fast rules about what degree of leverage is advisable—to a large extent, that's a matter of your personal risk tolerance—the documents should have something to say on the topic. They may or may not provide specifics on how much leverage is used, and in what instances. That's partly because the application of leverage can be a complex issue in both mathematical and investment policy terms.

At the very least, the documents should state whether the fund uses leverage and should give some indication of the degree applied. Don't make assumptions based on broad statements, though. All hedge funds are different, and you need to understand exactly how your particular fund views and uses leverage. After all, that's an issue fundamental to the most basic assessment of your fund's risk/reward profile. You also want to know how the fund's theoretical stance relates to its actual use of leverage, both currently and in the past. So don't be shy about asking any questions needed to fill in the blanks on this topic.

Potential Conflicts of Interest

Admittedly, this is a sensitive area. But to protect your own interests, you need to look at this issue objectively. Does the structure of the agreement give the general partners or certain limited partners any special advantages that are not openly disclosed? You would certainly hope not. But you wouldn't want to discover, somewhere down the road, that the fund is set up so the manager can siphon off the best investments for his own account, or pay himself a special fee for things he ought to be doing as part of his job. As always, the key phrase is "full disclosure."

My personal view is that the hedge fund business gives general partners enough profit potential that there should be zero tolerance for any complicated arrangements whereby general partners enrich themselves at the expense of limited partners, even if the money involved doesn't amount to much. To me, it's an issue of basic integrity.

Problems with cronyism or nepotism occasionally crop up. If the manager's relatives or school friends are on the payroll, is it because of their skills, or is it due solely to their personal ties? Don't assume the worst; there are a number of cases where investment managers have built effective, smooth-running organizations by working closely with a sibling, parent, or spouse. But anyone who works for the fund should have the credentials to warrant his or her position.

On the subject of broker/dealers, you should scrutinize any "soft dollar" brokerage arrangements. Since the mid-1970s, investment managers have been allowed to use their commission dollars as a form of payment for investment research and other services. The Securities Exchange Act of 1934, as amended in section 28(e), provides "safe harbor"—legal protection to those who pay a higher brokerage commission rate in exchange for some value-added services rather than the lowest available rate, as securities law normally requires.

The problem comes when the definition of "research" and the envelope of "other services" is stretched farther than it really should be. Some managers have given brokerage firms their business in exchange for everything from newspaper subscriptions and baseball tickets to office furnishings. A more subtle abuse is when managers receive research services that genuinely help them manage investments—but not the investments of those whose commission dollars have paid the freight.

Such problems aren't always easy to uncover, since fund managers may distribute their brokerage business with several objectives in mind. The quality of execution should be foremost, but managers may have good reasons for spreading their commission dollars around. For instance, they may want to tap various firms' research, or get broader access to initial public offerings (IPOs).

Soft-dollar issues are complex, and I won't burden you with all the details. But here's what you should know. Hedge fund managers don't have to rely solely on the "safe harbor" protection that all investment managers can claim under Section 28(e) because they have another way to protect themselves: All they have to do is disclose how they're using soft dollars in their offering documents. When you sign the agreement, you're giving your consent to whatever they've laid out. In a way, this is a double-edged sword. On the one hand, it means hedge funds might feel safe in pushing the envelope on soft dollars, going beyond the definitions normally considered allowable under the safe harbor provisions. But on the other hand, activities that cross the line are protected only if they're disclosed. So that makes it even more important that you go through the terms concerning soft dollars with a fine-toothed comb. If an investment manager does make use of soft dollars, try to evaluate whether the manager is distributing these soft dollars in ways that will benefit you and other limiteds, and not just himself.

These issues can be tricky, and sometimes conflicts of interest are in the eye of the beholder. But don't feel reluctant to raise questions about anything that doesn't look kosher. Even if there's only the potential for abuse, you should look for ways to ensure this potential is held in check.

Taxes

When you are a limited partner in a hedge fund, all tax consequences of the fund's activities pass directly to you. Therefore, you should assess whether the fund's investment strategies will generate primarily long-term capital gains, short-term gains, or some combination of the two. The fundamental question is how the fund's investment and trading policies might affect your own tax obligations. You should also ask when you'll be receiving your K-1 (Partner's Share of Income, Credits, and Deductions) form. However, funds are obligated to provide this information to you no later than March 31.

If you're the trustee of a foundation or endowment, you should be especially sensitive to the issue of unrelated business taxable income (UBTI). Hedge funds using leverage can generate UBTI, and even tax-exempt investors have to pay taxes on the incremental gains associated with leverage. That's not to say that an obligation to pay UBTI necessarily means the investment isn't worthwhile. If the fund's expected return is high enough, it may more than compensate you for any taxes you have to pay.

The bottom line is to make sure that your individual tax situation and sensitivities, viewed in light of your total financial picture, are congruent with the fund's accounting policies and practices. Remember, hedge funds don't take individual tax issues into consideration. If you have questions, you may want to consult with a tax adviser who's familiar with hedge funds.

Other Items to Consider

Here's a laundry list of remaining issues any would-be hedge fund investor should consider in reviewing an offering memorandum:

1. *Ceiling on assets.* See if the fund has a ceiling on the total assets it will accept. As I explained in a previous chapter, with hedge funds, bigger isn't necessarily better. Some hedge fund strategies invest in relatively narrow market niches, and their results may suffer if too much money is thrown at them. There's also the problem of market liquidity. A traditional manager investing in large-cap U.S. equities could handle billions and billions of dollars and have a negligible impact on the market. However, a hedge fund with a narrow mandate might well roil the market if it ever topped $500 million. Make sure the intended size of the fund is appropriate for the markets in which it invests.

2. *The fund's reporting policies.* You certainly don't expect the managers to notify you every time they buy or sell a security, but you do want to know what's happening with your money. How often are they going to send you reports? Monthly? Quarterly? And what will the reports contain? At a minimum, you should be shown the top 10 holdings and

some kind of sector weightings. You should also be informed about the ratio of long and short positions and the net equity exposure. The fund should report its performance over various periods of time—since the last report, year to date, last 12 months, since inception—rather than make you do these calculations. And, of course, performance should be shown both gross and net of fees.

Beyond formal reporting policies, it's useful to get a feel for the fund management's openness to conversations with limited partners. Just because they've got $500,000 of your money doesn't mean they should be expected to answer questions on a daily basis. But, on the other hand, since they have $500,000 of your money, they should be prepared to answer the telephone once in a while when you have a pressing question. In fact, it wouldn't hurt for them to buy you lunch.

3. *Succession.* Although it's not a welcome thought, you should know what provisions, if any, the fund makes for the death or incapacitation of a general partner. Because the success of a hedge fund investment is often inextricably linked to just one or two key people, the general partners should anticipate the possibility that, heaven forbid, something could happen to one of them. You'd hate to find out that the fund's resident genius was hit by the proverbial bus and your money is on autopilot until the next available withdrawal date.

4. *Service providers.* Read through the documents to find out who the fund's prime broker, attorney, auditor, and bank are. Obviously, the more reputable and recognizable those names, the better.

5. *"Tainted investors."* If you hold a professional position with a bank, investment firm, or brokerage house, you're known in hedge fund parlance as a "tainted investor" (as are the general partners), and you will have to sign something saying as much. The reason you're tainted is that rules of the National Association of Securities Dealers (NASD) prohibit you and members of your immediate family from investing in "hot issues," which are new public offerings that are in such high demand they're priced at a premium when trading commences. And contrary to everything you've read in the financial press, hedge funds actually report *three* sets of performance numbers: (1) performance of the hedge fund itself—the numbers you'll see in the databases, (2) performance of tainted investors (including general partners), which excludes the performance of any hot issues the fund may have invested in, and (3) performance of nontainted investors, who may get better numbers than the tainted investors

(and the fund itself) do, presuming the hot issues in the fund's portfolio perform as expected.

6. *The organization behind the fund.* While the hedge fund itself may not be registered with the SEC, the investment advisory organization behind the fund may be. If so, be sure to ask for Form ADV, which provides additional details about the investment organization. If there are any skeletons in the closet, this is where you should be able to find them.

SEPARATELY MANAGED ACCOUNTS

One other option is worth mentioning. If you find that you've gone through the process of selecting a hedge fund—you've found a strategy, firm, and manager that meet your objectives and preferences—but find one deal-breaking clause in your review of the documents, you may want to consider asking the general partners to run a separate portfolio. Instead of pooling your money into a commingled fund, you'd have your own stand-alone account with the flexibility to structure it to meet your own requirements. The biggest advantage of a separate account is that some of the terms of the hedge fund investment may be negotiable, including liquidity, tax management, and the frequency and content of reports.

You can't assume that the fund has the ability to offer a separate account option. That depends in part on whether the fund or its parent company is a registered investment adviser. Funds that are not registered are prohibited from offering more than a limited number of separate accounts.

Regulatory requirements aside, common sense tells you that a manager won't go to the trouble of running a separate account unless your account is large enough to make the effort worthwhile. A manager certainly won't bear the costs and administrative burden of managing a stand-alone portfolio (e.g., trading, accounting, reporting) for an investor who barely meets the commingled fund minimum.

A FINAL NOTE

A hedge fund's general partners are almost always significant investors in the funds they manage—and they should be, as this creates a powerful alignment between the interests of the managers and the investors. This is one of the big pluses of hedge funds. Unlike a mutual fund, you and the managers really become partners, both legally and in a financial sense. This is one of the reasons why hedge funds are so appealing to sophisticated investors. Having said that, it's only prudent to carefully examine the terms and guidelines of every aspect of the deal.

Chapter 12

Staying on Top
of Your Investment

Once you've made your initial investment in a hedge fund, you can kick back, relax, and just wait for the returns to start rolling in, right? Wrong. Every investment requires ongoing vigilance—and anyone who suggests otherwise is woefully naive.

In the early 1970s, there was a fad for what were called "one-decision stocks." Once you decided to buy them, your work was done; they required no attention beyond "file and forget." But the speciousness of this idea quickly became apparent. Both individually and collectively, these supposedly bulletproof investments went on to encounter all manner of perils. One of the immutable laws of financial markets is that they're always subject to the unpredictable and the unforeseen. That's just how things are.

It's no different with hedge funds. So if you've invested in a hedge fund, your job isn't over and in one sense, it's just beginning. After all, you've got a significant sum of money at stake and it's only prudent to keep an eye on it. By no means am I even hinting that you should be prepared to bolt at the first bump in the road, jumping in and out of hedge funds the way some people trade individual stocks. Hedge funds aren't that kind of investment. What I *am* saying is that you can't shift to cruise control after you've placed your money with a hedge fund manager. Quite the contrary. You need to be aware of every significant development concerning your hedge fund and the markets and securities in which it invests. What's more, you should be ready to respond with the appropriate action when the situation warrants. If a change is needed, the initiative will have to come from you. After all, you're not likely to hear a manager say, "I've done a lousy job; you really should fire me."

Surprisingly, most of what's written about hedge funds takes you up to the point of making an investment—and ends right there. The body of hedge fund literature is slim enough, but the material on monitoring and terminating hedge fund managers is virtually nonexistent.

So what's a hedge fund investor to do? If you put your money with a fund-of-funds manager, you've got it covered; postinvestment monitoring is part of the service you get for your management fee. It's the same if you opt to work with a consultant; keeping watch over your money is one of the prime ways consultants earn their keep.

But if you elect to fly solo, don't worry. Effective investment monitoring doesn't have to be a mystery. In this chapter, I'm going to share my philosophy for keeping tabs on your hedge fund investment and my tips for knowing when it's time to pull the plug.

HOW LARGE INSTITUTIONAL INVESTORS DO IT

When I was first struck by the paucity of information on monitoring of hedge funds, I thought back to my days in the traditional investment world. It seemed likely that some of the monitoring methods used by the investment executives who oversee big-name corporate pension plans, leading foundations and endowments, and major pools of public retirement money might well apply. After all, they're responsible for the long-term performance of billions of dollars in assets spread across dozens of managers and numerous asset classes. In essence, they're in the business of hiring and firing managers. So let's review their methods and then consider the extent to which they apply to hedge funds.

Quantitative Review

Institutional investors almost always have some hard-and-fast rules for determining whether a manager's performance is up to snuff. For instance, here is how a typical investment policy statement might read for a large-cap, core U.S. equity mandate:

The manager's objective is to:

1. Outperform the S&P 500 index by 200 basis points, annualized, over rolling five-year periods, net of fees.
2. Rank in the top third of a style-appropriate peer universe over rolling three-year periods with respect to performance, information ratio, and Sharpe ratio. The portfolio should not rank in the bottom quartile of any peer universe comparison for more than four consecutive quarters.
3. Invest the assets in a manner consistent with a large-cap, core equity style as measured by Zephyr Associates, Inc.'s StyleADVISOR.

Included in the guidelines might be a statement that failing to meet the performance standards or succumbing to style drift could result in a manager's losing a portion of his or her funding, being put on probation, or being terminated outright. This isn't as draconian as it sounds. Before the portfolio is funded, the manager usually gets the chance to sign off on the performance objectives and parameters governing the portfolio's style characteristics, and so has a chance to speak up if the guidelines don't seem realistic.

Qualitative Factors

Even if managers achieve stellar performance and have consistently stuck to their knitting, that doesn't mean they're automatically home free. Big institutional investors also look at qualitative factors when deciding whether to retain a manager. They review a number of things, including the impact of major organizational or personnel changes, whether the manager has religiously adhered to the investment guidelines, whether the firm is having big swings—up or down—in assets under management, and whether the particular investment style or strategy is still appropriate for the plan's overall objectives. If some major problem is identified—for instance, the investment strategy relies heavily on internal research and the firm loses its research director—and isn't resolved in a timely and satisfactory way, the manager may get the boot despite good numbers.

Communication

Most institutional investors meet face-to-face with their managers at least once a year and sometimes as often as once a quarter. Managers routinely spend an hour or so presenting performance, reviewing the investment process, going over holdings and transactions, providing organizational updates, and delivering their views on where the market's headed. The clients listen closely to make sure that the managers' words are consistent with their actions and that their explanations for what's going on in the portfolios make sense. Managers who lose the clients' trust or confidence, for whatever reason, will likely be fired.

In addition to formal meetings, traditional managers provide their institutional clients with a constant stream of information about their portfolios—holdings, transactions, performance, risk characteristics—you name it. Between this abundance of written information and regular in-person meetings, institutional investors have the input they need to judge whether a manager should be retained.

HOW WELL DO TRADITIONAL METHODS APPLY?

While individual investors should take a cue from the thoroughness and logic institutions bring to the task of investment monitoring, many of the specifics of the institutional approach don't really work for hedge funds—especially where quantitative analysis is concerned. And in the institutional world, quantitative analysis is viewed as the biggest part of monitoring; in fact, meeting cut-and-dried performance benchmarks is the first and primary test of a manager's worth. That simply doesn't apply to hedge funds; why would you compare a hedge manager's results to a traditional benchmark that the manager isn't setting out to beat in the first place?

You might instead want to compare a hedge fund's performance to a universe of similar funds, in order to see whether the manager's strategy has performed as well as it should under the prevailing market conditions. But while some consulting firms have developed strategy-specific hedge fund indexes, they're not widely available and, given the uniqueness of many hedge fund strategies, might not necessarily provide a valid, apples-to-apples comparison.

Yet another obstacle for quantitatively minded investors is the fact that hedge managers understandably don't release complete information on individual holdings or transactions. But without that data, there's no statistical basis for the kind of performance attribution analysis that institutional investors routinely review in order to determine why managers performed as they did.

The upshot is that the quantitative aspects of traditional monitoring and evaluation don't translate well to hedge funds. But you *can* learn from the qualitative standards that institutional investors apply. The challenge on the qualitative side is getting access to the information, since hedge fund managers generally aren't nearly as accessible or as open as their traditional counterparts.

STARTING OFF ON THE RIGHT FOOT

To establish the right framework for monitoring a hedge fund investment, you should communicate your requirements to the manager up front. It wouldn't be reasonable to ask him or her to sign off on a set of detailed investment policy guidelines as traditional managers do. If they're to deliver absolute returns, hedge fund managers need more flexibility than that.

What you *can* do, as soon as you've funded your investment, is write your manager a letter laying out your objectives and expectations. Your letter should spell out what you expect in terms of returns, risk level, and investment strategy. Explain which performance characteristics attracted you to the fund and outline precisely which circumstances would prompt you to withdraw your money. It's not that the fund is going to do anything differently because of your input—hedge funds don't tailor their portfolios to meet individual client objectives. However, putting your expectations in writing does provide a framework for future discussions and gives you a basis for analyzing the fund's results against your needs.

And make sure that you're aware of the fund's reporting policies. As I've noted, traditional managers provide a high degree of transparency; even mutual fund shareholders receive semiannual reports detailing each fund's individual holdings and the size of each position. That's simply not how hedge funds work. But while you can't expect full disclosure, you should expect a certain level of detail. At a minimum the fund should regularly provide you with a listing of the 10 largest holdings, sector weightings, information about the ratio of long and short positions, and performance numbers as described in the previous chapter. And even if you'll be receiving reports only once a quarter, make sure they break out monthly performance so you can track the fund on that basis.

ONCE YOU'RE UP AND RUNNING

Monitoring your hedge fund investment is easiest and most effective when you do it systematically. Here are my suggestions:

1. *Thoroughly review all correspondence from the manager.* This sounds obvious, but you'd be surprised how many people toss their quarterly reports into a pile of papers without giving them more than a glance. You should read reports in a timely manner and then file them where they can be quickly retrieved, should you need them for reference later on.

2. *Talk with the manager on a regularly scheduled basis—say, once a quarter.* It doesn't have to be an in-person meeting; a phone conversation will suffice. Be prepared to ask substantive questions about the most recent report you've received; don't launch off with some vague query such as, "How are things going?" I'd also recommend focusing each conversation on one specific topic of interest, such as performance, the organization, or the market environment and how it's influencing the strategy. If the manager won't get as specific as you'd like, ask broader questions that are relevant to the discussion at hand. But don't get into a cross-examining mode; keep things upbeat and friendly. Use these times not only to get information, but to build a relationship.

3. *Keep up your research and networking.* Your research efforts shouldn't end with the selection of a hedge fund. Build on what you've already learned by continuing to read, going to conferences, and staying in touch with your hedge fund semifinalists (you never know when you might want to give them some money, too). These are all good sources of information on what's going on

in the industry and how similar funds are doing. You've put in the effort to accumulate a body of investment knowledge; the last thing you need is to let it fade away.

SYSTEMATIZING YOUR REVIEW

In these volatile and uncertain times, inertia can be an enemy. After allowing for an initial grace period, make it a practice to revisit your hiring decision periodically. At some regular interval—say, whenever you review the manager's performance—or in between if significant questions or problems with the fund arise, ask yourself these questions: Has anything changed, either in the fund or in its market niche, since I made the decision to invest? Does my rationale for investing in the fund still hold true? Would I make the same hiring decision today?

Keep Performance Numbers in Perspective

One of the realities of monitoring a hedge fund is that you can check performance only periodically. It's not as though you can look up your fund's value in the newspaper each morning as you can with a mutual fund—and that's probably a good thing. It's important to remain focused on the bigger picture rather than short-term price movements.

As you look at performance, the obvious first step is to see how your fund's returns stack up against your own absolute return objective (in my case, 15 percent annually, net of all fees). This is the bogey that hedge fund managers must strive for—to me, it's the one return number that really counts. All other rankings and measures are secondary. Remember that while you should check your fund's performance on a monthly or at least quarterly basis, your target rate of return is an *annual* objective.

Remember, too, that returns are only one factor in the performance equation. You should always look at returns in the context of risk. Before you hired the manager, you should have evaluated at least 36 months' worth of performance data. As you receive new performance reports, compare these with the earlier data, so you can track any shifts in risk, return, and risk-adjusted return measures. What you want to determine is whether the fund's risk characteristics have stayed consistent.

If the performance results aren't good, this is the time to ask some pointed questions. Listen closely to the manager's views on market dynamics and trends. Does he or she make a persuasive case that the strategy remains valid despite a period of poor results? Has he adapted the strategy to the market's changing conditions? Is she repositioning the fund for an anticipated shift in climate? Is the manager out of step with the market, or does he have his finger on its pulse?

Even if it seems that a manager has stumbled, bear in mind that it's not at all unusual for hedge funds to do well for some time and then suddenly have a bad quarter, or even a bad year. That in itself shouldn't be a cause for disenchantment. If you find yourself getting nervous, it's helpful to look at things from a historical perspective. For instance, the February 1988 issue of *Town & Country* featured an article about what happened to some hedge funds in the 1987 stock market crash. John Lefrere, a managing partner of Delta Capital Management, which ran a $50 million hedge fund, recalled, "Two weeks before the downturn we looked dumb as hell because we were heavily committed on the short side and losing money on those investments." When the market plummeted, however, the value of Delta's puts shot up, in some cases tenfold. "They helped ameliorate our losses. We were very fortunate," Lefrere remembered.

The historical lesson is, don't jump to conclusions. Even the most brilliant manager will inevitably go through some rough patches. It's possible that the manager is right, but right just a little too soon. So I'd suggest you give a manager at least 18 months before you consider whether to retain or terminate the relationship based on performance. This time period, by the way, is relatively short compared to the amount of time you should allow for traditional managers to prove themselves. Because traditional managers are expected to adhere strictly to their chosen investment styles, they may be at the mercy of market cycles that play out over three- to five-year periods. But it's reasonable to expect that hedge managers will be more nimble and adaptable in the face of adverse market conditions.

LOOK FOR EARLY WARNING SIGNALS

Poor performance can be the result of market reversals, but it may also be symptomatic of problems with the fund's strategy or organization. The trouble is, it can take quite a while before those problems are reflected in the numbers, by which time the situation may already be toxic. So stay alert to early warning signs that can tell you when a hedge fund may be headed for trouble.

A Flagging of General Partners' Commitment

When any of the general partners pull a significant proportion of their assets out of the fund, that's an immediate signal that something isn't right. It's akin to insider selling in a public company: If people integral to the organization are bailing out of their financial commitments, you have to wonder what they know that you don't.

Keep an eye out for indications that personal problems, such as divorce or ill health, are undercutting a manager's commitment or abilities. Likewise, be alert to any personality or attitude changes that could prove damaging. For instance, a manager who achieves such spectacular performance as to make a bundle of money in a short period of time may lose his or her intensity. And while hedge fund managers aren't known for their humility, be especially wary of the overinflated ego. When egos spin out of control, the quality of decision making almost always suffers.

Organizational Upheavals

Changes in the manager's range of activities are another reason for investors to stop, look, and listen. If the management company repeatedly launches new funds or enters new businesses, both the rationale and the impact should be considered. While it's true that hedge fund managers don't punch a time clock, their time isn't infinitely expandable. So whenever a manager appears to be taking on a major new commitment, make sure he or she isn't spreading himself or herself too thin.

Find out whether the new venture is really a brand-new activity or just a repackaging of what the manager is already doing. Sometimes a manager will create a new fund that simply mirrors an existing one, in order to provide one vehicle for U.S.-based investors and another for offshore investors. The two funds have a different tax status, but their portfolios are *para passu*, as it's known in the trade—exactly the same. In this case, the new fund would have little or no impact on the manager's day-to-day activities.

Any significant shift in the fund's assets under management should raise a red flag. A rapid decline in assets suggests that other investors have been withdrawing their money; if so, you need to know why. A wave of investor defections is often a sign of serious underlying problems; moreover, such an exodus can create financial problems for the fund. A sudden surge in withdrawals may force a fund manager to raise cash by liquidating investments at unfavorable prices, possibly even having to sell some of the mainstays of the portfolio because liquidity in other holdings is drying up. When this happens, it can quickly lead to sagging performance, growing investor discontent, and another spate of redemptions, throwing the fund into an inexorable downward spiral.

By the same token, don't assume that a rapid increase in funds under management is such a wonderful thing. Gratifying as it is to think you were ahead of the curve in signing up with an up-and-coming manager, be forewarned: The challenge of putting a large pool of money to work may tax the manager's capabilities or leave him or her short of good investment ideas. Beyond that, the fund may be investing in a market segment that's too narrow to accommodate a huge influx of capital.

Take the example of a fund that invests in micro-cap stocks. It can invest only so much in any one idea, otherwise it would end up owning or controlling a whole collection of small companies. So what happens if this fund finds itself with huge sums to invest? Faced with a limited universe of good micro-cap opportunities, it may lower its standards and begin investing in less attractive situations. Or, it may modify its capitalization criteria, edging into small-cap or even mid-cap companies. In either case, you're not getting the same strategy you chose, and there's always the risk that the manager is venturing outside his or her realm of competence.

Joe Nicholas sums the problem up neatly (*Investing in Hedge Funds*, Bloomberg Press, 1999):

> Many of the hedge fund strategies profit from inefficiencies in niches of limited size. However, the high returns often attract more investor money than can be invested in the manner in which the original returns were generated. This may lead to more risky behavior by the managers to maintain return levels, such as an expansion into areas in which the manager has limited experience, or the increased use of leverage or more risky investments.

In short, investment strategies have varying degrees of scalability, and as I mentioned in Chapter 10, my personal bias is that funds of over $1 billion may be too large to keep their edge.

Turnover of Key Personnel

Hedge funds are typically run by one especially talented manager who puts his or her own stamp on virtually all decisions or by a small, close-knit group of individuals who have collectively evolved the fund's unique strategy. In either case, the departure of a key manager or analyst may leave a vacuum that's hard to fill. No matter how talented, a successor may not have the level of ability or the same feel for the strategy. Hedge fund strategies are often highly personalized, depending more on the brilliance and insights of one or two people than on a methodology that can be codified and replicated. If the fund is unable to carry on with the strategy as it was originally implemented, performance may suffer or the fund may depart from the winning strategy that attracted you in the first place—neither one an appealing scenario.

Departures from an Established Strategy

A hedge fund may deviate from its avowed strategy even when there's been no change in the cast of characters. The departure may be a conscious one: The fund managers may have concluded that their strategy must be altered in response to new economic realities, or they may have lost faith in it for some reason. On the other hand, problems such as organizational instability or an overload of assets may be leading the fund to stray from its established path.

Whatever the reason for a gradual or abrupt shift in strategy, it's a development that demands your attention. Remember, each investment plays a specific role in your portfolio. If a hedge fund is no longer fulfilling its assigned role—even if the returns are good—that can be deleterious to your overall investment objectives.

A Shift in Climate

Even if the fund's strategy doesn't change, the market environment may. Energy prices may go down instead of up; emerging markets may encounter political crises rather than economic booms; arbitrage spreads may move away from historical norms. No matter how compelling a fund's strategy was when you signed up, you need to reaffirm its viability and relevance as time goes by.

If fundamental conditions appear to be changing, it's time to reevaluate your investment. Are the changes cutting to the core of your strategy? Do the fund managers recognize the changes? How are they responding to them? If you're convinced the market has shifted and your manager thinks there's little cause for concern, you may want to back away from your investment. If the managers agree with your assessment and are doing something about it, decide whether you like the ways they're redirecting the fund. It's not unheard-of for hedge fund managers to conclude that their strategies are no longer viable and actually return investors' money. However, that usually doesn't happen until the fund's performance has already languished for several quarters.

The annals of hedge fund investing are littered with tales of strategies sunk by an economic sea change. Once again, Long-Term Capital Management is a case in point. That debacle occurred because the fund's strategy centered on exploiting historical relationships among various instruments, and those relationships changed in ways the managers didn't foresee and their mathematical models didn't take into account.

In early 2000, the hedge fund world was shaken when two legendary managers, Julian Robertson and George Soros, both stated publicly that their strategies weren't working as well as they had in the past. Renowned as one of the canniest value investors of his generation, Robertson led the Tiger Funds to returns averaging over 30 percent throughout the 1980s and 1990s. But in 1999, while the Nasdaq Composite Index rose 86 percent, Robertson's investments fell 19 percent. As he acknowledged in an October 1999 letter to investors, "These results stink." In January he had more bad news: Two of his biggest investments, U.S. Airways Group and Federal-Mogul Corporation, were "completely obliterated." Seemingly unattuned to the dynamics of the New Economy, Robertson in the spring announced that Tiger Management was closing down most of its operations and would liquidate the bulk of its investments. From a peak of $21 billion, his assets under management had dwindled to about $6 billion before he called it quits.

Around the same time, George Soros's flagship Quantum Fund announced major changes in both direction and management. In so many words, he said, "I no longer understand this market, and I'm going to lower the risk profile of my investments." As reported in the April 29 edition of the *New York Times*, Soros's right-hand man, fund manager Stanley Druckenmiller, also resigned.

The *Times* quoted one Wall Street analyst's take on what had happened to these legendary managers. "Julian said, 'This is irrational and I won't play,' and they carried him out feet first. Druckenmiller said, 'This is irrational and I will play,' and they carried him out feet first." Neither manager was able to adapt a formerly winning strategy to the technology-fixated climate of the late 1990s.

DECIDING TO EXIT

On what basis should you fire your hedge fund manager? It's never easy to terminate a relationship, especially one you entered with such confidence and high hopes. The best answer I can give is that the criteria for firing are the flip side of the ones you used for hiring. Sometimes a single factor, such as a breakdown in communications, diverging views of the market, or some breach of trust, however minor, is enough to warrant terminating a hedge fund relationship. While you don't want to make such decisions emotionally, it is both valid and important to listen to what your intuition tells you.

If you do decide to pull the plug, realize you won't be able to exit as quickly or easily as you could from a mutual fund. Typically you can withdraw your money only during a specified monthly or quarterly window, and you'll be required to announce your intentions several weeks in advance. So be prepared to wait before you're able to redeploy your funds.

But remember that a hedge fund investment need not be an all-or-nothing proposition. While liquidity is somewhat constrained, you can still increase or decrease your investment in a fund at the prescribed times. I'm not talking about trying to time the market; that's a bad idea in any case. But if you have concerns about a fund, it sometimes makes sense to pull back a bit while you get a better sense of how it's doing and where it's going.

You may also want to alter your exposure based on what's going on elsewhere in your portfolio. If you run a business that has become heavily involved in Latin America, for example, you may want to lighten up your holdings in a hedge fund investing in that region. Otherwise you'll end up with too much of your net worth exposed to events in one part of the world.

AVOID THESE CLASSIC MISTAKES

1. *Firing an absolute return manager for missing some relative return benchmark you've fixed upon.* That's not what you hired the manager to do.

2. *Having unrealistic expectations.* What's unrealistic? Comments like, "My goal is to be a hundred percent in stocks on the way up and a hundred percent short on the way down." Or, "I want relative performance in a bull market and absolute performance in a bear market."

3. *Succumbing to the "floating bogey" syndrome.* Don't change your mental benchmark based on the market segment that's recently been red hot. Be satisfied if your hedge fund is up 30 percent when the S&P 500 is up 20 percent, even though the Nasdaq has climbed 40 percent.

4. *Getting into an adversarial relationship with your manager.*

5. *Letting emotions cloud your judgment.* Keep the relationship friendly, but at arm's length.

6. *Developing "QP" (quarterly paranoia) about performance numbers.* If you get too wrapped up in short-term results, you'll inevitably lose sight of the big picture.

7. *Expecting constant hand-holding.* Your manager shouldn't be paying you a two-hour visit every month but rather should spend that time doing what he or she does best—making money for you and the other limited partners. Unless something unusual is going on, a 15- or 20-minute quarterly phone call should be all you need.

8. *Looking at returns while ignoring risk.* The true bottom line is the risk-adjusted return measures described in Chapter 10 including The Owen Ratio.

9. *Ignoring the net equity exposure of your fund on a month-to-month basis.*

10. *Paying no heed to the red flags right in front of you.* If key people are leaving the fund, the manager's time is consumed with new business

ventures, several major limited partners have pulled out, or communication is breaking down, do something about it. Find out what's going on, then make your decision. If the issues aren't being resolved, it may be time to exit.

11. *Getting greedy*. If your manager delivers the news that the fund is up 90 percent, it's not polite to ask, "Gross or net?"

FIVE RULES FOR LIMITED PARTNERS

1. Don't repeatedly call the manager to whine about the market or your financial disappointments.
2. Don't bring your personal woes into the hedge fund relationship.
3. Maintain objectivity about your investment.
4. Don't try to cadge off-the-cuff investment ideas for you and your friends.
5. Give credit where it's due. A little positive feedback goes a long way. Save your tough-guy persona for the times when you really need it. It will have more impact then, anyway.

THE END OF THE BEGINNING

This chapter reminds me of what Sir Winston Churchill said in 1943, when it seemed that the war would rage on interminably: "Now this is not the end. It is not even the beginning of the end. But it is, perhaps, the end of the beginning." Though the context is quite different, the same thought applies to hedge funds. Making the investment isn't the end of the process, but only the end of the beginning. It's your money that's at stake, and no one else has greater insight into your objectives—or a greater interest in making sure they're met.

As with every other step in the process, there's no simple formula or checklist for getting it right. But don't be frustrated that monitoring is more art than science. With a little initiative and persistence, you can make sure your investment stays on track.

Closing Thoughts

If only we had a crystal ball, we would know for certain where the stock market will be five years, or even one year, from now. Unfortunately, no one does have a crystal ball—not even the experts. As Yogi Berra would put it, "Forecasting is difficult, especially about the future." For every pundit who is convinced the Dow will hit 40,000, another warns that the bull market can't go on forever and a major meltdown is just around the corner.

I'm rooting for the optimists. But in the back of my mind I keep wondering, what if the doomsayers are right? One thing I know for sure: I'm too old to start building my net worth all over again if my portfolio drops by half in a bear market. Because we constantly hear such polarized, yet equally convincing views, of the market's outlook, I'm not willing to bet my money that either extreme will come to pass. That's why I'm taking a middle course—in other words, hedging my bets.

For every stock that's wildly overvalued and sure to come crashing down eventually, there's another company that's in the early stages of accelerated growth. I think it's a mistake to become so enamored of the growth opportunities that you become blind to the market's downside risks—or so convinced the end is near that you overlook opportunities to profit from the enormous changes taking place all around us. I believe that in the next few years, opportunities will abound to make money on both the long *and* the short sides of the market.

PUTTING THEORY TO THE TEST

Having looked at the opposing viewpoints, I've concluded that the principles embraced by A. W. Jones and his followers make a great deal of sense for any conservative investor—especially now. By investing for absolute return, embracing a flexible and opportunistic investment style, and being willing to raise cash and sell short in turbulent times, Jones-model managers can mitigate (though never, of course, eliminate) the damage a bear market can do, just in case the pessimists turn out to be right. On the other hand, by embracing change and being open to ideas outside the mainstream, they can also take advantage of newly emerging industries and companies.

Now, you may think this all sounds fine in principle, but still be skeptical about how well hedge funds fare in practice. And investors are right to be cautious. It's also true that during the strong bull market of recent years when almost everyone did well, it hasn't been so easy to put hedge fund managers to the test.

In the first six months of 2000, however, the investment climate shifted dramatically, giving investors a real opportunity to discern the differences between hedge funds and traditional, long-only managers. For the first time since 1994, four of the major market indexes—the S&P 500, Nasdaq, the MSCI World Equity Index, and the Dow Jones Industrial Average—were all down over the six-month period.

For the hedge fund industry, this period has been a real litmus test—and, it turns out, a profound validation. While the major market indexes headed south, from January 1 through June 30, 2000:

- The Hennessee Hedge Fund Index, which covers a broad range of nearly 20 hedge fund strategies, was up 7.1 percent.
- VAN Hedge Fund Advisors International Inc. reports that the average U.S. hedge fund was up 10.4 percent.
- Hedge Fund Research's HFRI Equity Hedge Index, which probably comes closest to a Jones-model approach, was up 10.56 percent.

Moreover, I strongly believe that the market's erratic behavior during this six-month period may well be representative of the market climate we're likely to see going forward. In other words, after enjoying abnormally high stock returns in the 1990s, we may be headed for a few lean years—even single-digit returns. This, to my mind, is what makes the recent divergence between hedge fund performance and the leading market indexes all the more compelling.

By the way, I'm not alone in this view of the market. In the July 10, 2000 *Wall Street Journal*, one of Wall Street's most outspoken bulls, Abby Joseph Cohen, chief investment strategist for Goldman Sachs, weighed in with her outlook. Pointing out that investors enjoyed "a marvelous period" in the late 1990s, she warns that while earnings are still good and inflation is under control, one crucial factor is different today. As the *Journal* put it, "Stock prices fully reflect just about all the good news she or anyone else can imagine." Cohen's conclusion: "Don't count on seeing those kinds of numbers again soon."

In a similar vein, a September 5, 2000 *Wall Street Journal* article headlined "A Weary Bull?" made a fairly strong case that tougher times may lie ahead. "A run as great as we had was an extraordinarily unusual and unique event," professor Jeremy Siegel of the University of Pennsylvania's Wharton School told the *Journal*. "To expect it to continue would be out of the realms of all probabiliy."

George Soros, who outperformed every other manager in the world over a period of some 30 years, believes the investment climate has changed so fundamentally that it's time to lower his expectations. As reported in the July 2000 issue of *Bloomberg* magazine, "George Soros has thrown in the towel on swashbuckling investing. Soros told investors he would stop making large, leveraged macro bets." And in June, he told reporters at a London press conference, "In my old age, I've become conservative . . . . I'll be happy if I average 15 percent rather than 31 percent"—a reference to the returns the Soros funds have averaged historically.

CONFESSIONS OF A HEDGE FUND MANAGER

I wrote this book in part because I wanted to puncture the myth that all hedge funds are risky. I hope that this book succeeds in making the case that conservative investors can benefit greatly from hedge investing. In fact, it's really an inherently conservative concept.

But a couple of things have bothered me since I began this project some two years ago. I don't want to be a promoter or an apologist for the hedge fund industry. I'd be the last one to say that all hedge fund managers know what they are doing and are guaranteed to make you rich. I've also worried about the possibility that, despite all my cautions and all the guidance I've tried to give in sorting out hedge fund strategies, I could inadvertently be leading investors into dangerous waters. I don't ever want to hear someone say that he or she read my book, put an entire $800,000 IRA into a hedge fund—and ended up losing every dime.

That's why this book isn't titled *The Only Hedge Fund Book You'll Ever Need* or *Why Every Investor Should Be in Hedge Funds*. I called it *The Prudent Investor's Guide to Hedge Funds* for two reasons. First, I myself am a resolutely conservative investor, and wanted to help others see the hedge fund industry through those eyes. Since you've picked up this book or even bought a copy, I presume that you are a conservative investor, too (or else an aggressive one who thinks it may be time to reform).

The second reason I put the word "prudent" into the title is because I want to emphasize the need for investors to be careful. While I want to get across the message that the hedge fund industry has much to offer a conservative investor, I have to be honest about the kind of trouble an unwary investor can get into.

THE COMPULSION TO WIN

While I was researching this book, and particularly as I got to know a number of hedge fund managers, I found myself thinking of Billy Kidd—an Olympic champion who is without question one of the greatest downhill ski racers the United States has ever produced. A good friend of mine used to tell me stories about Billy, because they grew up together in Steamboat Springs, Colorado; in fact, they were both on the high school ski team there. My friend assures me that from a technical standpoint, Billy was definitely *not* the best skier on the team. So why is it that he won race after race and went on to become a downhill skiing legend? It was because of his attitude toward risk.

In every downhill contest, as the racers hurtle forward at ever-accelerating speed, there's a point where anyone with any concern for life and limb will instinctively pull up just a bit. If you don't, you compound the chances of a bone-shattering injury ending your skiing days for good. But Billy never reached that point. While all the other racers pulled up, Billy would just go faster. Any normal person would have been incapable of overriding the animal fear that comes from our instinct for self-preservation. But Billy evidenced no fear whatsoever. Am I going too fast? What if I hit a bump? What if I lose control? It seemed these questions never crossed Billy's mind.

THE FUNDAMENTAL CHOICE

Some hedge fund managers are very much like Billy. They have a competitive drive—a compulsion to win at any cost—that makes them heedless of the risks. There's no doubt in my mind that the hedge fund industry attracts the best and brightest investment talent in the world. But I have to confess that some of these guys scare me. I'm talking about the ones who are never satisfied with a 60 percent return if someone else is earning 70 percent. Though they may have solid track records and delight investors with their spectacular returns, I'm just not convinced that they know when to pull up. Their greed and their desire to be on top drive them to attempt ever more daring maneuvers. That's why I've presented hedge fund strategies as being divided into two camps—"getting rich" and "staying rich"—and been explicit about my strong bias for the "staying rich" variety.

Now, I'm not saying that my way is right and other ways are wrong. You may conclude that it's not worth getting into a hedge fund unless it's the supercharged variety. If you're willing to take the risks, more power to you. I just want to make sure you know what you're getting into. Call it my own instinct for self-preservation or call it "wimping out," but my first-hand observations of fund managers tell me that when you combine high-testosterone personalities with the ability to leverage investments to the hilt and reap millions in performance fees, you're going to get a high-risk vehicle, no matter what you call it. For some managers, the temptation to push the envelope—to go for that next increment of return, regardless of the risks—is simply too great to resist.

Personally, I'm convinced that if you invest in a "getting rich" strategy, the odds are high that the manager will eventually crash and burn. I couldn't begin to guess whether it will happen next year or 10 years from now, and I can't deny that you might make a whole pile of money in the meantime. But I believe that at some point it will happen.

Does the market sometimes bail these guys out? Sure, it happens all the time. But what happens on the day when the market doesn't come back? A fund-of-funds approach will certainly ameliorate the risk that a certain manager will go too far out on a limb, but it doesn't neutralize the dangers of inherently risky strategies.

I'D RATHER STAY RICH

If I were 30 years younger, I might be more tempted to join the high-flying hedge fund crowd—the ones determined to get spectacularly rich, no matter what risks must be borne along the way. But at this stage in life I'm not really motivated by greed. I already have enough money to support the kind of lifestyle I want, and that doesn't include a personal Learjet. I simply want to maintain my current lifestyle and preserve the wealth I already have. So I've gone down the road as a conservative hedge fund investor. Along the way, I've learned quite a bit from "getting rich" managers, many of whom are enormously bright and talented.

Still, I'm putting my money on the "staying rich" approach, and if you, too, want most of all to keep the wealth you have, I'd counsel you to do the same. If you're systematic and smart about picking a manager, you'll get attractive returns. They won't be off the charts, and they won't make your golfing partner green with envy. But you'll sleep better at night. And one day, when your more adventurous friends at the club are bemoaning their losses, you'll just sit there quietly, knowing that you've come through just fine.

"Staying rich" managers are worriers, and Gen X-ers, who grew up with the bull market, will probably tell you they're missing a bet. Many dotcom disciples believe we've entered a new era, one in which the old economic laws and the lessons of history simply don't apply. But where a young investor sees a "new paradigm," an older and wiser one may see a "market cycle." Personally, I believe that worrying is an investor's best defense.

THE NEW GENERATION

For conservative investors, the good news is that finding "staying rich" managers has become considerably easier. In a rising market it's doubly difficult to figure out which funds are genuinely hedging their bets and which ones are in the game mainly for the sake of the 20 percent performance fee, running what amount to leveraged long-only portfolios in hedge-fund guise. In today's more turbulent times, however, performance numbers *do* tell the story. As frustrating as this market is for long-only managers, it's an environment in which managers who truly hedge can finally show their mettle. As the saying goes, "It's only when the tide goes out that you can learn who's been swimming naked."

I've also observed that lately there is a growing supply of hedge fund managers a conservative investor can feel comfortable with. In the early chapters of this book we traced the growth of the hedge fund industry through a period of especially rapid proliferation in the 1980s and early 1990s. The managers who adopted the private partnership structure back then found themselves riding the crest of a strong bull market. Many of them achieved enormous success and wealth by being smart, working hard, and making superior stock picks. But having operated for so long with the wind at their backs, relatively few felt any real need to hedge their portfolios against a market downturn—indeed, I suspect that few in this earlier generation of hedge fund managers are even conversant with hedging techniques. And who can blame them for ignoring the hazards of long-only investing? For the managers who prospered so greatly over the past 15 or more years, the risk taking has certainly paid off.

But times have changed. Today we're seeing the emergence of a whole new generation of managers who view high levels of market volatility as normal and are completely attuned to the notion of hedging their bets. They're not superstars who achieve jaw-dropping returns, nor are they ego-driven, celebrity wannabes as their predecessors all too often tended to be. They are simply skilled, pragmatic investment managers who anticipate a challenging climate and are fully prepared to cope with it.

This is not to say that today's new breed of managers cast their prospects in a pessimistic light. From conversations I've had, I can tell you that they see plenty of opportunities to make money in the months and years ahead. But according to their credo, what matters most is not how much money you make when times are good, but how much you keep when times are tough.

Consequently, the rising stars in this generation are disciplined, opportunistic, and above all adaptable, with their egos firmly in check. They're not so interested in being gurus; nor are they necessarily looking for spectacular wins. They just want to come out ahead, consistently, over the long haul. That's why they excel at true hedge investing.

A DIFFERENT PHILOSOPHY

So if you do decide to look at the hedge fund industry from a conservative vantage point, as I have, you'll find some very interesting "staying rich" strategies. If you want to know how to tell a "staying rich" from a "getting rich" strategy, I can tell you the difference. What distinguishes the two is a fundamental difference in philosophy.

While it's true that all hedge fund managers invest with an eye to absolute return—after all, they don't earn any performance fees if they don't achieve positive annual returns for their investors—they don't all pursue absolute returns in the same way.

Funds targeting annual returns of 20 percent, 25 percent, or even higher will unavoidably risk high volatility or even major losses; no investment manager, no matter how skilled, has ever figured out how to achieve such lofty gains without suffering an annual loss at some point. These funds aim for *maximum* absolute return. In their world view, the sky's the limit, and you simply accept whatever risks come along. But even when these funds are successful, the level of volatility can leave you gasping for air. When they don't manage to pull things off so well—then you're guaranteed some sleepless nights.

In constrast, managers of Jones-model funds, and those using other "staying rich" strategies, aim for a *target* absolute return. They consciously limit their goals to attractive, but reasonable level of annual returns, which to my mind means 12 to 15 percent. And why do they have such modest expectations, viewing anything more than 15 percent annually as pure gravy? It's because they want to avoid losses above all, while consistently achieving attractive returns in all market environments. They also want to avoid the high volatility that unnerves even the steeliest investors.

As explained in *Hedge Funds Demystified*, a 1998 report produced for the Pension & Endowment Forum by Goldman Sachs and Financial Risk Management Ltd., achieving consistency of return is all about controlling risk:

> While all hedge funds seek to generate positive returns in all market environments, there is a subset of hedge funds that FRM characterizes as "Absolute Return Funds." These funds place particularly strong emphasis on the disciplined use of investment and risk control processes, and as a result have consistently generated returns that have both low volatility and a low correlation with traditional equity and fixed income benchmarks. Relative to traditional active management, Absolute Return strategies target relatively more alpha and far less beta. Relative to other hedge funds, Absolute Return Funds tend to measure and control risk over much shorter time horizons and

are less tolerant of losses. . . . The incorporation of funds with these return characteristics should offer plan sponsors a means for improving the risk-adjusted returns of portfolios.

So it's the control of risk, in pursuit of consistent return rather than maximum return, that epitomizes the "staying rich" approach. And to me, the sweet spot in this range of strategies is around the ones targeting 15 percent a year. That target doesn't mean that in a good year you can't make 30 percent, 40 percent, or even 50 percent—but it does mean that you couldn't realistically expect to repeat that kind of performance two or three years in a row. It also means that there may be years when your returns, while still attractive in absolute terms, lag somewhat behind the gains from a roaring bull market.

If you, like me, are willing to give up some return in exchange for the expectation of consistent 15 percent returns and a measure of protection from market volatility, you can do that in one of two ways. You could hire a Jones-style manager or someone who follows the same principles. In my opinion, there's no better kind of hedge fund for a conservative investor who wants a stand-alone strategy.

Alternatively, if you want more diversification you can pursue the same goals through a carefully chosen fund of funds. When you start looking for an investment vehicle that blends very different kinds of strategies—from foreign nonperforming loans to distressed securities to merger arbitrage—you can find some fascinating combinations.

In my heart of hearts, I believe that hedge funds can offer great rewards to conservative investors who know their objectives and keep to the "staying rich" path. I hope that what I've learned and come to believe about hedge funds will help speed you on your own journey.

How I Made My Fortune

It was really quite simple. I bought an apple for 5¢, spent the evening polishing it, and sold it the next day for 10¢. With this I bought two apples, spent the evening polishing them, and sold them for 20¢. And so it went, until I had amassed $1.60.

It was then my wife's father died and left us $10 million.

—Anonymous Hedge Fund Manager

Index